DEMOCRACY, CAPITALISM AND EMPIRE IN LATE VICTORIAN BRITAIN, 1885–1910

Democracy, Capitalism and Empire in Late Victorian Britain, 1885–1910

E. Spencer Wellhofer
Professor of Political Science
University of Denver
Colorado

First published in Great Britain 1996 by
MACMILLAN PRESS LTD
Houndmills, Basingstoke, Hampshire RG21 6XS
and London
Companies and representatives
throughout the world

A catalogue record for this book is available
from the British Library.

ISBN 0–333–64313–5

 First published in the United States of America 1996 by
ST. MARTIN'S PRESS, INC.,
Scholarly and Reference Division,
175 Fifth Avenue,
New York, N.Y. 10010

ISBN 0–312–12916–5

Library of Congress Cataloging-in-Publication Data
Wellhofer. E. Spencer, 1941–
Democracy, capitalism and empire in late Victorian England.
1885–1910 / E. Spencer Wellhofer.
p. cm.
Includes bibliographical references and index.
ISBN 0–312–12916–5
1. Great Britain—Politics and government—1837–1901. 2. Great
Britain—Politics and government—1901–1910. 3. Imperialism—Great
Britain—History—19th century. 4. Capitalism—Great Britain–
–History—19th century. 5. Democracy—Great Britain—History—19th
century. I. Title.
DA560.W3 1996
941.081—dc20
95–43678
CIP

10 9 8 7 6 5 4 3 2 1
05 04 03 02 01 00 99 98 97 96

Printed in Great Britain by
Ipswich Book Co. Ltd, Ipswich, Suffolk

For Susan

Contents

List of Figures

xi

List of Tables

Preface

This project is an outgrowth of a long standing fascination with institutional responsiveness, adaptation and change. In one sense the project began when a graduate student returning from field research in Argentina found himself with a wealth of gathered information but little sense of a clear substantive problem. The events which followed in the Spring of 1968 at Columbia University concentrated the mind as a year and a half of field research had been unable to do. The subsequent work reflected those heady days with its focus on different facets of institutional responsiveness while developing an increasing concentration on political parties and democratic transition. Several questions underpinned these efforts: under what conditions do institutions become rigid, unable to accommodate the needs or demands for change? What do patterns of organisational evolution and elite recruitment have to tell us about the sources of and resistances to institutional responsiveness?

A more immediate impetus for this current project, however, lies in much more recent events in Europe and the former Soviet Union. As 1989 unfolded, I found myself, like most students of politics, deeply involved in discussions and debates on the likely outcome of the burgeoning efforts at democratic transition. These discussions were wide ranging and touched on all the current explanations and approaches to the study of democratic transition. However, one thought haunted me during these discussions: the historical and cultural boundaries of our language.

As my efforts turned to the current project and I indulged myself in the history of late Victorian Britain, it became increasing clear that the political leaders and intellectuals of that age faced conditions not unlike those more contemporary ones. Like ourselves, the singular question of the age centred on institutional responsiveness as demands for change followed the collapse of the previous ages' social ordering principles. Second, but of equal importance, however, these leaders and intellectuals were equally bound by the dominant ideas of their epoch as expressed in its contending languages. These languages provided the 'Flesh-Garment, the Body, of thought'. They determined the formulation of the questions, problems as well as the proposed solutions. Certainly some language reflected narrow economic or class or partisan interests, but more than crude determinism was at work. Language provided the conceptual tools and these were inadequate to the tasks at hand. Despite the apparent need for new social ordering principles, the interpretations of the age continued to employ contending languages and make predictions based on their logics, phrased in their words and cast up in their images.

The current project owes much to others for their assistance and support; indeed there are those without whom it would not have been possible. Friends and fellow scholars aided and encouraged the effort in numerous ways. Ken Wald generously shared his previous research and provided technical assistance for adding new data to his past efforts. Alan Ware of Worcester College, Oxford, and Lars Svsand of the Institute of Comparative Politics of the University of Bergen, Norway, encouraged the project with their interest and comments. James Caporaso, then of the University of Denver and now of the University of Washington, provided stimulation and advice both as Editor of *Comparative Political Studies* and as friend and colleague. Jack McArdle of the University of Virginia was most patient as I learned Latent Variable Path Analysis (LVPA). Closer to home Gregg Kvistad, Chair of the Department of Political Science, Marshall Haith, Director of Research, and William Zaranka, then Dean and now Provost, aided the effort by their financial support. Harold Perkin of Northwestern University kindly read some initial portions of the manuscript and his excellent comments formed the basis for revisions in the final work.

During various stages of the project financial support was provided by the Ford Foundation and the University of Denver. Major financial support for the project, however, was provided by the National Science Foundation under grant SES 79-25622. That funding underwrote a larger project of data acquisition as well as funding initial papers and articles of which this book is one component. The Foundation's continued support is gratefully acknowledged.

E. SPENCER WELLHOFER

1 'One Step Broken, The Great Scale's Destroy'd'

> Vast chain of being! which from God began,
> Natures aethereal, human, angel, man,
> Beast, bird, fish, insect, what no eye can see,
> No glass can reach; from Infinite to thee,
> From thee to nothing. – On superior pow'rs
> Were we to press, inferior might ours be;
> Or in the full creation leave a void,
> Where, one step broken, the great scale's destroy'd;
> From Nature's chain whatever link you strike,
> Tenth, or ten thousandth, breaks the chain alike.
>
> Alexander Pope, *Essay on Man*, 1733–4

> The proletarians have nothing to lose but their chains. They have the world to win.
>
> *Communist Manifesto*, London, 1848

> When he has been properly drilled by his Association he both votes and votes with his will. If the party nominees win, he wins with them as spontaneously as if the Association had not dictated his act. He is not aware that he is reduced to a mere cipher.
> ... to appear to themselves to be independent agents, yet exercise their franchise so that the party shall be victorious, electors must educate their volition to dance in their chains.
>
> *The Times*, 19 October 1885

> Language is called the Garment of Thought: however, it should rather be, Language is the Flesh – Garment, the Body, of thought.
>
> Thomas Carlyle, *Sartor Resartus*, 1833–4

Pope's vast chain of being is a metaphor for a social order of which few remnants remain. The history of its demise is the history of British politics and society in the nineteenth century and guides our endeavour. From a society devoted to ranks, orders and degrees grew individualism, self-

1

reliance and liberalism. From a polity secured by Crown, Church and Lords evolved popular sovereignty, partisan orthodoxy and public bureaucracy. From an agricultural economy secured by tradition emerged an industrial order based on *laissez-faire*.

Yet Pope's language is more than metaphor, if less than literal. For, if as Carlyle suggests, language captures the body of thought, then language offers us an understanding of the past. History's voices are important not only because they capture society's self-image, but because they cast up the designs and dreads by which men make their history. Three contending parables begin our story; in each, the chains chant a different allegory of social order. Pope's vast chain of being sings to us a pacific song of a changeless society created by God, hierarchical, fixed and eternal. Marx's chains intone of workers shackled to capitalist machines, but rejoice in a future of equality and liberty. *The Times'* dirge menaces us with a new dark age when masses of disciplined and regimented electors dance in their partisan chains.

If Pope speaks the eighteenth-century language of order, then Marx and *The Times* are dissident voices not only to Pope's order but to each other, as well as to the dominant language of nineteenth-century capitalism and liberalism. In the debates of history both defenders and dissenters provide us with insights into the past. Often the dissenters accurately portray the forces for change, but just as frequently are mistaken in projecting the outcome. Marx, for example, correctly identified the corrosive power of capitalism and class on Pope's vast chain, but did not foresee the regimented politics which *The Times* found so menacing. In the late nineteenth century Lord Salisbury and Friedrich Engels alerted us to the historical dynamics both uniting and dividing Britain but, with an equal measure of misplaced correctness, failed to predict the denouement of history. Salisbury, expressing himself in Pope's eighteenth-century language, called for the nineteenth-century polity to be a bulwark against both capitalist classes and democratic masses. Marx and Engels, speaking the new language of production, markets and classes, forecast the collapse of Salisbury's ideal.

The breaking of Pope's vast chain of being and its gradual and partial replacement by new mechanisms for ordering politics is the history of the transformation of British politics in the nineteenth century. The significance of this transformation cannot be underestimated, for not only did it give rise to the contemporary underpinnings of British politics, but it informed both its contemporaries and ours of the contentious debates on the successful linking of capitalism and democracy. In what follows we seek to understand this transformation in terms of the changing society and polity as expressed in society's self-image, as debated in the issues of the day and as evidenced in mass political behaviour of the time. To understand the transition, however, we must first understand what it displaced.

THE EIGHTEENTH-CENTURY REPUBLICAN IDEAL: HARMONY, HIERARCHY AND MUTUAL OBLIGATION

Our prelude lies in eighteenth-century society, a society characterised by the ideals of harmony and hierarchy linked together by the infinite chain of mutual social obligations, represented in Pope's metaphor. This 'vast chain of being' formed the essential language for describing both the nature of the hierarchy and its enduring omnipresence. As almost every commentator on the eighteenth century remarks, the legitimacy of the social order depended on the innumerable links of mutual obligations binding the social scale into an unbroken chain. From God in His Heaven to the lowest form of life, the order was ordained, clear, fixed and just. However imperfect the metaphor in practice, the language of the social order referred to 'ranks', 'orders', 'degrees', and 'corporations'.

Pope's metaphor, which can be traced back to ancient political thought, provided an ordering principle as well a moral justification for eighteenth-century English politics.[1] This principle revolved around three elements: harmony, hierarchy and mutual obligation. These formed the enduring rules for social order. Harmony was an ideal found in the natural order of things and that which the social order must emulate. Hierarchy was essential to harmony because individuals were endowed by God with unequal talents and character. Both harmony and hierarchy would be secure as long as each recognised his differences and sought only advancement commensurate with his talents and character. As Hobbes could affirm in the *Leviathan*, men believing themselves equal were the root of much disharmony in society. Finally, mutual obligation was necessary to the smooth running of the society. Those better off held an obligation to care for those less well off, just as the lower orders must understand, appreciate and reciprocate with obedience to those above.

In this aristocratic ideal, we are, of course, hearing echoes of classical political language, so much in evidence in Plato's republic, where great harm comes to the polis by 'meddling and exchange between the three great orders'. This ancient language for the social order existed well into the nineteenth century and continued to offer it appeals.[2] Perhaps foremost was its wide understanding and acceptance. Everyone simply 'knew' where they stood in the vast chain. As we shall see, such understanding and acceptance was a constant source of frustration to Marx and Engels. Second, the hierarchy was almost infinitely flexible and adaptable. New orders or ranks could be incorporated almost without end into the infinite gradations of the social order. We shall see just how such arguments sought to accommodate the expansion of citizenship in the nineteenth century.

In the reality of eighteenth-century society, in contrast to the ideal, admission to the upper ranks and orders was based on property; hence, the 'polity' was limited to a small elite who held their interests synonymously with the whole. In such a scheme, representation of the lesser orders, let alone individuals, was unnecessary, since all gained their representation indirectly through their superiors culminating in the aristocracy. As Arthur Young could remark in 1794:

> The principle of our constitution is the representation of property, imperfectly in theory, but efficiently in practice ... the great mass of property, both landed, moneyed and commercial, finds itself represented; and that the evils of such representation are trivial, will appear from the ease, happiness, and security of all the lower classes, hence possibly virtual representation takes place even where the real seems most remote.[3]

The republican ideal and the principle of property representation informed political debate well into the nineteenth century. In the debates surrounding the Third Reform Act, the Conservatives often presented their proposals in the language of Arthur Young and the images of the Classical Republican Ideal, while their fears cast up the Classical Republican Problem.

Cohesion across the ranks and orders of society in the eighteenth century was secured as much by the material as by the ideal foundations of the social order. The links of Pope's 'vast chain of being' were forged in the crucible of property and patronage and shielded from criticism by tradition and religion. The material base of all society, and rural society in particular, was property ownership, however widely or narrowly held. Consequently, the centres of both rural and town life were the great houses. So vast was the influence of the great house, so pervasive, so enduring that one author was led to remark that England seemed to be governed by 'a federation of country houses'.[4] Within the great houses and their lesser counterparts, the extended household formed the dominant social and economic unit of the age. The definition of the polity necessarily and naturally flowed from this relationship to property.

Representation through property, however, involved a reciprocal obligation under which those possessing property assumed some responsibility for the lot of those lacking it, while those lacking it accepted the guidance and benefice from those above. Hence, the language of ranks, orders and degrees held its counter-part in the principle of reciprocal ties captured by the couplets of 'duty' with 'charity', 'deference' with 'subordination'. Such reciprocal obligations were ordained by God. As Bishop Butler described the obligations embodied in the vast chain in a sermon in 1740 to the London Corporation:

> He who has distributed men into these different ranks, and at the same time united them into one society, in such sort as men are united, has by this Constitution of things, formally put the poor under the superintendency and patronage of the rich. The rich, then, are charged by natural providence, as much as by revealed appointment with the care of the poor.[5]

The ideal of eighteenth-century society drew much from classical language with its rhetoric of civic virtue and obligation. It premised a social order on harmony, hierarchy and mutual obligation. These principles were severely challenged in the nineteenth century, but their endurance is striking.

THE ENDURING IDEAL

Ideals have a passion for outlasting the conditions which give rise to them. The eighteenth-century ideal persisted even as its material and ideal foundations eroded. Despite the vast changes in the nineteenth century, official documents continued to espouse the ideals of the previous age. As late as the 1851 Census, the Registrar General's Department could state in its preface: 'the English family, in its essential type, is composed of husband, wife, children and servants; or less perfectly but more common, of husband, wife and children'.[6]

Likewise, the ideal for the upper class failed to recognise the changing economic basis of society. In an era of rising commerce and industry, declining agriculture and demands for popular democracy and class warfare, the ideal of the Victorian gentleman echoed that of an earlier age. Even as parvenus and Disraeli's 'bookstall men' edged their way into positions of rank and power in society, Gilbert Scott could write in 1857:

> Providence has ordained the different orders and gradations in which the human family is divided, and it is right and necessary that it should be maintained ... The position of a landed proprietor, be he squire or nobleman, is one of dignity. Wealth must always bring its responsibilities, but a landed proprietor is especially in a responsible position. He is a natural head of his parish or district – in which he should be looked up to as the bond of union between the classes. To him the poor man should looked to protection; those in doubt or difficulty for advice; the ill disposed for reproof or punishment; the deserving, of all classes, for consideration and hospitality; and *all* for a dignified, honourable and Christian example ... He is blessed with wealth, and he need not shrink from using it in its proper degree. He has been placed by Providence, in a position of authority and dignity, and no false modesty should deter him from expressing this, quietly and gravely, in the character of his house.[7]

As the gulf between the ideal of charity and reality of poverty widened in the nineteenth century, the perversity of obligation became as severe upon the beneficiaries as it became distasteful to the benefactors. As the vast chain corroded and its links slackened on the poor, many argued for hardened discipline forged to temper compassion. It is striking to think that in the same year that Marx and Engels penned the words of the Communist Manifesto and three years before Scott could wax eloquently on the noble obligations, J.S. Mill wrote in his *Principles of Political Economy*:

> the lot of the poor, in all things which affect them collectively, should be regulated *for* them, not *by* them. They should not be required to think for themselves, or give to their own reflection or forecast an influential voice in the determination of their destiny. It is the duty of the higher classes to think for them, and to take the responsibility of their lot, as the commander and officers of an army take that of the soldiers composing it.[8]

Mill's metaphor of an army is a striking one: The poor were to be disciplined, organised and regimented by modern organisational principles increasingly necessitated by the mass society (a comment echoed 40 years later in *The Times*).

Equally striking is that almost 100 years after Young's statement and 40 years after Scott's and Mill's work, Disraeli and Salisbury continued to proclaim the efficacy, efficiency and justice of the property principle in the franchise expansion debates of the 1880s. Disraeli and the Conservatives tenaciously argued that political representation expressed itself best and most efficiently through its 'natural relationship to property'. In the franchise debates of 1883, Salisbury bemoaned the loss of 'the bond of union between the classes'.

CHALLENGES TO THE 'VAST CHAIN OF BEING': CLASS, MASS AND THE SAVAGE CELT

> The bond of attachment is broken, there is no longer the generous bounty which calls forth a grateful and honest confiding dependence.

These words, written in 1829 by Robert Southey, poet laureate 1813–43, capture the sense of the fading ideal.[9] The last years of the eighteenth century and the first years of the nineteenth witnessed three challenges to the material and ideal foundations of the Vast Chain of Being: capitalism, democracy and nationalism. Capitalism, reflecting the continued expansion of commerce and industry and the growth of the factory system based on wage labour, found its expression in the growing language of markets, competition and class. The doctrine of *laissez-faire* offered a new ordering principle to society, replacing the eighteenth-century ideal of harmony. Democracy found its expression in the language of equality, mass and masses reflecting the growth of large urban centres with their swarming multitudes. The political doctrines of liberalism and individualism offered themselves up to society to contest the eighteenth-century ideal of hierarchy. Finally, nationalism, mirroring the increasing ethnic awareness and religious revivals of the nineteenth-century masses, offered its language of national self-determination. The doctrines of self-government and home rule challenged the language of mutual dependencies and obligations. Thus the eighteenth-century language of harmony, hierarchy and mutual obligation confronted that of capitalism, democracy and nationalism.

The material challenge to the old order appeared in the form of industrialisation and the rise of the great manufacturing towns. The attendant dislocations strained and often broke the links of mutual obligation sustaining the vast chain. Rising income inequality and declining agriculture produced corresponding increases in urban populations and disrupted even the best attempts to sustain the mutual obligations of the old order. Recent reinterpretations of mid-century inequalities indicate that in 1867 the top 5 per cent of population received 46 per cent of the income.[10] Moreover, the period witnessed a massive migration from the countryside to the new industrial centres, feeding both industry and poverty.[11] Under these conditions, the eighteenth-century language of harmony, hierarchy and obligation could no longer sustain the weight of the changing material circumstances.

By the 1830s 'the language of class' formed a nascent grammar of discourse on the nature of the social order. In contrast to Pope's references to an eternal hierarchy of rank, privilege and order, the new discourse found its referents in the sources of income introduced by Adam Smith in his *Wealth of Nations*: rent, capital and labour. The horizontal unity implied in the terms 'class' or 'classes' did not appear in its guise as a direct challenge to the hierarchy of the vast chain until well into the century. Rather, in its first representations class connoted a grouping or strata but without the overtones of a horizontal bonding or vertical conflict. Early commentators on the new term bemoaned it more for its connotations of equality and lack of deference than as a potential source of conflict in the social order.[12]

Paralleling the rise of the language of class with its potential for horizontal unities and vertical antagonisms was the breakdown of the principle of mutual obligations, raising the question: what would link the new classes together in society? In the absence of duty, obligation and mutual dependency, however unequal or malpractised, what mechanism would provide for harmonious running of the social order? The response came in the language of liberalism, utilitarianism and *laissez-faire* with its vocabulary of self-interest, contract, mutual dependency in the market and cashnexus.[13] Combined with notions of class, self-interest reformulated as class interest made a potent doctrine.

Although some commentators warned of such consequences earlier, the language of class did not assume its antagonistic character until the mid-nineteenth century when debates on suffrage expansion threatened to empower the lower orders.[14] Marx, whose name would become most associated with the notion of class conflict, was aware that he had neither originated the term nor invented the idea: 'No credit is due me for discovering the existence of classes in modern society nor yet the struggle between them. Long before me bourgeois historians had described the historical development of the class struggle and bourgeois economists the economic anatomy of the classes.'[15] Thus it was not class alone but class joined to the language of class interest that most threatened the old order. To this powerful mixture was added the language of democracy.

Particularly for the English, democracy raised the spectre of the mass and mob rule and presented three clear and eminent dangers: anarchy, mediocrity and tyranny.[16] Moreover, when united to the language of class, democracy imperilled the society based on property. The second language straining the vast chain of being therefore came in the idiom of democracy and equality. Anarchy was the most immediate threat posed by democracy. Earlier English reactions to the Revolution in France had given rise to a concern, if not outright phobia, of the undisciplined crowd. Canning gave voice to these concerns shared by many in 1820:

> Just so at the beginning of the French Revolution: the work of the Reformers was to loosen every established political relation, every legal holding of man to man, to destroy every corporation, to destroy every subsisting class of society, and to reduce the nation into individuals, in order to afterwards congregate them into mobs.[17]

Second, de Tocqueville, whose commentaries were widely read in Britain, posed a dilemma of democracy versus liberty, the latter being seen by the English as their central contribution to civilisation and the chief virtue of eighteenth-century society, as well as essential for society's creative genius. To the defenders of the vast chain, democracy threatened to repress the creativity of the aristocratic class with the crushing weight of the mass. De Tocqueville had spoken eloquently on the mediocrity inherent in American democracy where the passion for equality meant the ascendancy of ordinary men in public and intellectual life. Under such conditions, which Mill termed 'Chinese stationariness', intellectual conformity and mass taste would prevail.[18]

Finally Mill and others would write that the greatest threat to the individual was in democracy's 'tyranny of the majority'. As a consequence of progress in understanding politics and constitutions, Mill argued, tyranny in its classical form was less a threat than the new tyranny festering in civil society. Where once civil society was argued to be the bulwark against tyranny, now, for Mill and others, it became the breeding ground for even a more virulent French disease. For Salisbury and the Conservatives in the late nineteenth century, the polity must stand apart from the mass in order to preserve liberty; any attempt to subordinate the polity to society would ensure the new tyranny.

If the languages of class and mass were threats by themselves, their joining presented an even greater peril to the vast chain of being. For many writers such as Carlyle, capitalism with its language of class and democracy with the rhetoric of mass copulated to breed the mass society. Carlyle, who castigated The Gospel of Mammon as corroding the ties between men and emasculating the aristocracy of its social obligations, concluded:

> Our life is not a mutual helpfulness; but rather, cloaked under due laws-of-war, named 'fair competition' and so forth, it is mutual hostility. We have profoundly forgotten everywhere that *Cash-payment* is not the sole relation of human being; we think, nothing doubting, that *it* absolves and liquidates all engagements of man.[19]

Carlyle continued by stating that commerce and democracy had left the Aristocracy, that 'Corporation of the Best, of the Bravest' as a 'High Class without duties to do ... [was] like a tree planted on the precipices; from the roots of which all earth has been crumbling'.[20] For Mill the spread of commercial society and ideas of equality challenged the previous order and called into question how society would be governed:

> In the present stage of human progress, when ideas of equality are daily spreading more widely among the poorer classes, and can no longer be checked by anything short of the entire suppression of printed discussion and even of freedom of speech, it is not to be expected that the division of the human race into two hereditary classes, employers and employed, can be permanently maintained.[21]

In an age of the corrosion of the vast chain by the excoriating rhetoric of mass and masses and the rasping of language of cash and classes, governing the new order concentrated the minds of men. As the debates about the 1867 reform law intensified, the oratory grew more shrill, but did not end with the 'leap in the dark'. For Bagehot the 1867 reform act had transferred power to the lower classes while diluting that of the middle classes:' The middle classes have as little power as they had before 1832, and the only difference is that before 1832 they were ruled by those richer than themselves, and now they are ruled by those poorer.'[22]

The joining of the languages of capitalism and democracy to form the rhetoric of classes and masses intensified resistance among the Conservatives to franchise expansion where it was reformulated as the 'Classical Republican Problem'. No one expressed more deep reservations than Salisbury. Lord Salisbury, then Lord Cranborne, who would play a central role in the late Victorian period, eventually resigned from Disraeli's government over what he termed 'The Conservative Surrender' to the 'democracy of numbers' and the drift towards mass politics. For Salisbury, the franchise reform raised the 'Classical Republican Problem' in which the masses of poor would be agitated by demagogues and cast their ballots for the redistribution of property:

> The question of our destiny is one of extreme simplicity, and comparatively few years of trial will enable us to judge how it will be answered. A clear majority of the votes in a clear majority of the constituencies has been made over to those who have no other property but the labour of their hands. The omnipotence of Parliament is theirs, wholly and without reserve. Subject to them is a minority possessed in various degrees of a vast aggregate of accumulated wealth. If he were to set all considerations of conscience aside, each member of the poor but absolute majority would naturally desire so to use this new power as to make some portion of this wealth his own.[23]

Salisbury saw only two possibilities to avoid this outcome: 'Either the conscience of the working men will be so strong as to outweigh the suggestions of interest and the pressure of poverty, or they will not be clever enough to pull together for the purpose of gratifying their wishes.'[24]

Observing the same events from a different perspective, Marx delighted in the prospects of democracy as a stepping stone to socialism. In the 1867, again upon the passage of the Second Reform Act, he remarked 'that universal suffrage is the equivalent of political power for the working class of England, where the proletariat forms the large majority of the population'.[25]

However, neither Salisbury's dreads nor Marx's designs would come to fruition, although, as we shall see, Salisbury's would be closer to the mark. What neither Salisbury nor Marx could foresee was a third language straining the vast chain of being: the bravado of popular nationalism that would sweep across Europe in general and Britain in particular in the late nineteenth century. This tide would strain the links of the great chain in a different way, creating new collectivities based on common heritage, language and religion.

In the vast chain of being, religion linked with mutual obligation provided the justification for both duty and subordination. Religion, however, both united and divided eighteenth-century society. The religious wars of the previous epoch left their residues in all aspects of life, but were not equally resident across economy or geography. Perkin remarks on the 'familiar sandwich' of religion and social hierarchy in eighteenth-century England:

> From the Restoration settlement, when the Puritan aristocracy and gentry finally opted for the Church and left the sects to their social inferiors, the social structure of English religion became the familiar 'sandwich', with Anglicans (in some areas, such as rural Lancashire, Roman Catholics) at the top and bottom, and Dissenters in the middle.[26]

The rural and provincial character of life in the eighteenth century, however, meant relative isolation within the local area and, consequently, a significant degree of homogeneity. The result was that it was most common for the tenants of the great estates, as well as the freeholders and townspeople surrounding them, to follow the religion of the great house. Shared religion, then, reinforced the links of the vast chain.

> 'The arm of dependency was long, and even in the towns, especially in the market as distinct from the industrial towns, the tenants of local landowners, the professional men who served them, and those business men who hoped for some advantage, social, political or lucrative, from the association, tended to follow the landlord's religion.'[27]

Similar links of geography, economy and religion bound the Dissenters together. The Dissenters were found in the middle, geographically as well as socially. In the emerging industrial Midlands, Dissenters formed the new middle strata. In contrast to London, where the emerging commercial and financial strata came from or anxiously joined the Church, the middle strata of the future, great provincial cities were Nonconformist, a religious orientation they generally shared with their social inferiors.[28] Moreover, the Nonconformists' social reform zeal tended to forge bonds and links across the social strata in the industrial towns.

In the nineteenth century the uneven geography of religion became the basis for an ethnic revival among the middle class. In the early part of the eighteenth century, national traditions had languished in the Celtic fringe of Wales and Scotland, partly due to lack of interest and encouragement, but also to outright discouragement by the English. The last years of the eighteenth century and the first years of the nineteenth witnessed increasing interest among the middle classes in the national traditions and histories in the Celtic fringe of Britain.[29] Several factors fed the revival: the Romantic movement, religious revivalism and industrialisation. Ireland, of course, provides the most severe example of peripheral nationalism, but lies beyond the concerns of this research. However, there was considerable Irish migration to England and Scotland during the period, with important political implications. Irish migrants helped to generate a nativist reaction among other ethnic groups, furthering the rise of ethnic consciousness throughout Britain. Second, the question of Catholic emancipation became the focal point of much social tension. Catholic emancipation would mean Irish Catholic entry into parliament with all the attendant concerns of the Irish in both Ireland and throughout Britain. Harriet Martineau termed the question, 'the great political controversy of the day – the subject on which society is going mad'.[30]

Meanwhile, Scottish and Welsh nationalism evidenced stirrings. In 1778 the Highland Society was founded in London to encourage the preservation of Highland traditions, often of dubious authenticity.[31] Similar societies were founded in Wales at about the same time.[32] Their importance lay in seeking to uncover a distant and often indistinct past while promoting interest among middle-class urban intellectuals. In Wales, the movement was peculiarly linked to religious revivalism and Nonconformism. Morgan argues that evangelical Methodism between 1660 and 1730 was instrumental in both preserving the Welsh language as well as generating a reaction against the Methodist asceticism which found expression in a lust for a less moralistic folklore.[33] The result was a proliferation of societies interested in the Welsh past.

By the mid-nineteenth century nationalist revivalism was well under way in both Scotland and Wales, encouraged by similar movements in Ireland. Highland romanticism proved more pacific and less threatening to the English, particularly after Queen Victoria became so enamoured of its lore. Royal patronage did much to both promote and domesticate Scottish nationalism during the first two-thirds of the century. Queen Victoria's identification with Scottish lore was intertwined with her morose widowhood as much as Scott's romantic novels. On 15 October 1867, the twenty-eighth anniversary of her engagement to Albert, she had unveiled a statue of her beloved just above Middleston Lodge with an honour guard of the 93rd Highlanders. A year later, on 2 September 1868, she described her passage along the Loch Lomond Road in these terms:

> The scene today is all described in *Rob Roy* ... Most lovely ... Hardly a creature did we meet, and we passed merely a few pretty gentleman's places, or very poor cottages with simple women and barefooted long-haired lassies and children, quiet and unassuming old men and labourers. This solitude, the romance and wild loveliness of everything here, the absence of hotels and beggars, the independent simple people, who all speak Gaelic here, all make Scotland the proudest, finest country in the world.[34]

What Sir Walter Scott's writings and royal patronage did for the Highland lore, the Royal Commission's Blue Books of 1847 accomplished in a different manner for Welsh national identity. After decades of violence in Wales, reaching its crest in the 1830s with the Rebecca Riots, a government inquiry laid the responsibility upon dissenting religions and the Welsh language.[35] The reactions to the report and the on-going Anglicisation of Wales were strong, and intensified the nationalist fervour.[36] Moreover, linking rural protest to Welsh religion and language politicised the Nonconformist chapels as much as it alienated the intelligentsia, thereby militating against the domestication of Welsh nationalism along the lines of Scotland. Rising demands for disestablishment and home rule originate here. As Morgan states:

> By mid-century the growth of Nonconformity had come to create a fundamental line of division in Welsh life, polarising opinion in different areas in a way that class affiliations were not able to do. Nonconformity, not industrialism, was to form the basis of Welsh social and political development. As the gentry withdrew from national life, Nonconformist ministers became indisputable popular leaders, dominating press and pulpit.[37]

The spectre of Celtic nationalism, particularly in Ireland, raised grave concerns among the English and encouraged vulgar 'racial' theories of national character. By the 1840s such theories reached their nadir when the Celtic character was put on a par with the Gallic, and the English presented themselves as a civilised isle caught between Celtic savagery and the Gallic mob. In 1846 *The Economist* observed:

Thank God we are Saxons! Flanked by the savage Celt on the one side and the flighty Gaul on the other – the one a slave to his passions, the other a victim to the theories of the hour – we feel deeply grateful from our inner most hearts that we belong to a race, which if it cannot boast the flowing of fancy of one of its neighbours, nor the brilliant esprit of the other has an ample compensation in a social, slow reflective phlegmatic temperament.[38]

For the first two-thirds of the century England took scant notice of the rumblings in the periphery. Certainly Ireland was dealt with harshly when it was deemed necessary, but in most respects England assumed a posture towards the rising ethnic consciousness of the Celtic fringe similar to its other colonial possessions. Kearney appropriately describes these arrangements:

For much of the time the pattern of government within the United Kingdom rested upon alliances between Westminster and the local ascendancies of Wales, Ireland and Scotland. This situation began to change in mid-century when Irish Catholicism, Welsh Nonconformity and the Free Churches of Scotland formed an alliance with English dissent to bring pressure to bear upon the English establishment.[39]

However, by the latter part of the nineteenth century regional national movements demanded Home Rule. Joining the languages of classes, masses and races, late Victorian society confronted three challenges to the eighteenth-century ideal. These challenges were perhaps nowhere more evident than in the debates on the expansion of the political community.

EXPANDING THE POLITICAL COMMUNITY

Once joined, the rhetoric of classes, masses and races forged powerful new bonds in the social order and led to demands for participation in the polity. The expansion of the franchise, however, had two major consequences for political life, one more obvious than the other.

The less obvious effect of an enlarged electorate was the need for techniques to manage the multitudes. Since classical notions of the polity provided little guidance for incorporating large numbers of citizens, new mechanisms had to be developed to regulate and channel the participation of the greatly enlarged political community. Neither could existing techniques incorporate the multitudes into the polity. In the eighteenth century the power and awe of spectacle dominated and managed political life. The purpose of such spectacles was to bring the multitudes into public view where the power of the sovereign would be displayed. Such displays ranged from grand processions of the sovereign's wealth and might to bloody public executions exhibiting the sovereign's power over life and death. However, nineteenth-century society accommodated such techniques less fully for several reasons.[40] In general, the changing nature of society demanded altered disciplinary techniques: 'In a society in which the principal elements are no longer the community and the public life, but, on the one hand, private individuals and, on the other, the state, relations can be regulated only in a form that is the exact reverse of the spectacle.'[41] In particular, the technique of the spectacle did not lend itself well to a greatly enlarged electorate for, as soon became apparent, undisciplined mass politics was characterised by violence, high costs and fraud. Not that the technique of spectacle was immediately replaced; almost 50 years passed before the spectacle of public voting was supplanted by the secret ballot.

The language of the period mirrors these twin concerns: expanding democracy and managing multitudes. The debates of the period centre on the increasing worries of the political class for both its physical and financial security in mass elections. In addition, however, these debates reflected a deeper change in the relation of the citizen to the state. From the predominant concern of Classical political thought for the just and good citizen, the Renaissance gave birth to a new concern for the usefulness of the citizenry to the state's ends. No longer was the purpose of politics reflective of Plato's Republic, but rather the aggrandisement of state power. The citizenry became increasingly a means to this end, rather than the end of politics in itself. Political writings of the period evidence this change of concern. 'The increase and solidarity of this united power – not the freedom and virtue of the citizens, nor even their peace and tranquillity – was the ultimate goal set by these treatises.'[42] In this light, it is striking that Gladstone introduced his bill for franchise expansion in 1884 by arguing that each new citizen 'is an addition to the strength of the State'.[43]

However, even more striking were the mechanisms by which the new power could be realised. If the strength of the state were dependent on its citizenry, then it became important to ensure that new citizens performed in such a way as to fulfil this potential. The general problem was to effect the capacity latent in an unorganised multitude to become more economically efficient, more politically powerful and more militarily commanding than would be the mere sum of its components. The means of achieving this potential became the discipline of the multitudes. 'Discipline "makes" individuals; it is the specific technique of a power that regards individuals both as objects and as instruments of its exercise'.[44]

Before these concerns came to dominate democratic politics in the nineteenth century, they had their earlier parallels in other realms of society and economy. The resulting techniques sought to overcome the inefficiency of the mass, to master forces of unorganised multitude, to increase the effective utility of each individual in the multiplicity, and to replace weakened power from above with power relations within the multiplicity.[45] Two prominent English thinkers exemplify this thinking and both elaborated techniques for disciplining the individual to exploit the potential of the multitude: Jeremy Bentham and Adam Smith. It is significant that Foucault cites not a French example, but an English one, as the perfection of the new techniques: Bentham's Panopticon joined permanent surveillance by the authorities with discontinuous action by the inhabitants.[46] For, despite the self-view of the English ruling classes that liberty was the hallmark of England, others (from philosophers to philistines) were elaborating new disciplinary forms. Bentham's techniques, developed most fully in institutions such as prisons, schools, hospitals and factories, would only later (and in a limited degree) be applied to politics.

However, discipline raised a paradox when coupled to liberty, a paradox perhaps nowhere more evident than in Adam Smith's *The Wealth of Nations*. Smith is, of course, clearly identified with the market and his term 'the wealth of nations'. For some in the nineteenth century the market would become almost synonymous with liberty and guaranteed access to the market became a civil right. Moreover, Smith's use of the term 'wealth of nations' exemplifies the contradiction of liberty and discipline as well as the altered relation between the individual and the state, for the term 'wealth of nations' has two senses. First, the phrase was intended to convey not only the material well-being of the population, but second, and even more importantly, this material well-being as the basis for state power. Thus in Smith we see the clear shift to making the citizenry of the nation its principal source of strength. From here it is a small step to consideration of methods to harness the individual to this end. In the opening words of *The Wealth of Nations*, Smith clearly defines how the new wealth and hence state power will be created: by the division of labour, the segmentation of the tasks of production and their assignment to individuals. However, the division of labour entails not only the separation

of tasks into minute detail, but also the general organisation of labour
necessitating its collection, individuation, discipline, inspection and regi-
mentation. Smith describes precisely how the division of labour can best
be effected when 'those employed in every different branch of the work
can often be collected into the same workhouse, and placed at once under
the view of a spectator'.[47] In the same year that Smith published *The
Wealth of Nations*, Jedidiah Strutt built a new cotton mill at Belper. 'The
round structure embodied some revolutionary ideas. It was an attempt to
make a fire-proof building, the internal compartments being designed to
localise any outbreak wherever it occurred. Further, the foreman sat at the
hub of a wheel so to speak and could thence supervise the workers in each
compartment'.[48] In other words, it is the factory system with its disciplined work force where the potential of the division of labour is realised
for the strength of the state.

The methods developed by Bentham, Smith and others were never fully
applied to electoral politics. However, in the following chapter, we will
observe that the debates surrounding the franchise extension reflect both
these concerns: to enable the new citizens to participate in political life
and to ensure they participate in an orderly, disciplined but discontinuous
manner under the surveillance of the authorities. These dual concerns of
the expanded franchise and managing the multitude arose in unison
because the expansion of the franchise brought with it the problems of the
multitude which increased at an exponential rate: violence, cost and fraud.
As the number of electors increased so did the unruliness of elections.
Moreover, the massive bribery required to sway the great multitudes of an
enlarged electorate enormously increased the costs of office seeking.
Finally, the enlarged electorate created anonymous relationships in electoral politics and the resulting problem of determining who satisfied the
electoral qualifications. Two broad solutions evolved to meet these problems: first, the formal regulation of elections by the state to discipline the
electorate, reduce the costs of elections and determine the registry of
qualified voters; second, the rise of party, and party-affiliated, organisations to educate the new electorate to dance in their chains.

The more obvious consequence of the expanded franchise was the fuller
expression of issues of class and nationalism in electoral politics. The
debates surrounding franchise heightened the sense of these concerns in
politics. By the Second Reform Act of 1867 references to 'the people' and
'the mass' came to refer to the working classes rather than the middle
classes.[49]

Just as class entered the rhetoric of electoral politics, so too did ethnicity. Following the Second Reform Act of 1867, regional nationalism

began to find its expression in electoral politics as well. Liberal politicians quickly recognised its potential. In the 1868 election, the Liberals gained a foothold in Wales where three Nonconformists were returned to the Commons.

Following the 1868 election, Gladstone clearly understood the debt owed to a fuller expression of ethnic identities as well as the importance of organisation and discipline in an enlarged electorate. His statement, like Mill before him, uses the metaphor of an army, but now an army of ethnic voters summoned to support the party: 'our three corps d'armee, I may almost say, have been Scottish Presbyterians, English and Welsh and Irish Roman Catholics'.[50] With the passage of the Third Reform Act in 1884, class and ethnicity became the central concerns of British politics.

CONCLUSION

As the preceding discussion makes clear, the Victorian era forms a transition between the traditional order of the eighteenth century and the industrial society of the twentieth. Several languages of social order struggled for ascendancy. The outcome was an incomplete synthesis of the old order based on the language of rank, order and privilege and the newer society proclaiming the language of democracy, markets and ethnicity. The languages of masses, classes and races straining at Pope's 'vast chain of being' capture these dynamics.

To speak of change, however, is not to speak of abrupt disruptions in the definitions of the social order. Instead, important elements of the previous era's language of order continued well into the late Victorian period, with both the problems and the solutions couched in these terms. Neither did new definitions of the social order emerge fully articulated; instead, these evolved across the period. The language of Pope's vast chain, Carlyle's and Marx's capitalism, Disraeli's and Gladstone's democracy and Lord Salisbury's and Sir Walter Scott's empire overlapped and often conflicted with each other. As we examine the debates on franchise reform in the next chapter, we will see the influences of previous epochs.

Likewise, political behaviour evidenced similar incomplete synthesis. While political expressions of class and ethnicity became more possible under expanded democracy achieved by the reforms of 1883–5, these expressions were influenced by the language of the previous century's social order and, as would be expected, incorporated much of that vocabulary.

Thus, efforts to break the vast chain resulted neither in Pope's dire prediction nor in Marx's new world. Rather, the new classes began to 'educate their volition to dance in their chains'.

2 'A Deity of Equality' and 'Even a Safer Class of the Population': Debates on Expanding the Polity

The new philosophy [of equality] strikes further than at the existence of patriotism. It strikes at the home; it strikes at the individuality of man. It would reduce civilised society to human flocks and herds.

Benjamin Disraeli, 1872

We have made a little deity of equality. We have set it up as an idol and must take the consequences.

Robert Lowe, 1876

Those Radicals ... wish for equality right through, without qualification. They wish for equality among individuals: and therefore they are opposed to all honour or privileges which are transmitted by inheritance. From the same desire they are opposed to all inequalities in property: and by action of taxation, of succession laws, and of sundry other devices borrowed from the Socialist armoury, they hope to attain an absolute level, first in the ownership of land, and afterwards in all other kinds of ownership.

Lord Salisbury, 1883

I take my stand upon the broad principle that the enfranchisement of capable citizens, be they few or be they many – and if they be many so much the better – is an addition to the strength of the State.

William Gladstone, 1884

The language of the eighteenth century confronts that of the nineteenth in the words of Disraeli, Lowe, Salisbury and Gladstone. For Disraeli, Lowe and Salisbury democracy held the threat of mediocrity, anarchy and tyranny. In contrast, Gladstone saw in the masses an unrealised capacity for the State. These two distinct languages echo throughout the debates surrounding franchise reforms leading up to the 1883–5 milestones.

21

Despite their differences, however, a common concern united these two perspectives on democracy: the precise mechanisms by which the new citizenry could be incorporated, managed and, indeed, disciplined such that their potential could be realised. At each step in the democratic process, politicians were quick to see and exploit the potential of the expanding electorate. Each new sector of the electorate offered new concerns, issues and opportunities to office seekers. Moreover, the concerns of the political class about democracy were further tempered in Britain by the demonstrated power of a disciplined multitude in peace and war on the continent. However, would it be possible to realise this potential without succumbing to the French disease? This question became more pressing as it became more clear that further franchise expansion would exacerbate three inherent problems of mass electorates, which had already made their presence felt: unruliness, cost and anonymity.

In tracing the debates surrounding the expansion of the franchise culminating in the 1883–5 reforms, it is easy to underestimate the importance of their final passage. To do so is to miss a crucial turning point in British political history. While the reforms did not achieve universal suffrage, they did accept it in principle. While the measures clearly fell short of the 'arithmetic democracy' so feared by both Aristotle and Salisbury, they substantially moved British electoral politics towards the principle of 'one-adult, one-value, one-vote'. Second, the reforms secured the mechanisms for managing the mass electorate. Finally, the measures facilitated the expression of social and economic conflicts which would have been almost impossible under the old regime.

The importance of the 1883–5 reforms are highlighted by several scholars.[1] The shift from a hierarchical polity to a far more democratic one, which culminated in the 1883–5 reforms, began as a long series of electoral reforms following the First Reform Act of 1832. Three themes link these efforts: first, the reforms slowly expanded the size of the political community by admitting new property qualifications for citizenship. While these expansions altered the links in the vast chain, in many ways they also sustained the representation of property and the principle of hierarchy until well into the nineteenth century. Second, a series of measures, which responded to the increasing corruption and violence accompanying the enlarged electorate, culminated in the Ballot Act of 1872 and the Elimination of Corrupt Practices Act of 1883. These acts sought to regulate the sole legally recognised political act available to the mass of the new citizenry. The effect was to reduce the influence of the property and patronage that sustained the vast chain by privatising and disciplining political life. Third, the admission of new blocks of electors opened the

possibility for a fuller expression of issues of class and ethnicity in electoral politics. Thus, the history of British electoral reforms in the nineteenth century is an apparent paradox: the expansion of the political
community having direct representation while at the same time vastly con-
tracting the realm of political life.

'LOOK NOT TO PARLIAMENT, LOOK ONLY TO YOURSELVES'

It may seem odd to begin an analysis of electoral reforms and their consequences with a discussion of the Poor Law Reforms, however, these
reforms marked an important turning point in the concepts of citizenship
and civil rights. Richard Cobden's counsel[2] to the working classes in the
1840s captures this spirit which Marshall summarised thus:[3]

> [C]ivil rights were indispensable to a competitive market economy.
> They gave to each man, as part of his individual status, the power to
> engage in the economic struggle and made it possible to deny him social
> protection on the grounds that he was equipped with the means to
> protect himself.

The significance of the New Poor Law in our analysis is thus two-fold: it
embodied important notions of citizenship rights and it helped to launch
the market economy; both were crucial to corroding the vast chain.

The New Poor Law itself was less important than what it symbolised:
the re-writing of the labour code for Britain which greatly weakened the
hierarchical links in society. The existing labour code derived from three
laws dating from Elizabethan times. These laws provided the legal underpinnings for the ranks, orders and corporations of eighteenth-century
society by severely limiting the functional and geographical mobility of
labour. Even before the passage of the New Poor Law, many of the provisions of these three acts had fallen into disuse. Nevertheless, the passage
of the New Poor Law symbolised the removal of several of the most burdensome impediments to a free labour market, and for this reason its
importance often has been cited.[4]

Our immediate interest, however, lies more in the language and debates
surrounding the Poor Law reforms. The arguments for repeal of the Poor
Laws drew their language from the nascent notions of the market, equality
and citizenship. Repeal of the Old Poor Law was held necessary for
numerous reasons, including corruption, ineffectiveness and inefficiency;
however, present in the arguments was the still inchoate notion of the self-

reliant, self-governing individual as a 'free agent' in the market.[5] This view of the individual stood in stark contrast to the vast and permanent hierarchy fixed by the law since Elizabethan times.

The new political economy embodied the subversive and democratic notion that all individuals are equal in their 'propensity to truck, barter and exchange' and that it was the market, not their position in the vast chain of being, that generated the differences among them. Instead of the language of inherited ranks, orders and degrees, of which Salisbury would continue to speak over 100 years later, the new orders were defined by their sources of income.

As this notion gained currency, it was a small step to conclude that if the market were not permitted to function, the virtues of the lower ranks would be corrupted. Into this category fell the ill effects of the poor laws on the unemployed. Nassau Senior, later a member of the Royal Commission of 1834, remarked to Melbourne in 1831 on the 'idleness and improvidence occasioned by making up wages out of rates'.[6] The new political economy gained acceptance among the political elite as well; the chief sponsor of the bill, Lord John Russell, had read political economy at Edinburgh, not classics at Oxford or Cambridge as had most his contemporaries.[7]

Where as the Old Poor Law was premised on the right of individuals to a minimum standard of living, the New Poor Law limited such claims only to those lacking full citizenship. Citizens, that is, adult males, were held to be 'free agents' and enjoyed the protection of civil rights of contract. Nowhere was this more evident than in the conditions governing claims for relief. Upon claiming relief and entering the workhouse individuals declared themselves paupers, forfeited their civil rights of personal liberty and any political rights they possessed. Forfeiture of political rights in poverty remained until 1918. 'The stigma which clung to relief expressed the deep feelings of a people who understood that those who accepted relief must cross the road that separated the community of citizens from the outcast company of the destitute.'[8]

The second implication of the New Poor Law found expression in the representation of the market as an autonomous, natural sphere of activity subject to its own laws and best left unmolested. The New Poor Law reflected this thinking when it 'renounced all claims of trespass on the territory of the wages system, or to interfere with the forces of the free market'.[9] As Macaulay stated in the 1846 debate on the Ten Hours Bill: 'it is not desirable that the State should interfere with the contracts of persons of ripe age and sound mind, touching matters purely commercial'.[10] Standing behind this thinking was the logic that if economic dependency was not political, then each individual was free to enter or alter economic relationships. Moreover, since such relations were not political, redress of grievances was provided under the individual's civil rights exercised in the courts and was not the appropriate domain of state interference.[11] Finally, the 'principles of 1834' mandated that a poor person 'ought to be deterred from seeking relief and thus encouraged to fend for himself'.[12]

The New Poor Law challenged the vast chain at several links: first, it marked a fundamental shift in the concept of society from one based on rank, order and degree secured by the virtues of mutual obligations, service to society and responsibility for others, to one based on individual self-reliance and self-help. One historian called it the:

> most revolutionary economic measure of the early nineteenth century. The New Poor Law swept away the old principle of the right to work or maintenance, the idea that society has some responsibility for its members; it substituted the idea ... of treating human beings as individuals who must struggle for themselves or else succumb.[13]

Second, while it did not create, it permitted the expansion and flourishing of the market economy in labour. Thus, it functioned as 'an aid to capitalism because it relieved industry of all social responsibility outside the contract of employment, while sharpening the edge of competition in the labour market'.[14] Together these reforms ate away at the links of Pope's chain by legalising the autonomy of the market and providing it with, in Carlyle's words, the immunity from the duties 'mutual helpfulness' as 'it absolve[d] and liquidate[d] all engagements of man'.[15]

However, at the same time as the new law repealed the social rights embodied in the Old Poor Law, it also expanded and extended the civil rights of citizenship. By implication the labourer as citizen was empowered now with the rights of contract undergirded by his 'perfect liberty' as a free agent in the market. Finally, those possessing such liberty and adult capacities were deemed not to be in need of the support of the state. It was only non-citizens and those lacking in capacity who continued to receive the protection from the market. Parallel arguments were present in the franchise reforms.

'OF THE "ENLARGEMENT OF THE FRANCHISE", AND OTHER VAGARIES'

Mid-Victorian society was characterised by a sense of impending change. Signs were evident that the ancient links that bound society together were under stress, but little security was evident in the future of the these bonds. Throughout the period the economic order was usually portrayed as the causal force behind the impending political changes. Some, like Lord Ashley in 1848, were keenly aware of change, but found little solace in the new language of markets and democracy:

> All things are tending to change. We are entering on a new political dispensation; and many of us probably will outlive the integrity of our aristocratic institutions. Men are talking, they know not why, and they reflect not *how*, of *this* slight concession and *that*; of the 'enlargement of the franchise', and other vagaries.[16]

Intense intellectual efforts were consumed endowing the market as the new natural order of society while the political realm was portrayed as constructed from human weakness and necessity.[17] Moreover, when market arguments were coupled to progressive notions of development, political demands came to be seen as the natural outgrowth of economic progress.[18] J.S. Mill, for example, could formulate clearly that economic change gave rise to the need for political change and that politics should reflect the contributions of productive labour, as Smith called it, not merely tradition and privilege: 'Of the working men of Europe, it may be pronounced certain that the patriarchal or paternal system of government is one to which they will not again be subject.'[19] For the Chartists economic progress was linked to political rights and was expressed by Hartwell in 1837:

> It seems to me to be an anomaly that in a country where the arts and sciences have been raised to such height, chiefly by industry, skill and labours of the artisan ... only one adult male in seven should have a vote, that in such a country the working classes should be excluded from political life.[20]

THE FIRST REFORM ACT OF 1832

If there was some agreement that the language of the market and class had strained the links of the vast chain and necessitated some corresponding changes in the polity, there was less agreement on how the new links should be forged. Throughout the period 'democracy' remained a term of abuse and opprobrium; only Chartists and other radicals could speak in democratic terms.

In the debates surrounding the First Reform Act of 1832, the participants were keenly aware of the consequences of the expansion of political rights. The forces of economic change, domestic political agitation, partisan advantage and events in France all influenced the discussion, but these arguments were held in check by a commanding dread of 'arithmetic democracy'. The overriding concern focused on democracy's impelling logic which de Tocqueville articulated and Burke so abhorred: if once the principle of political equality were accepted, even in the slightest degree, there would be little argument for stopping its expansion. Moreover, with political equality, all the institutions of society would be in jeopardy engendering the unthinkable consequence that 'the great scale's destroy'd'. Peel expressed this openly and clearly when he stated his opposition to an expanded franchise: 'I was unwilling to open a door which I saw no prospect of being able to close.'[21]

Yet, if full democratic equality of persons was unacceptable, what alternative could be advanced to overcome the grievances articulated by Russell and Palmerston on corruption and misrepresentation of the current system while avoiding the 'state of diseased and feverish excitement' so evident across the Channel? The answer appeared in the guise of arguments on the nature of property taken from the eighteenth-century ideal: remedies lay not in the representation of individual citizens, but in the representation of communities and interests overwhelming defined by 'the natural relationship to property', as Disraeli expressed it. Thus the principal objections to the existing legislation could be incorporated into contemporary language: the deficiencies of the current state of affairs lay in the fact that some interests remained underrepresented, not that individuals *qua* citizens were not represented.[22] The salient point for the Whigs was that economic change gave rise to new forms of property found in the commercial and industrial interests which should be represented in the polity. This can be seen quite clearly in the manner of re-allocation of two-member seats; 'the essential feature was the principle of selecting substantial interests and real communities for enfranchisement rather than attempting to build a uniform structure on a numerical basis'.[23]

The principle of community interests was even more evident in the debate on the representation of the universities which clearly emboldened the principle of representation of corporations. The government recently had enfranchised Trinity College, Dublin, on the grounds of representing the community and interests of the Church of England. As Althorp, Chancellor of the Exchequer, explained to O'Connell speaking on the representation of the universities:

It was deemed expedient that Oxford and Cambridge should possess their present elective system as a means of protecting the interests of the Established Church; and in conformity with that principle it was thought but fair that the interests of the Established Church in Ireland should be equally protected in that House. On that ground too, he must tell the honourable and learned member from Waterford, that franchise ought to be confined to Protestant scholars.[24]

While the representation of interests and communities remained the central organising principle, it was the 'natural relation to property' which determined the principle in practice. Property itself came to be seen as a surrogate for including the most meritorious of the population in political decision-making. What is essential in this view of representation was the notion that electors represented communities of interests, not their self-interests alone, and that, as electors, they spoke for those interests.

This very notion of electors as representatives of community interests reaffirmed the principle represented by the vast chain of being as well as provided a powerful argument in favour of public voting and against the secret ballot. Since electors cast their ballots as representatives of the community, it was held desirable that the community should know their vote. If the ballot was secret, electors would be immune from the scrutiny of their communities and might exercise their judgement irresponsibly.

'It was said he paid a thousand pounds for five votes'

Thus complained Edward Seymour upon his son-in-law's loss of a seat at Horsham in 1847.[25]

Expanded suffrage in the name of new property forms and public elections in the name of responsibility gave rise to extreme corruption. Politics increasingly became an intensely public spectacle, open to a remarkable range of influence and potential abuse.[26] Efforts to stem corrupt practices and undue influence followed almost immediately the expansion of franchise in 1832 as the potential for corruption was realised. Proposals for the secret ballot were defeated on the grounds that they countermanded the principles of the constitution of the country and would encourage corruption of the principle of indirect representation.[27] The early acts of 1841 and 1842 aimed at reducing corruption were generally ineffective. A major step was taken with the Corrupt Practices Act of 1854 which, while hardly completely successful, marked the beginning of series of reform measures.[28] What is so essential to note about elections under the open system was the acute politicisation of public life, often accompanied by considerable bribery and violence. It would not be lost on reformers of a later period that, in the absence of a secret ballot, the politicisation of the electorate would only increase as the electorate was expanded, threatening the very legitimacy of the state. As one witness before the parliamentary committee in 1842 remarked, violence had become so widespread that given the 'inconvenience of the innocent electors of an election ... the electors would be glad if the town was disfranchised'.[29]

THE SECOND REFORM ACT OF 1867

> There is a principle in the county franchise when you deal with it, and it is this – the franchise must be a county franchise. It must be a suffrage exercised by those who have a natural relation to the chief property and chief industry of the county. Those who are to exercise it ought to be members of the same community, and not strangers.

Thus Disraeli expressed the Conservative position in speaking to the county franchise reform of 1867.[30] Disraeli's comment reaffirmed the Conservative principles underpinning the franchise. Lord Elcho, leader of the influential Adullamites, echoed Peel: once the qualifications for suffrage were lowered there would be no stopping short of complete household democracy. In this he had the support of Disraeli who maintained as late as 1859 that,[31] 'It would be injudicious, not to say intolerable, when we are guarding ourselves against the predominance of a territorial aristocracy, that we should reform Parliament by securing the predominance of a household democracy.' As Cowling notes, the parliamentary debates over the 1867 reform bill contain 'no general advocacy of the democratic franchise, electoral districts or equality between the worth of one vote and another'. Rather there existed 'an overwhelming anxiety to establish that nothing should be done to destroy the alliance of responsibility, respectability, wealth and status on one hand and the possible new electorate on the other'.[32]

Maintaining this responsibility and respectability would be ensured by the continuance of the principles of representation of natural communities embodied in the 1832 act. Abstract equality of individuals embodied no such natural community. From this reasoning equality of representation does not follow. 'The idea of electoral districts, or of distribution of seats based on upon exact equality of population, was bitterly decried by both parties.'[33] Thus Russell, Walpole and Disraeli could reject population as a guide to representation because it would subvert the natural relationship to property and thus the principle which ensured the harmony and hierarchy, the balance and moderation, the privilege and responsibility of the constitution. The representation of individuals would subvert the constitution by shifting the power to a numerical majority sharing no natural community and would usurp the rights of representation of other constituencies. On this principle the advantages of small boroughs rested with only the Radicals protesting.

If the 'natural relation to property' was the organising principle of representation, however, the exact nature of that property was more contentious. Debates over the borough franchise centred on the amount and nature of the property holding rather than on 'the chief property' as the basis of community of interests. Central to this debate was the character of those enfranchised by various schemes, with opposition to the propertyless working classes as a consistent theme. Eventually the notion of 'household franchise' appeared and, once introduced, the inevitability of democratic logic made it difficult to withdraw. 'As Gladstone admitted, once the phrase had been advertised as its battleground, its force was irresistible.'[34] The important elements of the final bill were several: the number of electors in the boroughs more than doubled, enfranchising a significant portion of the working class and leading to the predictions of Marx and Engels for their triumph. However, the overall impact was checked by the balance of the county franchise and the continuation of numerous anomalies to democratic logic. More important was the move away from the principle of community of interests based on the natural relation to the chief property embodied in the household franchise, and this marked 'the first decisive event in what has been called the "transition to democracy"'.[35]

Resistance to arithmetic democracy remained strong within some elements of the Conservatives. Salisbury was so distraught by the prospect embodied in the 1867 reform, he resigned from Disraeli's government. In 1869 he reflected on the atmosphere leading up to the bill's passage:

A vague idea that the poorer men are the more easily they are influenced by the rich; a notion that those whose vocation it was to bargain and battle with the middle classes must on that account love the gentry; an impression – for it could be no more – that the ruder class of minds would be more sensitive to traditional emotions; and an indistinct application to English politics of Napoleon's (then) success in taming the revolution by universal suffrage; all these arguments, never thought out, by floating in men's minds, and accepted as motives for action at a time when the party battle was too hot to admit for close reflection, went to make up the clear conviction of the mass of the

Conservative party, that in a Reform Bill more Radical than that of the Whigs they had discovered the secret of a sure and signal triumph.[36]

Despite popular agitation for manhood suffrage, Salisbury's scepticism had triumphed and the principle never stood much likelihood of success in the debates; a similar fate awaited efforts to secure the secret ballot. *The Times* had noted that electoral morality had reached a nadir in the previous election of 1865. It was not unusual for upwards of one-third of the electorate to receive or give bribes in the contest.[37] The reform bill, however, had been given precedence over the Corrupt Practices at Elections Bill; the latter was not introduced until the former had gone to committee in April of 1867. The result was the Corrupt Practices Act of 1868. Its most significant feature was the transfer of electoral petitions of alleged corruptions from the House Elections Committee to the judiciary to be tried in the local courts of the petition instead of London. It was generally held that the new procedures helped to reduce corruption, but hardly eliminated excessive expenditure, riots and intimidation.[38] The public character of elections brought forth considerable violence and pointed up the consequences of an expanded electorate forced to declare themselves in public.[39]

THE BALLOT ACT OF 1872

It seems to me that [the secret ballot] might succeed in counteracting some of the most legitimate influence exercised by one class over another, but that it will leave the poorer classes open to all the influences of corruption by which they can be moved.

Thus, Lord Argyll, a Liberal, declaring his opposition to the secret ballot, wrote to Gladstone in 1870.[40]

In the same year a parliamentary Select Committee held hearings on the need for the reform of electoral corruption. The committee considered four solutions to corruption, but alighted on the secret ballot as the best remedy. The proposal required Gladstone to alter his previously held position that the franchise was held in trust by the elector and thus should be made public. Instead he argued that the vast expansion of the electorate in 1867 created conditions in which this was no longer practical, an apparent reference to violence provoked by public voting. Moreover, Gladstone continued, since universal suffrage was inevitable the ballot made good sense. This remark provoked a major reaction, reflecting as it did the logic of the inevitability of democracy.[41] Meanwhile, the opposition held fast. Lord Argyll continued: 'The motives under which men act in secret are as a general rule inferior to those under which they act in public.'[42] Nevertheless, the final version of the bill included provisions for complete secrecy on the grounds that only by eliminating any possible proof of how the elector voted could the sale of ballots be terminated.

The secret ballot broke the vast chain of being by privatising the only officially recognised form of political participation. In the absence of public spectacle and observation by the upper orders, the links could not hold. In principle, the secret ballot meant that the elector must be seen in a new light: as the representative of his own self-interest rather than as trustee of a community of interests, a striking parallel to the view of the individual in the labour market. The representation of individuals as *citizen units* shifted away from the historic principle of Disraeli's that politics must represent communities and interests with a 'natural relation to property'.

The Act was remarkably successful in achieving its stated purposes. First, the secret ballot almost eliminated direct corruption since, however much he wanted to advocate the community's interests, the elector had no means of proving he had done so. Second, the privatisation of the vote altered the nature of elections from a public spectacle to a solitary political act divorced from the community. In this respect the act achieved its second aim: the reduction of violence and intimidation surrounding the public spectacle of voting.

However, by cutting off the voter from the influence of his superiors, the ballot not only severed yet another link in the vast chain of influence and privilege in politics: it also sequestered the economically dependent from his peers. For if the landed, industrial and commercial classes no longer could intimidate and buy the votes of their tenants and workers, neither could the tenants and workers exert direct influence on each other in the voting booth. Once in the voting booth the elector could cast his ballot for any reason or non-reason.[43]

The long run effects of the privatisation of the vote was the depoliticization of elections. Even by the first elections under the new law, *The Times* noted: 'No bands of music paraded in the town. No colours or banners were seen in procession. The church bells were silent ... . Both at Pontefract and Knottingley the topic was the dullness of the election. 'It hardly seemed like an election,' the tradespeople said; and they were right.'[44] Similar reports soon came from elections in Preston, Leeds, Liverpool and Manchester: 'The excitement and riots which had characterised the open nomination and polling were largely eliminated, and the factor of violence disappeared almost entirely from the electoral contests.'[45]

THE REFORM ACTS OF 1883–5

> The safe workings of the household franchise in Boroughs has removed, in the judgement of your Majesty's advisers, all, even the most shadowy, grounds for apprehension from the disfranchisement of what may be considered as even a safer class of the population.

Thus wrote Gladstone to the Queen in January of 1884, informing her of the cabinet's decision to seek electoral reform in the coming year.[46]

For some time reform pressures had been building to alter the relationships of dependency in the polity further. Under the electoral reforms of 1867 the franchise had been extended, but the principles of representation remained unaltered. The 1870s witnessed the increasingly anomalous position of the individual to the polity. Three general causes lay behind the need for reform: first, the enormous change in society and economy had dramatically altered property relationships; second, the effects of the previous political reforms, particularly the Second Reform Act of 1867 and the Secret Ballot Act of 1872, had enlarged the electorate and altered the traditional relationship among the links of the political chain, a condition which all had found increasingly difficult to live with; finally, the various electoral reforms between 1867 and 1872 led to a series of anomalies in representation. These three factors favoured the passage of the three great milestones in British political history: the Elimination of Corrupt and Illegal Practices Act of 1883, the Third Reform Act (Franchise Expansion) of 1884, and the Redistribution of 1885. The significance of the acts lay in their transformation of political life: the final breaking of the great chain, the expansion of the political community while restricting the formal channels of participation and the opening of electoral politics to the voices of class, mass and the savage Celt.

The Elimination of Corrupt Practices Act, 1883

> I am afraid I am in a small minority in the Party in the House of Commons – who only think of one thing – lessening the cheque to be drawn on their bankers.

So wrote W.H. Smith, Disraeli's 'bookstall man'. complaining to Salisbury on the rising costs of election campaigning in 1883.[47]

The Ballot Act of 1872 had divorced voting from direct outside influences, dramatically reducing direct bribery, violence, personation and intimidation. However, if the direct cost of individual votes declined markedly, the costs of collective bribery rose equally. Instead of directly buying individual votes, candidates resorted to the extensive use of collective corruption: for example, great treats, picnics, entertainments, excursions, and so forth. In addition, candidates' typical expenses included funds to maintain the electoral register, usually requiring the retention of a solicitor, moneys to support all charities and institutions in the constituency, as well as funds to build club buildings and libraries.[48] Coupled to the expanded electorate these costs became increasingly burdensome.

The burdens borne by the candidates were the remnants of the vast chain of mutual obligations embodied in the 'natural relationship to property' and were particularly heavy in the rural and small town constituencies where the traditional bonds between lord and tenant continued. The Ballot Act of 1872 bared these relationships for, if these expectations continued from one side of the relationship, the reciprocity of those less well-off could no longer be observed as a result of the secret ballot. The exceedingly high expenses of the 1880 election, coupled to several incidents of extreme corruption, were the immediate causes for placing corruption reform on the parliamentary agenda.

However, it was not merely a matter of the probity, but the bankruptcy, of the political class, particularly the gentry whose position was already diminished by industrial and commercial expansion and the decline of agriculture. Electoral expenses were bound to increase as the size of the electorate grew, either by natural increment or franchise expansion. Sir Henry James (Liberal Attorney-General) noted both these causes during the second reading of the bill:

If the expenditure were to be increased, and were to continue to increase, even if there were no great abnormal change in the way of additions to constituencies, it was manifest that the effect must be that men of position in the country would be driven to refuse to become candidates. The old influence of a man's name or position, or worth, was gradually being destroyed by the mere fact of wealth, and often the unmeritorious wealth, of his opponents.[49]

Hence, one drive behind the legislation was not to lower electoral expenses in order to admit less well-off candidates, although the Radicals thought this might develop and no doubt W.H. Smith would have appreciated it, but rather to preserve the traditional place of the landed classes in the political landscape. Nevertheless, the unintended consequence of the Act unlocked political offices for a new class of potential candidates; and, when coupled to the changing sources of wealth and the emergence of new organisations and collectivities, a major step toward democracy ensued.

A second reason given for needed reforms was that excessive expenditure corrupted and incited the electors and contributed to the violence of the process. As the electorate expanded, fear of its unruliness increased proportionately. Thinkers such as Bagehot and Lowe complained bitterly of the threat of 'a great seething and swaying mass' and its threats to the polity.[50] But as distasteful as it might be, if the franchise was to be expanded, then the electorate must be disciplined by lessening exorbitant expenditures. Expenditures should be limited to those necessary to educate the voters. As Gorst stated: 'All that was really required was that the constituencies should have the means of amply being informed, or informing themselves, of the character, qualifications and political views of the candidates.'[51] All other expenditures were excessive.

The provisions of the Act specified three areas governing electoral expenses: (1) persons who might be legally employed for promoting the candidacy, (2) additional expenses beyond personnel for advertising and printing, (3) penalties, classification of illegal practices and expense maxima determined by the number of electors.[52] The effect of the Act was to reduce expenses by about half compared to the 1868 and 1880 elections.[53] 'Not merely did the provisions prove practical, but because of them electioneering was radically transformed', and both the costs and corruption were dramatically reduced.[54] Despite an 80 per cent increase in the electorate in 1884, electoral expenditures decreased by 41 per cent between 1880 and 1885.[55] In addition, incidents of reported corruption declined and were dealt with more harshly.[56] Although it is impossible to calculate exact figures, an estimate of the cost of the average election still presented insurmountable financial barriers to all but the most affluent and remained well beyond the typical wage earner. The cost of a typical election was about 100 times the yearly earnings of the average wage earner in 1886, but this was a marked decrease from a factor of 1000 in 1880.[57]

The Third Reform (Franchise Expansion) Act, 1884

What do the public interests require the Government to undertake ... ? I entertain no doubts that the equalisation of the suffrage is the question of questions for the time.

With these words Gladstone undertook his campaign for franchise reform in 1884.[58]

When the Conservatives had passed the franchise extension in 1867, Disraeli and the Young England movement had expected to benefit from the influx of new electors, much as the Whigs had benefited from the 1832 reforms. Franchise appeared as a means of incorporating and taming the demands for change, thereby shackling them with the vast chain of being, an argument which, as we have seen, Salisbury violently disputed. By the mid1870s Salisbury's warnings appeared to bear fruit: it was becoming increasingly clear that the poorer class was not always guided by their betters. As often as not the lower orders were deeply suspicious of the interventions and offerings, however well intentioned, of the ranks, orders and corporations above them.[59]

The 1884 act increased the eligible electorate by 80 per cent to about 17.5 per cent of the total population, 29.7 per cent of the adult population and 63.3 per cent of the adult male population. Blewett considers even these figures an exaggeration, adjusting the figure to 59 per cent of the adult male population.[60] Certainly, the Act did not achieve universal male suffrage and it continued a variety of anomalies, such as plural voting and cumbersome registration requirements. Two groups remained systematically excluded: resident servants and sons living with their parents. The largest class in the new electorate became the household franchise, consisting of 84 per cent of the electorate in 1911.[61]

The Registration Act of 1885

> The existing registration law in this country is utterly bad. It belongs to a time when a vote was a privilege not a right, and when it had the effect of keeping people off the registrar.

Thus James Stuart, a Radical, observed in the debate in the House in 1892 over an attempt to reform the electoral registration laws.[62] Registration in some form had been part of the franchise since the 1832 Reform Act, which empowered the 'overseers of poor' to determine the qualifications of the electors and to deprive those on relief of their political rights. Between the First and the Third Reform Acts, the difficulties of the registration procedures became increasingly apparent.[63]

Following further expansion of the franchise in 1867, complexities in administering the law and its manipulation for political purposes increased demands for change, and in 1878 the proposed substance of the 1873 law was passed. By simplifying the registration process and limiting challenges to electors, the law significantly expanded the electorate. Seymour estimates that these procedures expanded the electorate more than the

Second Reform Act itself.[64] However, the 1878 Act applied only to the boroughs; its extension to the counties had to wait until 1885. The Registration Act of 1885 made the registration procedures identical for the counties and boroughs.

Of equal significance the 1885 Act facilitated and formalised the information to be provided to the overseers, increased the frequency of voter qualification reports and generally continued the gradual intrusion of state power into the social realm. The obvious purpose of registration was to ensure that only qualified electors participated. However, the evolution of the procedures corresponded with the need to deal with a greatly expanded electorate whose qualifications were not obvious. To overcome this problem it became necessary to gather and co-ordinate more information on the electorate.

The greater significance of the registration process lay in its long term effects of quieting and disciplining the electorate. Seymour summed up the importance in these words:

> But the more satisfactory operation of the registration system was not entirely a result of the rather slight amendments introduced in 1878 and 1885. In all probability time rather than the statutory change had been a great settling factor. It must be remembered that registration was new to England in 1832 and it would have been surprising had the process proved acceptable before the rough edges had been worn by years of practice. Slowness is a characteristic of the English and the halfcentury does not seem too long a period in which to accustom the newly enfranchised people to the mechanism of registration.[65]

The Registration Act, therefore, figured as another important element in the creation and disciplining of the mass electorate. The Ballot Act had made the vote a private matter, thereby removing voting from the public spectacle and helping to reduce corruption and violence at the polls. The Elimination of Corrupt Practices Act sought to reach areas not covered by previous efforts by regulating electoral practices more closely. Coupled to the Registration Act these made possible the expansion of the electorate in 1884, while limiting the scope of political life. One element remained to facilitate the fuller expression of social divisions in electoral politics.

The Redistribution Act of 1885

> It is not satisfactory; but, it is probably all that can be had ...; but one thing strikes me painfully – that no one seems to have any knowledge or

intelligent forecast of what will be the result of all this. It is another leap in the dark.

So wrote Lord Carnarvon, echoing Dilke's famous remark on the 1867 reforms upon reflecting on the Conservative acceptance of the Redistribution Act.[66]

To secure passage of franchise reform, the Liberal government agreed to take up the redistribution of parliamentary seats and promised that the new franchise would not be acted upon until such time. The redistribution represented a compromise between traditional forms of representation and democratic principles. Its essential features, reached in the Arlington Street Compact among the party leaders, retained the established representation principles with the overrepresentation of Scotland, plural voting, some plural member districts and representation of the universities. It advanced towards 'arithmetic democracy' with an increase in single-member districts, more equal representation of the boroughs and counties and the disenfranchisement of smaller centres.[67] Most importantly is reduced the ratio of the smallest to the largest electorates to 1:8 from 1:250.[68] Attempts to make the reform more democratic by proportional representation failed.

The importance of the Redistribution Act lay in its creation of more homogeneous districts. Combined with the principle of single-member districts, it shifted 'the emphasis in politics from the interests which all classes in a particular community hold in common to the interests which particular classes had in common with similar classes in other communities'.[69] The result was increased partisan voting with parties advocating more narrowly articulated appeals. As Cornford noted in commenting on increased party voting for the Conservatives:[70]

What happened between 1880 and 1885 was not a mass conversion [to Conservatism], but the Redistribution Act, with its allocation of seats and its single member constituencies. Where Conservative supporters had formerly been swamped in huge constituencies, they were now high and dry on an island of their own.

What fitted the Conservatives was equally applicable to other parties as well. Indeed, in the debates on redistribution, G.J. Goschen warned precisely of this situation:[71] 'Let us beware that the single member constituencies do not develop into single class constituencies, whose members will come here feeling themselves responsible, not to the whole people of the country, but to the particular class living in the district by which they are returned.'

The three reforms of 1883–5 created conditions which permitted the political expression of a deeply altered society in late Victorian Britain. Corrupt practices reforms restricted, but did not eliminate, the more direct influences of the upper classes on the economically dependent. The expansion of the franchise, however limited, expanded the political community while at the same time opening the way to challenges to its definition. Finally, the redistribution act brought the representative system closer to the newly forming collectivities.

REACTIONS TO THE 'DEITY OF EQUALITY'

The Conservatives and democracy

Alas! How right we were in 1867!, we have been in the full tide of democracy consequent on the 1867 Bill, for many years, without knowing it.

Thus concluded Lord Eustace Cecil in a letter to Salisbury upon the Conservative defeat of 1880.[72] While Cecil and Salisbury perhaps represented the most extreme Conservative views on suffrage reform, they perhaps also articulated deeply felt fears of the party leaders.

For the Conservatives preservation of the remnants of the vast chain was their aim. By the 1880s the Conservatives realised they had lost out to 'arithmetic democracy' in the boroughs, but still hoped to avoid its consequences in the counties where the links of the vast chain still held sway. In 1883 Lord John Manners could assert that there existed two franchises which must be kept separate: 'the Counties represent property, the Boroughs, persons'.[73] By 1884, Manners sought, in the redistribution debates, to link Disraeli's 'natural relation to property' to an increase in the number of agricultural districts, an obvious effort to ensure a base for Conservative support: 'If it is thought necessary to increase the representation of the peasantry, nothing could be more easily or more satisfactorily accomplished than by increasing the number of agricultural boroughs.'[74] However, industrialisation and urbanisation had significantly eroded the property basis of Conservative support, even in the counties.[75]

Increasingly aware of their inability to resist the rising tide of democracy, the Conservatives explored various responses to it. First, following the Second Reform Act of 1867 until their defeat 1880, the Conservatives, reflecting Disraeli's influence, hoped to civilise the newly enfranchised lower orders through social reform coupled to appeals to tradition. Second, with a stinging defeat in 1880, Disraeli's death in 1881 and Salisbury's ascendancy in the leadership, the party abandoned social reform and retreated more to its traditional appeals to Crown, Church, Lords and Empire.[76] Third, after Salisbury's ascendancy was complete, he added his own strongly principled opposition to 'arithmetic democracy' while renewing appeals to tradition.[77] Finally, while never accepting popular politics, Salisbury reluctantly acceded to younger Conservatives' demands for a party effort at mass organisation, the Primrose League.

In 1872 Disraeli had set the agenda for the Conservatives for the coming decades with his speeches at the Crystal Palace and in Manchester. To the traditional triad of Church, Crown and Lords, he had added Empire and social reform. In the addition of Empire, Disraeli had recognised the increasing strains on the 'integrity of Empire' to which any franchise expansion would give vent. His concern for empire reflected the rising apprehension about the heightened ethnoregional identities, shortly to manifest themselves in the renewed 'Irish problem' and the Home Rule question. The Conservative response was to re-emphasise tradition.[78]

Under Disraeli's guidance the Conservatives sought to co-opt the working class via social reform. Disraeli proposed social reform designed to improve the lot of the working class in order to civilise them. In a letter written after the passage of the labour legislation of 1875, Disraeli described his intentions to Lady Chesterfield: 'This is the greatest measure since the Short Time Act and will gain and retain for the Tories the lasting affection of the working classes.'[79] Disraeli's and the Conservatives' aims were clearly to domesticate the working classes or, as Disraeli remarked in 1872:

> You have established a society of classes which give vigour and variety to life. You have not only a middle class, but a hierarchy of middle classes, in which every degree of wealth, refinement, industry, energy and enterprise is duly represented, while the working classes have been civilised by increased means and increased leisure, the two civilisers of man.[80]

Years of social reform followed; however, no matter how hard the Conservatives sought to win the working classes, they found it impossible to abandon their notions of hierarchy and accept equality. 'Conservatives could not envisage any relationship between party and people other than that of guarded benevolence on the one side and grateful deference on the other, nor did they wish for anything different.'[81] Appeals to tradition were far more compatible; in both ideology and organisational hierarchy, the Primrose League better expressed the party's view of the lower orders.

The Conservative emphasis on tradition found its most fulsome expression in the Primrose League whose language echoed Pope and whose hierarchical organisation derived from medieval ranks, orders and degrees. The League's name derived from Queen Victoria's remark on Disraeli's supposed love of that flower, though the only known reference he made to the species was that it made 'capital good salads'. Founded in 1883 on the eve of suffrage expansion, 'the league's strength as a Conservative organisation lay in its refusal to apologise for being traditional'.[82] The League's self-stated purpose was the defence of the three pillars of the realm – Church, Constitution and Empire – by creating 'a feeling of respect and sympathy for the virtues, the struggles and the aspirations of those born to toil', and to illustrate to the less well-off that 'people who, by accident to birth, are rich or highly placed are not the soul-less, selfish beings depicted by the political stump-orator'.[83]

Some contemporary observers scoffed and dismissed the League as simply 'an antidote of the Caucus'.[84] Nevertheless, the potential for the blatant and conscious manipulation of tradition was certainly realised by the League. When one observer remarked that the League's activities might be a bit lowbrow, Lady Salisbury responded: 'Vulgar? Of course it's vulgar, but that is why we have done so well.'[85] The League sought harmony and hierarchy in created tradition; however, the difficulty in doing so lay in tradition's variation across territory and in the fact that varied traditions did not lend themselves equally to the Conservative view in an age of class, mass and ethnicity.[86]

With urbanisation and industrialisation Conservatism had retreated increasingly to rural areas. Hence, it became more important than ever to retain control of rural districts, to resist the redistribution of seats and to counter the new collective identities. In 1877 Goschen would oppose rural franchise on the grounds that their ignorance and level of social development made agricultural labourers opposed to the laws of political economy.[87] In 1878 the Conservative member from Gloucestershire remarked, 'the agricultural labourer is only a stalking horse for the trade unionist' and extending them the franchise would send them on 'a worse wild-goose chase after high wages by Act of Parliament than ever led by trade unions'.[88] By 1883 Lord George Hamilton commented on the effects in Ireland of expanded suffrage:[89]

> If the Land Act is now to give satisfaction to anybody, it will be to Tenant farmers or existing voters. But just as we have satisfied them, we are going to bring in a new class of voters who are pretty sure to support the most extreme Nationalist candidates.

Conservative adaptation to democracy and capitalism was challenged on other fronts as well. The 'Great Depression' and increasing foreign competition for industry meant difficulties for the party's newer business supporters and weakened its commitment to social reform. As early as 1872 Disraeli, the author of *Sybil* and leader of the Young England movement in the 1840s, implicitly recognised that his efforts at social reform were antagonistic to the party's attraction of capitalists. While the Conservatives were committed to social improvement, they must do so 'without violating the economic truth upon which the prosperity of all States depends.'[90] As the depression worsened, Conservative leaders considered, but backed away from, relief efforts which would do violence to the principles of political economy or weaken the economy's performance in light of increased foreign competition. In the late 1870s the party came under pressure to repeal earlier reform legislation. In the 1880s any expansion of franchise was seen as likely to increase the demand for amelioration of working-class conditions and further reduce capital accumulation.[91]

Conservatism's increasingly principled opposition to equality derived from fears that democratic equality would dissolve traditional social bonds. However, the leaders' ability to argue from principle was weakened by Disraeli's earlier pragmatism. In 1876 he set the tone for Conservative opposition to franchise: 'The distribution of political power is an affair of convention and not an affair of abstract and moral right.'[92] For the better part of the next decade this position was successful, but it placed the party at a strategic disadvantage with the advance of principled equality advocated by the Radicals in the 1880s.

Nevertheless, some Conservatives like Salisbury attempted to evoke principled opposition; as early as 1879 he warned against 'extreme democracy'.[93] By 1883 Salisbury, in an unsigned article entitled 'Disintegration' in *The Quarterly Review*, had elevated opposition to one of uncompromising principle. Echoing Burke, he feared democracy would destroy the very impartiality of the state and bring about disintegration of the Empire by class warfare and territorial conflict. In the words cited at the beginning of this chapter, Salisbury particularly condemned the Radicals in the Liberal party for their advocacy of democratic equality.[94]

Moreover, Salisbury argued that the logical extension of democratic equality was 'self-government', but in a community 'which is not homogeneous ... self-government is not only a bad metaphor, but becomes flagrantly deceptive'. He criticised Gladstone for engaging in the 'haggling of the market' to gain Irish support in exchange for Home Rule. He concluded that:

One issue there is which, in the judgement not only of the Conservative party, but in that of the great majority of Englishmen, is absolutely closed. The highest interests of the Empire, as well as the most sacred obligations of honour, forbid us to solve this question by conceding any species of independence to Ireland; or in other words, any licence to the majority in that country to govern the rest of Irishmen as they please.[95]

Other Conservative leaders sought to draw their principled opposition to equality from the party's defeat in the 1880 election. Despite Disraeli's attempts to defend his 'Angels in Marble', some party leaders concluded the Conservatives had lost the urban working-class vote and were suffering the hidden harvest of the 1867 reform.[96]

Electoral defeat also focused attention on the 'new foreign political organisation', as Disraeli referred to the Liberal's caucus system.[97] In 1878 the Conservatives spoke disdainfully of the caucus system as imposing itself on the liberty of Parliament, but the 1880 defeat wonderfully concentrated their minds on the potential of party organisation. In a notable change of mind, the faults of the caucus system lay in, as Lord Dunraven commented, 'the manner in which the machine is worked, not in the nature of the machine'.[98]

Disraeli's initial hope was that franchise expansion, coupled to re-invigorated party organisation, would facilitate playing off one collectivity against another. He sought to divide both class and ethic identifications using the working-class support to counter threats to Imperial integrity. But the inability to finance such reforms, the rising hostility in Ireland, the decay of Conservative party organisation and the consequential drift of the party to into a 'Peelite' reliance on 'old landed property and the newer industrial and commercial wealth, and drawing an increasing amount of its strength from the urban middle classes' constrained the strategy.[99]

The Liberals and democracy

I am not now prepared to discuss the admission to the franchise as it was discussion [sic] fifty years ago ... It [enlargement of the franchise] is not now a question of nicely calculated less or more.

With those words Gladstone opened the first night of debate on franchise reform in June of 1884.[100] For the Liberals, although franchise had been considered at various levels for some time, 1876 had marked a turning point. In that year Chamberlain won a parliamentary seat in the by-election, shortly to be joined by Morley. Tensions in the party mounted as franchise and representation became reified into principled opposition. It was the Conservative, Lowe, who noted the changed logic of the franchise question: From franchise as a privilege granted only to those who qualified, Chamberlain and Morley favoured it as an abstract right from which exclusion had to be justified.[101] Franchise opposition suffered a major set back in the party when Gladstone in 1877 came out in favour of some extension of suffrage. On the eve of the 1880 election, then, the party was committed in principle to reform, although divided internally on the extent of that reform.

The Liberal ministry found itself preoccupied with Ireland for its first three years following the 1880 election, and the franchise question became entwined in the Imperial integrity. When franchise re-emerged as a crucial question in 1883, factional lines had hardened. Chamberlain stood for the principled position with his 'one man, one vote' to be accompanied by redistribution and payment of the members of Parliament. A few months later Chamberlain, Bright and Morley, with the support of organised labour, went even further at the Leeds Liberal Conference, urging reform of the House of Lords.[102] Gladstone attempted to maintain a middle course.

If the Conservatives had seen franchise extension as a prelude to social and imperial dissolution, the Liberals portrayed it as means of saving both. For Gladstone, franchise expansion represented a means of incorporating new groups into political life and strengthening the state, not destroying it.[103] His logic rested on the assumption that by giving a larger voice to all qualified individuals, the fragmentation of society would be diminished, a conviction originating from both conscience and convenience.

A central tenet of the Liberal party was a faith in the continual progress of society and consequently the continued improvement in the human condition. This Liberal conscience was admirably stated by the eminent Victorian economist, Alfred Marshall, in his address to the Cambridge Reform Club in 1873. Marshall accepted that while all men would never achieve equality, their improvement could be continuous:

> The question is not whether all men will ultimately be equal – that they certainly never will be – but whether progress may not go on steadily if slowly, till the official distinction between working man and gentleman has passed away; till, by occupation at least, every man is a gentleman. I hold that it may, and that it will.[104]

To the Liberals, economic progress was synonymous with social progress and the continual improvement of the working class sprang from the economic changes taking place. Moreover, advancement of technology brought forth the development of a skilled artisan class, an aristocracy of labour as Engels called it while despairing of its consequences, who, freed from the servitude of physical labour,

> are steadily striving upward; steadily aiming at a higher and more liberal preparation in youth; steadily learning to value time and leisure for themselves, learning to care more for this man than for mere increase of wages and material comforts; steadily developing independence and a manly respect for themselves, and, therefore, a courteous respect for others; they are steadily accepting the private and public duties of the citizen; steadily increasing their grasp of the truth that they are men, and not producing machines. They are steadily becoming gentleman.[105]

Thus, the Liberals in general, and Gladstone in particular, were prone to see 'sober and orderly habits' growing among the lower classes. The responsible working class, if brought into political life, would not contribute to the 'Classical Republican Problem' so feared by Salisbury, but instead demonstrate their support for the changing social order. One scholar goes so far as to conclude that 'the main force behind the reforming legislation of 1884–5 was the Liberals' firm faith in the continuing and extensive improvement in the manners and the morals of the working classes'.[106]

However, it was not conscience alone which motivated the Liberals. As Disraeli before him, Gladstone sought the tactical advantage Disraeli had hit upon in 1880: expansion of the franchise to weaken the threat to Empire by diffusing the growing nationalism in the periphery. Referring specifically to Ireland, but clearly understanding the implications for Britain as a whole, Gladstone in 1884 echoed Disraeli's earlier strategy: franchise expansion might dilute the forces for Home Rule by raising the class issue: 'Is not the admission of another class, the labourer, by household suffrage, *quite* as likely to establish a dual current in the constituencies, as to increase the volume of that single force which now carries all before it?'[107]

For the Liberals the new identities derived from class could be seen as potentially useful. With good reason some Liberals, particularly the Radicals and Chamberlain, could expect support from the emerging class divisions. In the 1870s the Labour Representation League had sought closer ties with the Liberals, but found little response partly because of some Liberal indifference and partly because of the effects of the Great

Depression.[108] The growth of trade unionism during this period alerted some Liberals to a potential appeal.[109] With the ascendancy of the Radicals in the Liberal party, Gladstone was increasingly forced to accommodate the labour movement. Even in rural areas the Liberals stood to benefit from the enfranchisement of the working classes. The Amalgamated Labour League, representing rural labourers and thus a potential ally in Conservative strongholds, congratulated Gladstone on his victory in the 1880 general election: 'We are preparing for the day of our political liberation by forming each branch of our organisation into a Liberal Club.'[110]

In the area of party organisation the Liberals also sought to realise this potential. The success of the caucus led many Liberals, particularly the Radicals, to see great political advantage in expanded franchise.[111] Chamberlain clearly recognised the potential for Radical success under expanded franchise. He could confidently confide to a friend that 'agitation on Franchise [is] the card to play which would give the Liberals a majority at the next elections'.[112]

CONCLUSION

The First Reform Act of 1832 and the New Poor Law of 1834 initiated a series of changes culminating in the three milestones of political reform of 1883–5. In the broadest sense the earlier reforms laid the foundations for that distinctive triad of liberal democracy: defining the boundaries of the polity, the economy and civil society as well as seeking to regulate the relations among them. The New Poor Law built upon the notion of the market as an autonomous self-governing sphere which all adult males entered on equal terms. Regardless of the realities of the market, grievances were left to the courts where in principle all adult males held rights of contract. The implications for politics were soon forthcoming. Demands for franchise reform shortly were erected on similar foundations. However, expansion of the franchise initially could not assume an autonomy of the political sphere parallel to the economy, a condition which led to increasing costs of elections and widespread corruption. It took 40 years to discipline the popular political sphere, from the First Reform Act of 1832 to the Ballot Act of 1872. With the secret ballot, the single officially recognised political act was privatised and removed from public scrutiny. The effect was to greatly weaken the remaining links in the Pope's vast chain.

The weakening of the traditional bonds, coupled to changes in economy and society, opened the way for new identities in politics. Industrialisation, urbanisation, labour organisation and national identities thrashed at and strained the bonds of Pope's vast chain. However, it was change in the electoral regime between 1883 and 1885 which permitted their expression more clearly than ever before. While the new electoral institutions sought to channel the forces of class, mass and ethnicity into electoral politics, the outcome was not predetermined. The processes by which this was achieved are now the focus of our concern.

3 'Not only a Bad Metaphor': Classes, Masses and Races in Late Victorian Politics

> But the matter [of self-government] assumes an entirely different aspect, when we come to apply the word to a community which is not homogenous. If it consists of different elements that have not been fused together; if large masses of citizens are separated into jealous or hostile sections, by deep divisions of creed or race, or even by interest, the word 'self-government' is not only a bad metaphor, but becomes flagrantly deceptive.
>
> Lord Salisbury, 1883

Salisbury's[1] words, although directed at Home Rule for Ireland, reflect the Conservatives' deeply felt fears that the extension of the franchise would loosen the chains of hierarchy and unleash passions capable of destroying the harmony of the eighteenth-century social order. At the heart of Salisbury's concern was the increasing fragmentation in the polity. In this chapter we uncover the diversity and depth of the social divisions which Salisbury so feared. In some instances the bonds of the vast chain retain their power; while in others, the evidence indicates such bonds were hardly existent before the extension of the franchise. However, politics rarely operates at the reified level implied by the vast chain; rather, everyday politics revolves around more ephemeral issues which, however, reflect enduring sources of change and conflict. We therefore devote some discussion to the political issues of the period which captured the latent divisions of the late Victorian polity.

This chapter then embraces several objectives: first, we seek to provide a context for late Victorian British politics, a task which embodies mapping the contours of political life defined by the dominant identities of the age and the political issues reflective of these identities. The interpretation which places religion at the centre of the politics, portraying a polity divided between established and non-established churches, is found wanting. First, the emphasis on religion obscures the increasing salience of class during the period. Second, religious interpretations of politics stumble over the uneven spread of religion across class. Third, the stress on religion fails to acknowledge adequately the increasing intrusion of territorial identities as a separate force in politics. In the latter part of this chapter, this more complex interpretation is developed into a statistical model illustrating and grounding the socio-economic contours of the period.

Next, we seek a clarification of the impact of the franchise expansion and reforms of 1883–5. Then, we focus on the organisational efforts seeking to educate the newly enfranchised electorate to dance in their chains: in particular, the Conservative Party's Primrose League and trade unionism. Finally, the long run political trends of the 1885–1910 period are modelled statistically. The chapter establishes the broad contours of religious, economic and political change in the 1885–1910 period. In subsequent chapters, these four elements – social groupings, enfranchisement, organisational efforts and long run political trends – are brought together into statistical models to examine the contending explanatory powers of religion, class, territory, enfranchisement and organisations in the transformation of late Victorian politics.

THE BACKDROP TO LATE VICTORIAN POLITICS

Changes in late Victorian politics emerge from a previous age of earlier political accommodations which form a backdrop for their unfolding. The newer forces unleashed by capitalism, democracy and nationalism are channelled, modified and muted by existing social and political divisions. How these earlier divisions influenced later ones requires us to examine the religious and class context of late Victorian society.

Late Victorian society is often portrayed as undergoing a shift from an agrarian and early industrial economy with an emphasis on religious differences to a fully industrialised class-based polity following the First World War. The principal evidence for this interpretation is the decline of the Liberals and their displacement by Labour. While this is not necessarily incorrect, it is perhaps incomplete and overly determined, since it fails to consider the subtleties of the late Victorian period, the means by which the new order arose and the possibility of alternative outcomes.

RELIGION, CLASS AND EMPIRE IN LATE VICTORIAN BRITAIN

Three contextual elements moulded the politics of late Victorian Britain: religion, class and empire. The traditional interpretation emphasises the established and non-established churches as the basis of political life.[2] Into this mix, it is argued, were thrust class distinctions, but such divisions remained in the background until the post-First World War era.[3]

Several explanations exist for this transition, sometimes called 'The Strange Death of Liberal England' question after George Dangerfield's work.[4] The 'Strange Death' question centres on the inevitability of the decline of Liberal England and its embodiment, the Liberal Party. To account for the decline of the Liberals and the corresponding rise of Labour, interpretations range from the intra-party machinations highlighted by Dangerfield to 'the long-term social and economic changes which were simultaneously uniting Britain geographically and dividing her inhabitants in terms of class'.[5] In between are to be found the importance of franchise expansion,[6] the decline of Nonconformity,[7] the central role of deference,[8] the changing structure of the British economy,[9] the processes of socialisation,[10] and finally more recent crises of the state theories.[11]

POLITICAL ISSUES IN LATE VICTORIAN BRITAIN: RELIGION AND POLITICS AND THE TRIAD OF Es: ESTABLISHMENT, EDUCATION AND ENTERTAINMENT

In the traditional interpretation political life is represented as revolving around a 'Triad of Es' – Establishment, Education and Entertainment – reflecting the religious basis of politics.[12] Establishment centred on the challenges of Nonconformist groups to the privileged and official position of the Church of England. By the middle to late nineteenth century, non-established denominations had made some progress in reducing the influence and position of the established Church. In 1828 the Test and Corporations Act had opened civic life to non-Anglicans. In 1869 the Liberal government of Gladstone disestablished the Church of England in Ireland. In 1885 the radicals in the Liberal party demanded a similar treatment in Wales, a demand incorporated into the Liberal Party platform in 1892.[13]

Education formed the second political controversy and was closely tied to the religious question in society. Here the issue was school financing and religious instruction. Prior to the Education Act of 1870 primary schools were largely supported by churches, a condition obviously favouring the wealthier church organisations, usually the Church of England. The Education Act of that year put in place a system which supplemented but did not replace church-sponsored schools. Initially the change was welcomed by the Nonconformists who sought to use the Liberal Party's electoral machinery to gain control of the local school authorities. However, in 1906 the Conservatives went a step further and proposed supporting all schools, non-denominational as well as church sponsored, 'on the rates', a condition clearly seen by Nonconformists as state support for church schools, including Roman Catholic schools, as well as a step towards re-establishment of the Church of England.[14]

Education resurrected the question of the position of the Roman Church in Britain, a question made more manifest by the extensive Irish immigration after the 1840s and the resurgence of interest in ritualism and Catholicism in late Victorian Britain, particularly the Oxford Movement and the passage of several prominent intellectuals to Catholicism. Roman Catholics made up a significant portion of the population.[15] These conditions heightened fears of 'papism' in which school financing seemed to propose putting 'Rome on the rates'.[16]

Entertainment formed the third 'E' of the 'Triad of Es'. Particularly for the lower orders, entertainment in Victorian society centred on drink; consequently, the debate over entertainment focused on temperance.[17] The Conservative alliance with the 'trade' was well known and attacked by the Liberals as the compact of 'Parsons and Publicans'. The issue arose anew in 1904 when the Licensing Bill proposed a system of compensation for lost licenses, a provision which led Lloyd George to call the bill 'a party bribe for gross political corruption – an act which Tammany Hall could not exceed'.[18]

THE LIMITS OF THE RELIGIOUS INTERPRETATION OF POLITICS: EMPIRE AND CLASS

While focusing on the 'Triad of Es' captures some of the dimensions of politics in late Victorian Britain, it cannot claim the full riches of the period's politics. First, the concentration on religious divisions between the Church of England and Nonconformism tends to underplay the importance of the sizeable Roman Catholic population in political life. Second, and more important, the traditional interpretation ignores two central political issues during the period – class and imperial integrity – and their relationship to religion. Moreover, paradoxically, by focusing on the divisiveness of religion, the traditional interpretation also emphasises religion's unifying effects. The paradox arises because, by portraying religion as the central issue in late Victorian Britain, the interpretation stresses religion's role in cross-cutting both class and territorial questions, thereby reducing the latter's political salience. The fallacy of the traditional religious interpretation lies with its assumption regarding the relationship of religion to class and territory.

The following analysis augments the traditional 'Triad of Es' with two dimensions of conflict: Empire and class.[19] The conflicts were at times cross-cutting and at other times reinforcing. Class represents the most recent addition to the mix and its place with the others has been the subject of considerable controversy.

Empire and the territorial structuring of politics

Empire marks the fourth 'E' figuring in late Victorian politics. Although an independent dimension, it involved elements of the three previous Es. The late nineteenth century witnessed the rise of popular ethnic-linguistic consciousness increasingly coupled to territorial identities. These new found identities were particularly strong where geographic concentrations of culture encouraged territorial identities.[20]

Hobsbawm[21] notes the nationalism of the late nineteenth century differed in three major respects from previous national identities:

> First, it abandoned the 'threshold principle' which, as we have seen was central to nationalism of the Liberal era. Henceforth, *any* body of people considering themselves a 'nation' claimed the right to self-determination which, in the last analysis, meant the right to a separate sovereign state for their own territory. Second, and in consequence of this multiplication of potential 'unhistorical' nations, ethnicity and language became the central, increasingly the decisive or even the only criteria of potential nationhood. Yet there a was third change which affected not so much the non-state national movements, which now became increasingly numerous and ambitious, but national sentiments within the established nation-states: a sharp shift to the political right of nation and flag for which the term 'nationalism' was actually invented in the last decade(s) of the nineteenth century.

The new nationalisms were moulded, if not manufactured, by middle-class intellectuals. Commenting on Scottish nationalism in the nineteenth century, Trevor-Roper[22] remarked: 'Indeed, the whole concept of a distinct Highland culture and tradition is a retrospective invention.' Prys Morgan[23] remarks on a parallel process in Wales in the late nineteenth century. Kenneth O. Morgan[24] notes: 'By the 1880s, then, the concepts of

Wales and Welshness were beginning to assume a more coherent form.'
The case of Ireland was, of course, even more extreme.[25]

The rise of ethno-national consciousness and religion were intertwined.
Englishness was associated with the official Church, while Irishness found
its expression in Catholicism and Welsh identity in Nonconformism.
While this characterisation is generally correct, Nonconformism also
found adherents among the English, particularly in the Midlands.

Heightened ethnic consciousness took several forms, but typical manifestations can be found in two rural revolts of the period: the Welsh Tithe
War of 1886–95 and the Highland Land War of 1881–96. The Welsh
Tithe War appeared in the less Anglicised areas of Wales where Welsh
language and tradition were more intact. In the 1880s this ethnic tension
was seized upon by the Nonconformist small-town bourgeoisie to challenge the long standing ascendancy of the Anglicised landlords and the
Anglican Church in Wales. Later such discontents were moulded into the
Anti-Tithe League and, still later, into the Welsh Land League forming a
base for disestablishment and Home Rule demands in Wales. The latter
allied themselves to the Liberal party.[26]

The Highland Land War in Scotland evidenced a similar pattern. Small
town elites, especially in the later stages, were able to arouse rural holders
against the absentee Anglican landlords with appeals to cultural identity
and religious dissenting traditions. Like its Welsh counterpart, the
Highland revolts became a source of support for Home Rule demands.[27]

Both wars suggest the importance of ethnicity and rural versus urban
divisions in late Victorian politics. However, ethnicity was not coterminous with regional territory: inter-regional labour migration meant
that significant ethnic populations resided outside their indigenous terri-
tories. These territorial dimensions are explicitly considered in Chapter 6.

The salient point for our current discussion is that Britain experienced
the stirrings of peripheral nationalism in Ireland, Wales and Scotland and
these represented a major challenge to Imperial integrity. While the
intensity of the nationalisms differed across the Celtic periphery, the
general pattern was ethnic resistance to the core, represented by England
(particularly Home County England), and it revolved around the question
of Home Rule.[28] Home Rule represented economic, political and cultural
conflicts between the core and the Celtic periphery, and it challenged the
nation building process under way for several centuries.[29]

The positions of the political parties on these issues were well defined.
The Conservatives and their allies in the Unionist camp clearly stood for
Imperial integrity and resistance to autonomy for Ireland, Wales or
Scotland. Even before the 1886 split, the Liberals championed the cause of

Home Rule on numerous issues from disestablishment of the Church of England, local option for drink and local control of schools.[30]

Religion and class in late Victorian Britain

The traditional interpretation of the religious base of political life rests on the assumption that religion was more or less equally spread across class. An alternative view argues that organised religion in late Victorian Britain was principally a phenomenon in the middle class.[31] For the working classes generally, apathy rather than religious belief or activity was the norm. In this interpretation the established Church in particular held little appeal for the working class. Engels[32] remarked on the religious indifference in his 1844 study, *The Condition of the Working Class in England*:

> The workers are shielded by their defective education from the preju-
> dices of religion, and do not worry about things of which they are ignor-
> ant. They are quite free from the religious fanaticism which holds the
> bourgeoisie in its grip. If any of the workers do possess some veneer of
> religion, it is only a nominal attachment to some religious body, and
> does not indicate any spiritual conviction. All bourgeois writers are
> agreed that the workers have no religion and do not go to church.
> Exceptions to this are the Irish, a few of the older workers and those
> wage-earners who have one foot in the middle-class camp – overlook-
> ers, foreman, and so on. Among the mass of the working-class
> population, however, one nearly always finds an utter indifference to
> religion.

Observers of the late Victorian period found little reason to disagree with Engels' earlier assessment. Charles Booth noted in his 1902 study:[33] 'The great section of the population, which passes by the name of the working classes, lying between the lower middle class and the 'poor', remains, as a whole, outside all the religious bodies, whether organised as churches or as missions.'

Efforts to minister to the working classes met with little success.[34] As one contemporary observer noted, the Church of England represented 'essentially Christianity developed by a middle class soil ... It puts ortho-doxy in place of reverence for truth, and substitutes pecuniary subscriptions for active personal exertions.'[35] Similarly the Nonconformist religions often abandoned the working class for their more affluent middle-class adherents. As a Wesleyan minister remarked in 1859: 'The tendency of dissent is to deal with the middle class, and when the middle class forsake a given neighbourhood, the chapel is removed as the seat-holders are gone.'[36] Similarly, Pelling[37] concluded, 'the growth of suburbs and the closing of the chapels in the dingier districts of the cities as the middle-class Nonconformists moved away showed how little permanent strength there was in the religious commitment of the working classes to any Protestant denomination'.[38] This situation was found generally throughout Britain. In Wales religious practices were similar. Despite overall greater involvement in religion, urban Wales displayed a condition similar to English urban centres: the middle class was more active in church life than the working class.

Two exceptions existed to this general pattern: rural areas and working-class Roman Catholics. In rural areas, despite the general decline of religious life and a thinning of the rural population, rural dwellers remained bonded to the vast chain and were more incorporated into the church's organisations.[39]

The second major exception was the Roman Catholic Church's attempt to minister to urban working-class Catholics. One contemporary report, paralleling Engels' remarks above, stated: 'The poor (except the Roman Catholic poor) do not attend service on Sunday, though there are a few churches and missions which gather some, and forlorn groups can be collected by a liberal granting of relief.'[40] The influx of Irish migrants beginning in the 1840s had created an large reservoir of Catholic unskilled general labourers in British industrial cities such as Manchester, Liverpool and Glasgow. These Irish migrants suffered the dual burdens of the lowest position in the hierarchy of industrial society as well as religious and ethnic discrimination. As migrant labourers they led itinerant lives as the last hired, first fired and were often employed as strike breakers. In 1879 Marx[41] despaired of Irish-English working class antagonism:

And most important of all! Every industrial and commercial centre in England now possesses a working-class *divided* into *two* hostile camps, English proletarians and Irish proletarians. The ordinary English worker hates the Irish worker as a competitor who lowers his standard of life. In relation to the Irish worker he feels himself a member of the *ruling* nation so turns himself into a tool of the aristocrats and capitalists of his country *against Ireland*, thus strengthening their domination *over himself*. He cherishes religious, social and national prejudices against the Irish worker ... The Irishman pays him back with interest on his own money. He sees in the English worker at once the accomplice and the stupid stool of the *English domination in Ireland*.

The Roman Catholic Church further hindered the social assimilation of the Irish migrant into British society, while at the same time it promoted their economic competition. The Church's staunch opposition to inter-marriage encouraged the social isolation of Irish Catholics from the larger society; intra-marriage among Irish Catholics remained the highest of all migrants hovering around 80 per cent during the period.[42] At the same time, the Church's educational efforts and temperance crusades helped to improve the Irishmen's ability to compete in the labour market.[43]

The class variation of religious incorporation has important implications for the traditional interpretation of late Victorian politics. If religious adherence varied by social class, and if industrialisation had produced a sizeable urban working class, then a substantial portion of the new indus-trial working class may have lacked religious affiliation and not have been incorporated into organised religious life. This is not say the urban working class was secular or antagonistic to religion, merely that they were 'untouched' by religious organisations. The importance of this for the current research lies in the existence of an 'un-ministered' and 'unchurched' industrial working class: if such a class existed outside organised religion, then religion is not a likely explanation for their poli-tics. The principal exception was the Roman Catholic working class.

Any weakness of religion among the lower orders is important for another reason as well. Religious organisations were important disciplin-arians in society. Foucault,[44] after examining the regulations concerning charitable and religious organisations, concluded: 'Religious groups and charity organisations had long played this role of "disciplining" the popu-lation.' As Foucault continues, the goals of organised religion were not only 'religious (conversion and moralisation)', but also 'economic (aid and encouragement to work) or political (the struggle against discontent and agitation)'. This role of religion in disciplining the working class and in sustaining the established order is affirmed by Thompson,[45] who sum-marised the benefits of the Sunday school movement:

> Generations of working-class children learnt the value of orderliness, punctuality, industry, and cleanliness in Sunday schools ... These values were the same as those instilled in the respectable working-class home, with the added authority of church or chapel. They reinforced each other, as mutually supporting strands in the working-class culture into which the Sunday school had been incorporated.

However, what if the Sunday school culture had not been incorporated by all elements of the working class? What if the burgeoning working class were beyond the reach of organised religion? What if, instead of incorporation into religion, the swarming multitudes of the cities lived outside the disciplinary mechanisms described by Thompson and Foucault? This was precisely the concern of numerous contemporary commentators. After noting the lack of religious involvement by the working class, Horace Mann, the reporter for the 1851 religious census, concluded in language echoing Disraeli's two nations comment:[46]

> The masses, therefore, of our large and growing towns – connected by no sympathetic tie with those by fortune placed above them – form a world apart, a nation by themselves; divided almost as effectively from the rest of us as if they spoke another language or inhabited another land. What Dr. Chalmers calls 'the influence of locality' is powerless here: the area is too extensive and the multitude too vast.

In such a situation, the working class would be ripe for appeals from new orthodoxies ranging from the Salvation Army to Socialism.[47] Later in this chapter we investigate the influence of religion on the politics of the working class; however, the potential for political unity among the working class also depended on the changing nature of that class.

The nature of the working class

Rapid industrialisation intensified class divisions. Changes in the production process including the concentration of capital, labour and markets, as well as the performance of the economy and the growth of militant trade unions, heightened the awareness of class distinctions. Between 1850 and 1900 the British economy underwent a second industrial revolution marked by a shift from light manufacturing, particularly textiles, to coal, iron and capital goods manufacture.[48]

The resulting demands for labour were in large part met by the decline in agricultural employment. The new labour market's need for largely unskilled labour was met by drawing such workers from agriculture. Agricultural employment decreased by 630 000 between 1851 and 1911, or from 21.7 per cent of the labour force to 8.3 per cent.[49] Reduced domestic agricultural production, accommodated by the opening of international markets in food products, bolstered arguments for free trade. The opening of British agriculture to international competition was an important factor in the agrarian unrest in the 1870s and was instrumental in the resurgence of the 'Irish Problem' which was to haunt British politics during the entire period.[50] The consequence was that large reservoirs of migrant, unskilled,

manual labour emerged in Victorian cities.[51] Moreover, the decline of
landed wealth eviscerated the traditional economic base of the political
class.[52]

A second revolutionary aspect of the new industrialisation was the
changing organisation of labour. No longer was industry characterised by
small firms; instead, a series of mergers meant the emergence of large corporate entities. 'As late as the 1870s the immediate employer of many
workers was not the large-scale capitalist enterprise but an intermediate
sub-contractor who was both an employer and an employee.'[53] By the
1880s both size of industrial plants as well as size of corporate enterprises
had increased rapidly.[54] The increased scale of production and the
mechanisation of labour accompanied changing social relations of production. No longer was the industrial worker accompanied on the shop floor
by his employer, instead the application of new disciplinary techniques
emboldened by scientific management dominated the organisation of
labour.[55] These industrial organisational changes were accompanied by a
shift from time to piece wages.[56]

Concomitant with the changing organisation of labour was the organisation of markets. Increasingly small manufacturing firms were replaced by
larger units of production and marketing.

> Between 1888 and 1914 an average of at least sixty-seven firms disap-
> peared in mergers each year, and in three peak years of high share
> prices and intense merger activity between 1898 and 1900 as many as
> 650 firms valued at a total of 42 million pounds were absorbed in 198
> separate mergers ... All most all of these claimed, and many of them
> achieved, market shares of 60 per cent to 90 per cent.[57]

Coupled to the economic decline after 1870, these changes carried
severe consequences for the working class. Several factors are usually
cited for the economic decline: first, increasing international competition
with the emergence of the USA and Germany as competing industrial
powers after 1870 challenged Britain's monopoly on industry.[58] The
resulting slowing of economic growth due to reduced exports was only
partially offset by domestic demand. In 1886 unemployment averaged
10.2 per cent, but reached 13.5 per cent in heavy industries such as engineering, shipbuilding and metal-working. In that year 22 per cent of the
membership of the Boilermakers' and Iron-shipbuilders' unions reported
unemployment. The decline also held regional consequences with unemployment rates of 32 per cent reported in the Clydeside.[59] Second,
changing production, accompanied by the growth of a large unskilled,

non-unionised and poorly paid working class for whom unemployment was a constant threat, created a new class in society.[60] Both resulted in growing class inequalities. Writing in 1885, Engels[61] had reached a similar conclusion and added his own optimistic forecast for Socialism:

> The truth is this: during the period of England's industrial monopoly the English working-class have, to a certain extent, shared in the benefits of the monopoly. These benefits were very unequally parcelled out amongst them; the privileged minority pocketed most, but even the great mass had, at least, a temporary share now and then. And that is the reason why, since the dying-out of Owenism, there has been no Socialism in England. With the breakdown of that monopoly, the English working-class will lose that privileged position; it will find itself generally – the privileged and leading minority not excepted – on a level with its fellow-workers abroad. And that is the reason why there will be Socialism in England.

Economic inequalities in Victorian Britain were considerably greater than inequalities in comparable societies in similar stages of development. In 1867 the top 10 per cent of the population received 52.4 per cent of the income, while the bottom 40 per cent received 15.2 per cent of the income; in 1880, the figures were 54.2 per cent and 17 per cent respectively; in 1913, figures were 49.8 per cent and 17.2 per cent. During the period, then, the lowest 40 per cent had increased their share by about 2 per cent; in an expanding economy this could be, and indeed was, interpreted as general improvement in the well-being of the working class.[62]

However, economic inequalities were not only large in absolute terms but, as more recent analyses indicate, were increasing during the period. Earlier optimistic interpretations for the period[63] argued that the years 1880–95 witnessed 'the rapid general improvement in the conditions of life of the nineteenth-century worker'. Moreover, it was held that the depression reduced the cost of living disproportionately benefiting the poorest workers. Thus Hobsbawm[64] concluded: 'Clearly the last quarter of the nineteenth century was a time when life became very much easier and more varied for the working class.' This misreading of the contemporary statistical studies continues in the literature.[65]

What these optimistic appraisals ignored, however, were three things: the biases of contemporary statistical gathering, the existence of more accurate contemporary studies as well as recent re-analyses of both. In an extensive analysis of the biases of the gathering of official statistics, Davidson concludes that official statistics greatly understated poverty.[66]

Moreover, it was not only official statistical sources which underestimated the extent of poverty. As Perkin[67] points out, the contemporary studies[68] consisted of limited samples, 'subjectively selected wage rates' and shifting populations. Finally, the interpretation that real wages were rising ignores two excellent contemporary studies.[69]

In light of the limitations of much of the existing data, it is even more striking that under closer analysis, these statistics reveal at least the stagnation, if not decline, of working-class living standards during the late Victorian period. Bowley's[70] more detailed study of official wage statistics in the late Victorian period concluded that while wages generally increased between 1860 and 1891, after that time they stagnated with some occupations showing rapid and wide fluctuations in wages. Similarly, Perkin's[71] re-analyses of the Levi data for 1850–80 lead him to conclude that profits were rising faster than wages and that the 'distribution of income was becoming more unequal not only between the business and working classes but within the business class itself'.

Seeking to reaffirm the more optimistic interpretation of improving conditions of the working class, some authors[72] have argued that the working class fared well in the late Victorian period despite stagnating or declining wages because declining prices during the 'Great Depression' improved their purchasing power. However, again, both earlier and more recent analyses of the late Victorian and Edwardian periods refute this interpretation. Bowley estimates 'average real wages were nearly stationary during these twenty years [1896–1914]'.[73] A more recent analysis offers the same conclusions.[74] These analyses provide substantial support for the deteriorating condition of the late Victorian working class and argue for heightened class conflict during the period. However, several factors mitigated class conflict in a pure form: differing rates of unemployment as well as increasing skills and organisational differentiation within the working class.

While there remains some variance of opinion on the size and condition of the new industrial labouring class,[75] there is general agreement that the changing organisation of labour could not be accommodated by the organising principles of the mid-Victorian political economy. 'Data collected by the trade unions suggest that following the Great Depression skilled workers faced greater economic uncertainty, with longer and more frequent spells of unemployment.' In addition, '[t]he "new unions" formed among the unskilled workers at the close of the 1880s were strongly influenced by the militant outlook of the revolutionary socialists'.[76] Yet the language of the period had little capacity to recognise the problem.

The term for 'unemployment' did not come into common use until after 1895, and even as late as 1910 unemployment was seen principally as a concern of charity and relief. Yet as early as 1886, H.S. Foxwell stated his 'conviction, continually increasing in strength, that uncertainty of employment is the root evil of the present industrial regime'.[77] However, lacking a doctrine to comprehend the phenomenon, it was essential to accommodate unemployment into the orthodox political economy embodied in the Poor Law Reforms 50 years earlier. The response was more rigorous enforcement of the law accompanied by a restriction on outdoor relief premised on the earlier arguments of Senior.[78] The result was a continuous decline in the number of recipients under the Poor Laws.[79]

The first notable break with the doctrinal orthodoxy of the period was the 'Chamberlain circular' of 1886 in which Joseph Chamberlain in his capacity as President of the Local Government authorised a nascent scheme of public works projects for the unemployed. It marked the first recognition that orthodox political economy was inadequate and that the state has some responsibility for those left behind.[80]

Changes in the industrial order held the potential for both cohesion and division within the industrial working class as well. While in general the industrial order made work similar and increased income differences, the principle of division of labour also engendered distinctions within the industrial working class. Increasingly industrial labour was distinguished by skill level as well as type of industrial enterprise. These effects of industrialisation gave rise to the much contested distinction of the 'labour aristocracy' which we explore in detail in Chapter 7. On one side stood Marx and Engels, whose theory predicted class polarisation but who found themselves bemoaning the 'infinite fragmentation of interest and rank' and 'innumerable gradations'. On the other side stood men like Marshall who saw labourers becoming 'gentlemen'.[81]

RELIGION, CLASS AND ETHNICITY: CROSS-CUTTING AND REINFORCING

The traditional representation portrays the religious and class divisions as cross-cutting so that one mollifies the intensity of the other. Thus, Nonconformity could blur the emerging class differences by bringing together those of different classes in a shared religion. Similarly, polarisation and cohesion along religious lines is weakened by developing class distinctions which veil religious differences in emerging class groupings.

For this interpretation to function, however, it is essential that religious life is equally engaging and organised across classes.

A parallel argument exists for the ethnicity: if ethnicity cross-cuts class and religious divisions, ethnic identifications can ameliorate the latter antagonisms. On the other hand, if ethnicity is associated with either class or religious groupings, it can reinforce these, heightening the salience of both.

Observing religious, class and ethnic divisions in late Victorian Britain

In this section we ground the above arguments in the socio-economic data for the period. We begin by identifying the religious and class contours and configurations which form the backdrop against which class dynamics evolve during the period. Two general outcomes appear possible: first, religious activities are equally spread across classes and ethnics as suggested in the traditional interpretation; or second, religion, class and ethnicity co-vary in some fashion to generate distinctive groupings. Data are drawn from an earlier study consisting of 115 surrogate constituencies.[82]

Factor analysis generates latent variables displaying the religious, class and ethnic relations. If religious activity is evenly spread across class and ethnicity, then the resulting factors should draw on all measures. If, as suggested by others, religion, class and ethnicity are predominantly middle-class and rural phenomena, this should appear as uneven association with the factors.[83]

Factor analysis generates the four factors or latent variables which demonstrate quite clearly that religious incorporation varies with social class. The four configurations below describe the contours of religion and class in late Victorian Britain.

1. *Anglican Alliance*: The core of this alliance is the Church of England particularly in areas of high ministering and church attendance. Ancillary educational organisations provide additional support. The alliance draws upon both commercial, non-production occupations in the cities as well as agricultural workers. It loads negatively on Scottish born and demonstrates very low loading for Welsh and Irish born.

2. *Irish Roman Catholic Working Class*: Religious and ethnic measures contribute most heavily to this factor: maximum Roman Catholic Sunday church, day school and Sunday school attendance as well as Irish born. In addition non-agricultural general unskilled labour shows a moderate loading.

3. *Nonconformist Alliance:* Core support for this factor derives from the Nonconformist ministrations, Sunday service attendance and school attendance. In addition the factor obtains a moderately high loading on middle class and a strong loading on Welsh born with a lesser loading from agricultural workers. While similar in its class base to the Anglican Alliance, the Nonconformist Alliance differs in its religious and ethnic base.

4. *'Unchurched' Working Class*: This factor loads highly on manual and industrial workers and less on skilled workers. Including skilled workers in this factor generates a gross measure of the working class which initially rules out discussion of the 'labour aristocracy' thesis; however, this factor can be decomposed later to evaluate the thesis. Finally, the factor demonstrates little relationship to any of the religious factors indicating the 'untouched' character of the industrial working class.

These four groupings identify the social contours of late Victorian Britain and clearly illustrate the differing associations of religion, class and ethnicity. Figure 3.1 presents these results in graphic form. Following the conventions of Latent Variable Path Analysis (LVPA), we represent latent variables (LVs) or factors by circles, observed or manifest variables (MVs) by rectangles, variances of the LVs as smaller circles attached to the LVs, initially set to 1.0, residual variances of the MVs as smaller circles attached to the MVs. Single headed arrows are directed relationships which are pointed outwards, indicating we consider the MVs to be observed manifestations of the LVs. Curved double-headed arrows indicate undirected co-variances.[84]

ELECTORAL REFORM AND THE EXPRESSION OF RELIGION, CLASS AND ETHNICITY

Franchise reform in 1884 increased the electorate by 67 per cent and brought greater balance between the counties and the boroughs. In England and Wales the Act enlarged the electorate by 162 per cent to include two-thirds of the adult males. In Scotland the franchise included three-fifths of the adult males.[85] The redistribution of the seats corrected the overrepresentation of England where previously two-thirds of the House had been elected by one-quarter of the electorate. Under the new law, the largest group of qualified electors became those holding the property, occupation and household franchises. The former referred to those

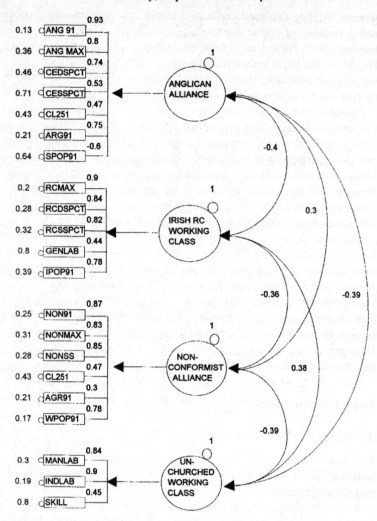

Figure 3.1   Latent variable measurement models for social configurations

who owned or rented any land or tenement with a value over £10; the
latter to those who inhabited a separate dwelling. These two categories
accounted for 84 per cent of the electorate in 1911.[86] The largest occupational group enfranchised were probably the agricultural labourers.[87]

Excluded were still some 70 per cent of the adult population and 40 per
cent of the adult male population. The largest single exclusion constituted

women. Among excluded males, the lowest economic classes predominated because of the property value qualifications and the residency requirement.[88] These figures belie the statements by several scholars that late Victorian Britain achieved close to universal male suffrage, but do support the statement that: 'By the legislation of 1883–5 the electoral system was brought nearer to its present form.'[89]

Inequities and anomalies persisted in other facets as well: the overrepresentation of Ireland (and to a lesser extent Scotland and Wales); plural voting; disproportionate representation of rural districts; difficult registration procedures; and the persistence of many small boroughs with electorates of less than 5000 even following redistribution and redistricting.[90] Nevertheless, the reforms did provide the opportunity for the greater electoral expression of the newly forming identities. Thus were set in motion forces which moulded British politics in the succeeding 25 years.

The reforms provided for greater expression of class voting by more homogeneous districts, by reducing bribery and setting maximum electoral expenses, by lowering the thresholds to participation among house holders and by increasing seats allocated to such industrial cities as Liverpool, Birmingham and Glasgow.[91] Yet the mobilisation of class divisions became intertwined with religion, ethnicity and territory. Popular politics in late Victorian Britain evidenced territorial stresses emanating from pre-industrial struggles over nation-formation and state-building, developed in Chapter 6 as a centre – periphery conflict dimension.

Organisational responses

The National Liberal Federation

Expansion of the electorate also engendered organisational efforts by political parties eager to mobilise the newly enfranchised as well as to counter the attempts of their rivals. The best known organisational form to evolve in the period was Chamberlain's National Liberal Federation which became a much noted and controversial model of party organisation.[92] While modern party organisation was elaborated by a Liberal, in an ironic twist the Liberal party itself failed to benefit from its use. With Chamberlain's bolt to the Unionist Alliance in 1886, the Liberals never developed strong organisations.

The Liberals never seem to have contemplated a formal party structure, and the notion of party membership would probably have been seen as illiberal. It is true that organisation was taken more seriously after 1906, but then fitfully and only by part of the leadership. As Sir Robert Hudson pointed out in 1907, the Liberal habit in many places of having agents only at election time was hazardous, and he complained publicly in 1910 that the first retrenchment was always in organisation.[93]

In consequence, despite the extensive literature on the Liberal caucus system, the party developed little formal organisation and consequently failed to benefit from it. Also as a consequence, little systematic information exists for quantitative analysis.

The Primrose League

Previous Conservative attempts at strong party organisation had met stiff resistance from arguments against constituency interference. By the 1870s, however, even the modicum of Conservative party organisation, built by Disraeli in response to the previous franchise reform of 1867, had fallen on hard times. The rise of the Liberal caucus system, followed by the defeat of the Conservatives in the 1880 election, provoked a period of deep and severe quarrelling and demoralisation. Moreover, with Disraeli's death the following year, party leadership was divided between Sir Stafford Northcote in the Commons and Lord Salisbury in the Lords. Four party members in the House – Churchill, Gorst, Wolff and Balfour – led a movement to challenge Salisbury, in part by demanding a more open party, and by reinvigorating Disraeli's 'Tory Democracy' based upon popular appeal. These efforts bore fruit in the foundation of the Primrose League in 1883.[94]

For reasons of personal ambition as well as political realism, this younger group of Conservatives, dubbed the 'Fourth Party', took up the cause of party reform in 1881 and received Disraeli's endorsement.[95] Gorst, Disraeli's adviser on party organisation following the 1867 reforms, was now persuaded by W.H. Smith to undertake a re-examination of the party organisation in the light of the 1880 defeat. Salisbury's resistance to the Fourth Party's advocacy of mass organisation was partially overcome when the Fourth Party directed its vitriolic attacks against Northcote, Salisbury's chief rival for control of the party, and by the fact that Balfour was his son-in-law.

The Fourth Party became even more appealing to Salisbury as he slowly and reluctantly came to the realisation that the Conservatives must face the consequences of expanded suffrage, class tensions and rising peripheral nationalism. In 1883, against Salisbury's wishes, the Fourth Party launched the Primrose Tory League. The League's original purpose was contradictory, embodying both elements of a secret society of younger, more lively Conservatives (echoing Disraeli's Young England Movement), as well as a mass popular organisation. Churchill's own direct experience with the Liberal Caucus in his Birmingham election in 1880 probably confirmed his perception of the importance of mass organisation.[96] Gorst, among others, realised that the passage of the Corrupt Practices Act had immensely altered the means available for swaying the electorate (soon to be greatly expanded under the Third Reform Act).

Moreover, the League represented a unique compromise and advantage to Salisbury in several respects: first, it facilitated a renewed effort at Conservative mass organisation, but did so in a manner with which Salisbury could feel most comfortable. Its stress on hierarchy, tradition and loyalty to Empire were central to Salisbury's view of both party and government. Salisbury was never comfortable with the League's mass appeal, but did serve as Grand Master from 1885 to 1903 when his son-in-law, Balfour, assumed the position. As Grand Master, Salisbury's responsibility was limited to a yearly address to the Grand Habitation each April; for the most part, then, he was able to avoid what he termed 'something so filthy in the humiliations' that required the popular politician 'to swallow the most claptrap pledges as a condition of [popular] support'.[97]

Second, under the management of Middleton (who replaced Gorst in 1885), the League proved an effective tool for mass organisation and represented 'the direct result of a combination of the Home Rule and "Imperial" issues, and upon which the Conservative leaders sedulously played'.[98]

Third, Salisbury's distrust of mass democracy and organisation and his fear that Parliament would be 'enslaved by the caucus' was short-circuited by the organisation of the League. There was never any question of the League being internally democratic or presenting a challenge to the party leadership. The leadership of the League was always dominated by titled aristocrats who usually held positions in the National Union and Parliamentary Party as well.[99]

Finally, in the most immediate sense the creation of the League played into Salisbury's hand by enabling him to invite Churchill into the government while subordinating the latter's creation to party discipline.

It should be remembered that Salisbury served as Prime Minister from 1885 to 1886, 1886–92 and 1895–1902 as well as Foreign Secretary from 1874 to 1878. The adoption of mass organisation by the Conservatives and their consequent survival into the modern period were accomplished during his leadership.

The Primrose League sought to build popular support for the Conservatives by blurring class distinctions with appeals to the three

bulwarks of Tory society: Church, Empire and aristocracy. In this sense
the League echoed the principles of the previous era's social order:
harmony, hierarchy and mutual obligation. In their founding document
they stated:[100]

> Having in view the failure of Conservative and Constitutional
> Associations to suit the popular taste or to succeed in joining all classes
> together for political objects, it was desirable to form a new political
> society with should embrace all classes and all creeds except atheists
> and enemies of the Empire.

Similarly the constitution of the League stated: 'That the objects of the
League are the promotion of the Tory principles – viz. the maintenance of
religion, of the estates of the realm, and the ' "Imperial Ascendancy of
Great Britain." '

The League sought and achieved the most blatant, conscious, and
remarkably successful creation and manipulation of tradition. Its core style
might be termed 'ritualistic medievalism' which elaborated an intricate
hierarchy of offices informed by medieval titles, costumes, songs, oaths
and manners of address. The League's activities focused on the social
events which brought together members of widely divergent backgrounds.
This often necessitated entertainment less appealing to the upper social
orders and, some party regulars charged, diverted funds from more
explicitly political party activities, yet this was one of the League's most
successful tactics. The League also permitted the Conservatives to avoid
some of the campaign spending limits of the Corrupt Practices Act.[101]

Under Salisbury and his electoral adviser, the League became a central
element in the Conservative electoral machine which, 'serviced by professional agents ... was distinctly more effective than its Liberal counterpart'.[102] The League was all the more effective because it 'built up a
membership among working class women which Labour could not match',
since Labour depended so heavily on organisation in the workplace rather
than the residence.[103]

The organisational foundation of the League was its 'Habitations' or
centres, which by the 1890s had spread throughout all of Britain and numbered over 2300, claiming just over one million members.[104] Detailed occupational data for members is not available, but Pugh's[105] analysis of the
Cleveland Habitation shows that about three-quarters of the members came
from the emerging bourgeoisie and working class. While not officially part
of the Conservative Party's National Union, the League was very closely
associated with the Party and its leadership was drawn from the aristocratic

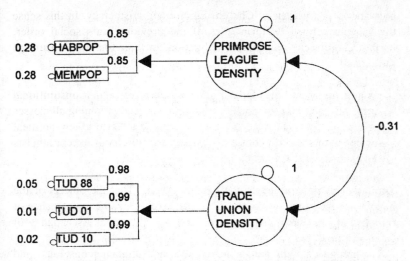

Figure 3.2   Latent variable measurement model for organizational density

and official ranks of the Party; typical leading office holders included Lord Randolph Churchill, Salisbury, Curzon, Balfour and Baldwin. Primrose League strength is measured by the density of organisation and member-ship.[106] Figure 3.2 presents the measurement model; the result produces a strong measure of the League's membership and organisational density. As we shall see the League added a crucial element to Conservative success.

The Trade Union Movement

In addition to the major parties, the Labour movement began to elaborate organisational strategies for mobilising the working class.[107] Union growth increased rapidly after 1890 displaying a 25 per cent increase between 1892 and 1905, and unionism was essential for Labour party electoral mobilisation.[108] Although trade unions had grown rapidly after 1850, the reform of the labour law in 1871 and again in 1875 provided new impetus for continued growth. In the 1880s the 'new unionism' gained among industrial workers.[109]

Of even more important political consequence was the rise of the New Unionism after 1886 which rejected the ideology of 'Labourism' and opted for greater militancy.[110] The ideology of the New Unionism was decidedly more antagonistic to capitalism, as Tom Mann declared in 1886 in his attack on the 'old unionism':[111] 'The true Unionist policy of *aggression* seems lost sight of; in fact the average unionist of today is a man with a fossilised intellect, either hopelessly apathetic, or supporting a policy that plays directly into the hands of the capitalist exploiter.'

Despite declines of membership and organisational failures due to employers' counter-attacks and deteriorating economic conditions, the New Unionism stimulated union organisation in general, bringing new blood into the trade union movement. Their ideology contributed to the growing disenchantment with *laissez-faire* as well as with the Liberal Party, which became increasing preoccupied with questions of Empire (first with Gladstone's obsession with Ireland and, after his resignation in 1894, with Rosebery's turning to Liberal Imperialism).

Our indicators measure trade union density in 1888, 1901 and 1910.[112] Beginning the data in 1888 means the measure particularly taps the New Unionism rather than the old line craft unions which dominated trade unionism until the 1880s. The results of the measurement model are presented in Figure 3.2, which generates a powerful and coherent measure of trade union density and is independent from the Primrose League density, our other measure of the organisational response.

ELECTORAL AND PARTY ALLIANCES

The dominant parties of the late Victorian period, the Conservatives and Liberals, struggled to come to terms with the emerging class society and peripheral nationalism. In addition, the period witnessed the birth and initial successes of the Labour party as well as the ending of 'Lib-Labism' in which the Liberals and Labour co-operated in electoral efforts.

Electoral trends of party vote are constructed for each party's vote across time. The logic behind this technique is quite straightforward. In 1898 A.L. Lowell[113] commented:

> The results of any particular election can, no doubt, be explained by reference to circumstances under which it took place, to the nature of the issues presented, to the reputation of the candidates and to the state of prosperity or depression of industry at the moment; and yet if the phenomenon is repeated with great regularity for a considerable period of time we should be justified in concluding that it is due to some enduring cause, and that the form in which the issues are presented is itself a result of that cause.

A central aim of this research is to examine both the 'enduring causes' and the short run changes in electoral politics which altered the political

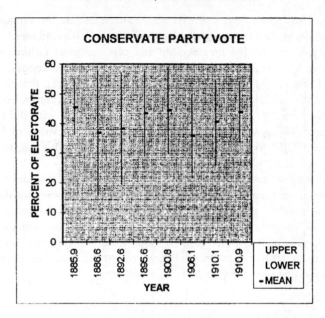

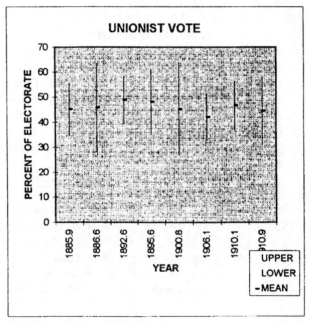

Figure 3.3   Changes in party vote 1885–1910

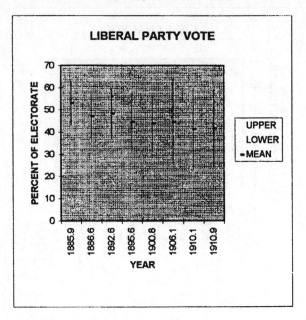

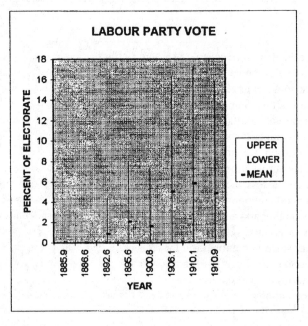

Figure 3.3   *(cont.)*

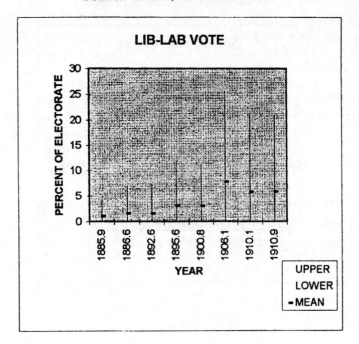

Figure 3.3 *(cont.)*

balance in Britain between 1885 and 1910. The eight elections between 1885 and December of 1910 provide multiple time point measures to capture these changes. Figure 3.3 presents the mean and one standard deviation above and below the mean for each party's votes across time. The mean vote alerts us to the general electoral trend, while the standard deviations suggest some dynamics of change across time.

In addition we are interested in capturing the growth and decline dynamics across time. To accomplish this we need to develop a measure which can assess the across-time change. All change processes contain two general components: an element which is constant from one observation to another and a second which constitutes the change from one observation to another. Here and in Chapter 4, we treat these processes as singular since in combination they generate a growth curve. In Chapter 5 we decompose these two components to develop models of short run fluctuations around the trends in electoral politics.

Since initially we are interested in only an overall measure of electoral change, we develop Latent Growth Models (LGMs) for party vote. LGMs capture the underlying dynamics generating the growth curve. The technique is appropriate to longitudinal repeated measures of the same units of observation for the same variables in the same units of measurements. Principal component factor analysis of the data generates a series of coefficients indicating that observation's contribution to the growth curve. Graphed across time, they present an image of the latent growth curve for the phenomenon in question. The slope of the curve indicates the change in party vote. Figure 3.4 presents the latent growth curves for the

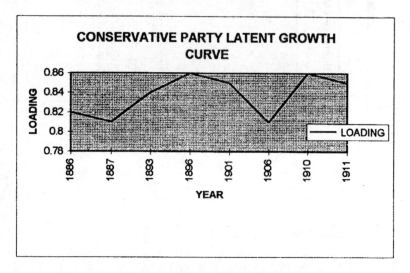

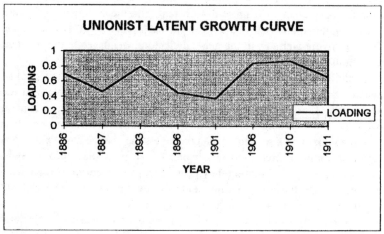

Figure 3.4   Party vote latent growth curves

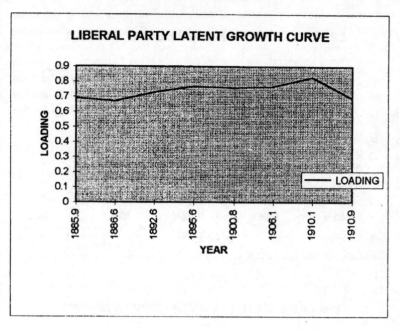

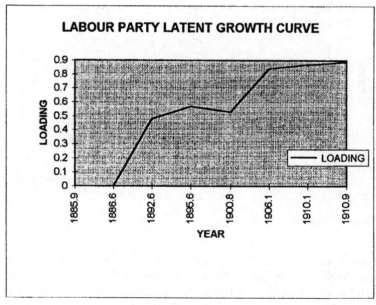

Figure 3.4   (*cont.*)

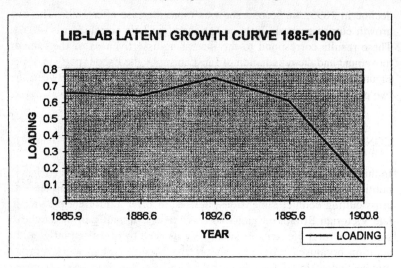

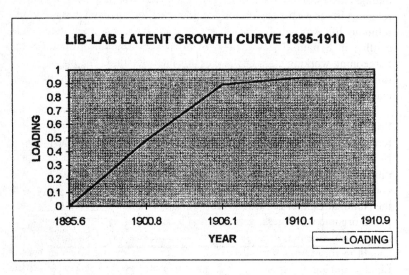

Figure 3.4   *(cont.)*

Unionist, Conservative, Liberal, Lib-Lab and Labour party vote for the eight elections across time to display the trend line.[114]

The general pattern is similar to the descriptive statistics presented in Figure 3.3, with one major exception. The Lib-Lab vote breaks into two growth curves: the first demonstrates an initial rise, followed by a steep decline in 1895; the second shows a rapid increase after 1895. The two growth curves generate little co-variance (the LVs correlation is –0.02). These results correspond to the increasing assertiveness of the Labour movement and the repudiation of Lib-Labism by the Labour party in 1906. Figure 3.4 suggests a dramatic change in the Lib-Lab vote between the two periods.

CONCLUSIONS

In this chapter we established the broad contours of late Victorian British politics. While the traditional interpretation portrays religion and class as cross-cutting conflict dimensions, our results offer a different picture. In late Victorian Britain religion and class cohere primarily in the country-side where rural life remains strongly influenced by organised religion. In addition organised religion is associated with the urban and suburban middle classes. In contrast, among the industrial working class, organised religious life is weak. The traditional interpretation assumed that organised religious life was equally shared among all classes and ameliorated class conflict in Britain. The weakness of organised religious life among the burgeoning working class challenges this interpretation. The major excep-tion to this finding, however, lies in the Irish Roman Catholic working class.

Two major organisational thrusts are captured in the analysis: the Primrose League and the trade union movement. The League was a crea-ture of the Conservative Party explicitly designed to blur class distinctions by appealing to time-honoured principles of social harmony, hierarchy and mutual obligation. The League grew to impressive proportions and was considered by some analysts to be a more important political force than the National Liberal Federation. If the League sought to resurrect the sup-posed organic wholeness, harmony and hierarchy of medieval society, the labour movement portrayed society as wracked by class conflict and sought to forge links within the working class. Trade unionism increased rapidly during the period, first among more established and skilled workers, and later in the New Unionism of the 1880s which sought to organise the industrial as well as the unskilled general labourers. If the Church of England and the Primrose League formed the bulwark of the Conservative response to industrialisation and franchise expansion, the trade union movement underpinned the inchoate Labour Party.

Finally the analysis illuminated the broad shifts in party vote for the 1885–1910 period. The Unionist alliance, consisting at its core of the

Conservative Party augmented by unofficial Conservatives and Liberal-Unionists, shackled themselves to Pope's vast chain represented by the Constitution, imperial integrity, 'natural relation to property', and the traditions of harmony and hierarchy and mutual obligation. The Conservatives maintained stability and coherence during the period. In contrast, the Liberal Party, which originally sought to embrace the universalisation of political and social rights through its support for suffrage expansion, found itself challenged by Home Rule and a militant labour movement. These challenges form those enduring causes giving rise to the changes in the party support evident in the electoral trends. Shifts for the minor parties are also evident from the analysis. The Lib-Labs show a sharp disjuncture in support between 1895 and 1900. Support for Labour shows a dramatic growth over the period.

In the following chapter the analysis turns to exploring the enduring causes behind these party electoral trends. Causal models link the socio-economic and organisational factors to the political trend lines in an effort to account for these changes. The outcome determines the predictive power of the religious, class and organisational latent variables.

4 'Comfortable Contemplations': The Effects of Franchise Expansion on Long Term Social-Partisan Alignments

I see in the Church of England an immense and omnipresent ramification of machinery working without cost to the people – and daily and hourly lifting the masses of the people, rich and poor alike, from the dead and dreary level of the lowest and most material cares of life, up to the comfortable contemplations of higher and serener form of existence and destiny. I see in the Church of England a centre, and a source, and a guide of charitable effort, mitigating by its mendicant importunity the violence of human misery, whether mental or physical, and contributing to the work of alleviation from its own not superfluous resources.

R. Churchill, 'Trust the People', 16 April 1884

And the backbone of the party has been – to speak historically without partisan reference – the religious, Protestantism and Puritarianism of England. For very good reason, because a party whose object is to rule men's actions by a moral principle in legislation and government derives its force from conscience, and from the omnipotence which is behind it ... The strength of the Liberal Party is, and always has been, in the force of the individual and social conscience. It is a power which, like a mighty river in flood, must eventually carry everything before it, since it is the nature of right to win at last.

Nonconformist and Independence, 1 January 1880

The object of the party is to establish a Socialist State, when land and capital will be held by the community and used for the well-being of the community, and when the exchange of commodities will be organised also by the community, so as to secure the highest standard of living for the individual.

Programme of the Independent Labour Party, January 1893

The franchise reforms of 1883–5 brought forth many 'comfortable contemplations' as the political classes entertained the consequence of expanded franchise. These reforms had greatly weakened, if not broken, the vast chain of being which underpinned the traditional order. But if the formal links were weakened, informal bonds, both long standing and newly developing, endured and would become the means to educate the volition of the new electorate to dance in their chains. For the Conservatives, Churchill's Birmingham speech of 1884 reflected the optimism that 'Tory Democracy', as evolved by Disraeli, could win over the masses. A reliance on the traditional symbols of the Constitution (particularly the Church of England), coupled with a pragmatic faith that the utility of such institutions could be made self-evident to the new electorate, might prove a winning combination. Through the continued reliance on the traditional values of hierarchy, harmony and obligation embodied in the established ranks, orders and degrees, the Conservatives could effectively mould good Englishmen. Churchill's chief vehicle to this end was the Primrose League, established on the eve of franchise expansion in 1883 and appealing precisely to such symbols. Under Salisbury's leadership the party remained decidedly cool to popular appeals to the demos, but did effectively employ the symbols Churchill supported.

For the Liberals, their unbounded faith in the ultimate triumph of their cause was both a source of great strength as well as a major weakness because it increasingly figured in their alienation of the important newer elements of the electorate. The Nonconformist conscience was certainly the guide for the Liberals, particularly under Gladstone. Through the early years of the period, the Liberal conscience served the party well. Eventually, however, the increasing size of the working class, coupled to the appearance of the New Unions, brought a strata into political life in which the Liberal rhetoric found little resonance. At the same time a religious revival among the middle classes, particularly in the periphery, sounded a siren to the Liberals who were lulled by its seductive allures. In combination these two factors dramatically shifted the political support of the Liberals. The more the Liberals relied on their Nonconformist conscience as their guide, the more isolated they became among the peripheral, religious middle classes.

What the Liberals failed to grasp and what Conservatives found so fearful, but could only marginally counter, was the rise of class in politics. To the Liberals, the gospel and altruism of their principles was so self-evident; it was difficult to contemplate why good men should not follow them. What the Liberals could not know was that for large segments of the growing working class, organised religion was at best a distant, and perhaps a unappealing, beacon in their politics. Among these strata the Labour movement found its greatest support.

EXPRESSIONS OF RELIGION AND CLASS IN LATE VICTORIAN VOTING, 1885–1910

The traditional representation of late Victorian politics portrays a polity in which emerging class divisions are subordinated to, and cross-cut by, religious differences. Such analyses are premised on the assumption that religion was equally spread among all classes. Chapter 3 challenged this characterisation by demonstrating that organised religion varied across class and urban/rural location, with the urban middle class and rural areas more thoroughly incorporated into organised religious life. The sole exception was found among the Irish Roman Catholic working class, where efforts by the Church were successful. The non-Catholic urban working class, on the other hand, subsisted largely beyond the reach of organised religion. If religion is portrayed as a retarding effect on the development of class politics, then the absence of religion should be a key factor in accounting for the rise of class politics.

Religion was not the only orthodoxy contending for souls in late Victorian society. Two new organisational forms emerged during the period guided by political elites seeking to mould the new citizenry: trade unions and party organisations. Trade unions formed the most important working class movement during this time and directly contested organised religion's efforts to channel working-class discontent into non-violent, other-worldly expressions.[1] Political party organisations formed the second organisational thrust, as embodied in the Conservative Party's Primrose League.

This chapter focuses on capturing the dynamics of broad political changes in late Victorian Britain by developing statistical models to explain the electoral trends illustrated in Chapter 3. That chapter established three groupings of latent variables: socio-economic, organisational and party vote trends. In this chapter these groupings form the basis for LVPA, in which the factor loadings developed in Chapter 3 work as the starting values for the statistical models.

The analysis developed in this chapter assumes that organisational efforts intervene between class and religion and the vote trends. The simplest representation of this model is Figure 4.1. We know, of course, that religious divisions preceded industrialisation in Britain and that they formed the basis of political life before industrialisation. We also know

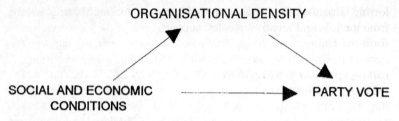

Figure 4.1   Conceptual model of electoral change

that the working class appeared before the development of trade unions. Thus the ordering of the variables in Figure 4.1 seems obvious.

The next step entails examining this model against the data.[2] The locus of our investigation in this chapter follows the logic of Figure 4.1. The organisational efforts of trade unions and the Primrose League intervene between the socio-economic information and the vote trend LVs. Figure 4.2 substitutes the measured LVs developed in Chapter 3 for the generic constructs in Figure 4.1. Thus, the LVs of Anglican Alliance, Nonconformist Alliance, Irish Roman Catholic working class and 'unchurched' working class are incorporated as exogenous LVs and placed on the left of the figure; Primrose League density and trade union density form the intervening organisational variables and are placed in the centre, while party vote trends form the endogenous LVs. The factor loadings link the manifest to the LVs and are the starting values in the LVPA model.

The success of the models in Figures 4.2 to 4.6 is judged by their ability to reconstruct the trend lines defined in Chapter 3. In general the models do well at predicting the trend lines. Below we discuss the substantive findings supported by the models and the statistical results which sustain these interpretations. This chapter focuses on the long-term changes of the 1885–1910 period; the following chapter links short term changes to particular issues and elections.

THE UNIONIST COALITION AND CONSERVATISM

In most interpretations of the late Victorian era, Unionism and Conservatism are firmly linked to the Church of England via the religious questions revolving around the 'Triad of Es': Establishment, Education and Entertainment. The fourth E, representing the question of Empire, became increasingly important with the rise of the Home Rule debates following Gladstone's embracing of Home Rule and Chamberlain's bolting from the Liberal Party followed by his alliance with the Conservatives to form the Unionist coalition. The model's results certainly support this general interpretation, but also provide additional insights into the dynamics across the period.

For the Unionists their support, as expected, is greater in the presence of the Anglican Alliance, consisting of both urban and rural Church of England strongholds (see Figure 4.2). In addition, however, the Conservative-Unionists benefit from the Roman Catholic working class and the organisational efforts of the Primrose League. In contrast, the coalition does worse in the presence of the Nonconformist middle classes and trade

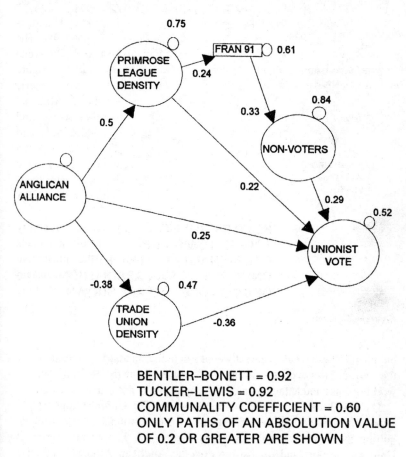

BENTLER–BONETT = 0.92
TUCKER–LEWIS = 0.92
COMMUNALITY COEFFICIENT = 0.60
ONLY PATHS OF AN ABSOLUTION VALUE
OF 0.2 OR GREATER ARE SHOWN

Figure 4.2   LVPA model for Unionist vote trend 1885–1910

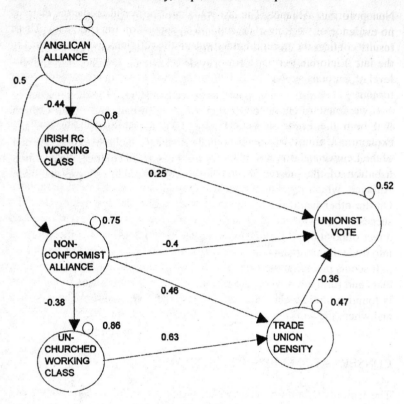

BENTLER–BONETT = 0.92
TUCKER–LEWIS = 0.92
COMMUNALITY COEFFICIENT = 0.60
ONLY PATHS OF AN ABSOLUTION VALUE
OF 0.2 OR GREATER ARE SHOWN

Figure 4.2   *(cont.)*

unionism. These results generally conform to the standard interpretations of the period. However, the strength of support from the Roman Catholic working class and antagonism of trade unionism is not usually stressed.

The religious, social and economic sources of Unionist support and opposition, as well as the importance of organisational efforts in channelling these, are clearly evident in Figure 4.2. The social origins of Unionist support and opposition are: the Anglican Alliance, the Irish Roman Catholic Working Class and, with a negative coefficient, the

Nonconformist Alliance. The last is the most powerful predictor. There is no evidence of working-class support or opposition for Unionism. These results confirm the general agreement on the religious base of politics in the late Victorian period. Enfranchisement has an indirect effect on the level of Unionist support, with Unionism doing better in areas of low voter turnout.

If we now turn our attention to effects of organisational efforts, we see that both the Primrose League and trade unionism are important in explaining Unionist success. Unionist support is increased by the presence of the League and diminished by the presence of trade unionism. The contribution of the League is in addition to that made by the Anglican Alliance, which remains the most important source of Unionist support. On the other hand, the presence of trade unionism diminishes Unionist success. The evidence is clear that, while the working class showed no direct opposition to Unionism, when the working class was incorporated into trade union organisation, powerful opposition to Unionism results.

It seems plain that the sources of Unionist support are found in middle-class and rural areas where Anglicanism is strong; opposition to Unionism is found in middle-class and rural areas where Nonconformism is strong and where the working class is organised into trade unions.

CONSERVATISM VERSUS UNIONISM

The Unionist coalition, however, consisted of an alliance of the several minor parties with the Conservatives, particularly the Liberal Unionists under Chamberlain after 1886 as well as lesser groupings such as the Independent Conservatives. We may further refine the model above by examining the Unionist support after removing the effects of the Conservative vote. The question is: what additional support did the Unionist groups bring to the Conservatives? The answer appears in Figure 4.3, which shows the differences between the Conservatives and the other parties in the coalition. From these results we see that the Anglican Alliance and the Roman Catholic working class are far more strongly tied to the Conservatives than the Unionists, while the opposite is true for the Nonconformist middle classes. Trade unionism is equally opposed to both.

This model clarifies a blatant anomaly in Figure 4.2: Irish Roman Catholic support for the Unionist alliance. Why should Irish migrants support an alliance of parties strongly opposed to Irish Home Rule? The answer to this question lies in the nature of the Unionist alliance and the intricacies of the religious education question. At the core of the Unionist

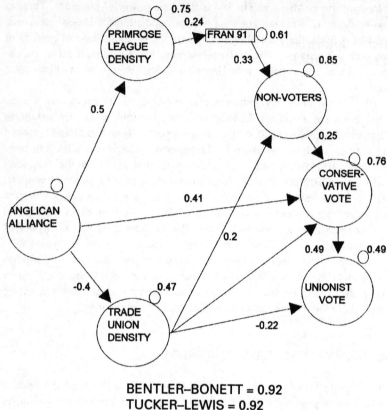

Figure 4.3   LVPA model for Unionist and Conservative vote trend 1885–1910

alliance was the Conservative Party. The Conservative position on Home Rule was opposed by the Liberals and, of course, the Irish Nationalists. The Home Rule question, however, was cross-cut by the religious education controversy reflected in the Education Act of 1870. What we see at work in the model are the cross-cutting effects of two of our four Es: Education and Empire.

The Education Act of 1870 had recognised two types of schools: 'voluntary schools', usually associated with churches, and board schools, set

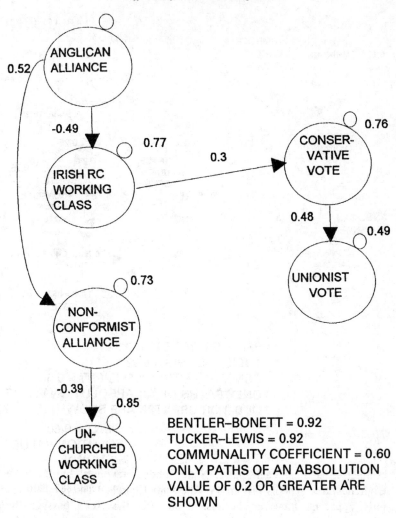

BENTLER–BONETT = 0.92
TUCKER–LEWIS = 0.92
COMMUNALITY COEFFICIENT = 0.60
ONLY PATHS OF AN ABSOLUTION
VALUE OF 0.2 OR GREATER ARE
SHOWN

Figure 4.3   *(cont.)*

up by the local boards of education to administer privately initiated schools when voluntary schools could not meet the need. The purpose of the Act was never, however, to promote secular education, but merely to aid in previously established schools. However, while the Act did permit religious observances in schools, it forbade denominational observances. Over time this arrangement formed a paradox: 'Two classes of schools

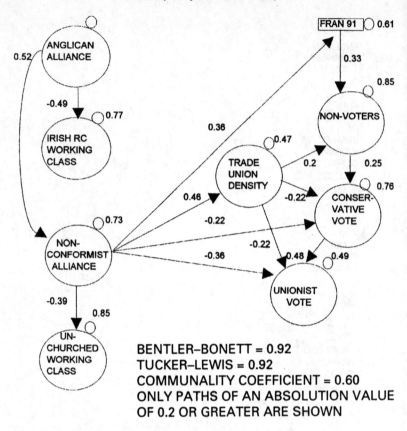

Figure 4.3   *(cont.)*

competing against each other: State schools favoured by the Free Churches; free schools favoured by the State Church.'[3] The paradox was only apparent, however, because soon after the Act's passage the Nonconformists recognised that the non-denominationalism favoured by the Act was similar to their own views of religion.[4] Moreover, with the growth of primary education and the expansion of the franchise to those less incorporated into organised religion, Anglicans and Catholics saw the balance of voters, who elected the local boards of education, shifting against them. This led to strenuous efforts on the part of the Church of England to increase state subsidies to church affiliated 'voluntary schools', which would also include Roman Catholic schools. The Roman Catholic Church was keenly aware of these implications:

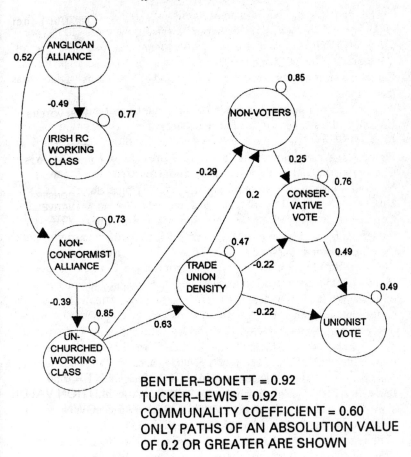

BENTLER–BONETT = 0.92
TUCKER–LEWIS = 0.92
COMMUNALITY COEFFICIENT = 0.60
ONLY PATHS OF AN ABSOLUTION VALUE
OF 0.2 OR GREATER ARE SHOWN

Figure 4.3 *(cont.)*

For they also maintained voluntary schools and were even more determined than the Anglicans to preserve their denominational character. It was for the sake of their schools, that the Irish Catholics, after compromising the Liberals on the question of Home Rule, betrayed them on the morrow of the election [of 1895] and made terms with the Conservatives on the question of education.[5]

The issue influenced party alignments throughout the period reaching its high point in the debates on subsequent Education Acts of 1889 and 1902.

The division of the Roman Catholic working class between the Unionists and Conservatives demonstrates nicely the cross-cutting pressures of Education and Empire. After removing the influence of Conservatism on the Unionist Coalition, we see that the Irish Roman Catholic working class gives clear support to the Conservatives, but not to the Unionists.

A second significant difference between the Conservatives and their Unionist allies appears in the intensity of the opposition of the Nonconformist Alliance *to both*. When the coalition is aggregated in Figure 4.2, Nonconformism is the strongest predictor of Unionism. When Conservatism and Unionism are disaggregrated in Figure 4.3, Nonconformism is still the most powerful negative predictor of Unionism, but its force is slightly reduced and mediated by opposition to the Conservatives as well. Since the Nonconformist Alliance is highly influenced by its Welsh variant, these results reflect the intensity of both the Education and Empire issues.

A final difference between the Conservative and Unionist support in Figure 4.3 appears in the influence of enfranchisement and voter turnout on each. While Conservatism is unaffected by levels of enfranchisement or turnout, Unionism benefits in areas of greater enfranchisement and lower turnout. Such characteristics working in favour of the Unionists are not surprising: such districts would likely be more rural and less competitive. Matthew, McKibbin and Kay[6] conclude the same: 'The geographical pattern of pre-1918 enfranchisement – and the lack of it – is, therefore, fairly clear. It was high in rural areas, county boroughs, suburban divisions, spas, and watering places. It was particularly low in cities, in constituencies of high mobility, and low generally in industrial areas.'

In sum we can see what additional support the Unionists and unofficial Conservatives brought to the Conservative fold: to the core of Conservative support derived from the Anglican Alliance, the Unionists attracted spirited opposition to Home Rule and support for Empire, while providing the Irish Roman Catholic working class with the possibility to vote Conservative on the education question and avoid the most vehement anti-Home Rulers. Lastly, the coalition partners aided the Conservatives in those areas least integrated into competitive electoral politics and, hence, more traditional.[7]

Despite the breaking of the formal links in the vast chain with the reforms of 1883–5, these results suggest the powerful influences of the informal bonds represented by religion in explaining Conservative and Unionist support. However, the models also suggest the newly forged links of class begin to work to the detriment of Conservatism. Working-class opposition, mediated through trade unionism, shows growing opposition to Conservatism. Meanwhile, middle-class Nonconformism remains in opposition to Unionism, but with a weaker relationship to Conservatism.

These results illustrate the cross-cutting character of the three conflict dimensions of religion, class and territory in late Victorian Britain. The Conservative position on religion unites the Anglican Alliance with the Irish Roman Catholic working class in support of religious sponsored schools at the same time as it alienates the Nonconformist middle classes.[8] The Conservative Party's position on class issues strengthens its ties to the middle-class element in the Anglican Alliance, but estranges the 'unchurched' working class and the trade union movement. Finally, the Unionist coalition's stance on territorial integrity garners additional support from the Anglican Alliance through the Primrose League while it dissociates non-English ethnics. For the Conservative Party these relationships are strengthening across time; for Unionism these relationships fluctuate across time.

THE DILEMMAS OF LIBERALISM AND REALIGNMENT

Between 1885 and 1910 Liberalism struggled to adjust to a changing Britain in which the old links were corroding and new bonds emerging. In 1886 the Liberal Party entered a prolonged crisis as it struggled to reconcile Gladstone's 'old liberalism' with the emerging collectivist conflicts over religion, class and territory. Gladstone himself fought to retain the party's traditional individualism in an age of increasing collectivist solutions to these questions.[9] Gladstone's support for franchise expansion in the early 1880s clearly reflected his democratic principles; yet it was the expansion of the political community which unleashed the very forces favouring new collectivities based on class, religion and territory. In religious matters, Liberalism followed the principle of individual conscience against established church privilege. It opposed denominational schools and supported the disestablishment of the Church in Wales. These religious issues were central in accounting for the increasing support from Nonconformism as well as Liberalism's rejection by Roman Catholics and Anglicans.

On class issues Liberalism's principles led to ambivalence on state interference in the market, the rejection of Chamberlain's 'gas and water socialism', the endorsement of free trade and a hesitancy towards organised labour, particularly the 'New Unionism' of the later 1880s. At the same time, however, the party attempted to court the newly enfranchised working class through Lib-Labism. The party's adherence to economic liberalism eventually alienated both the working class and protectionist capitalists.

Perhaps more than any other issue, however, territorial integrity tore at Liberalism's principles and lost the party broad support during the period. Territorial integrity had two facets, one political and one economic, and centred on two issues: Home Rule and Tariff Reform. Gladstone's support for Home Rule, splitting the party in 1886, was foreshadowed by his moral crusade against the 'Bulgarian Atrocities' and Disraeli's pro-Turkish policy between 1876 and 1880. It was also consistent with his emphasis on individual self-expression and national self-determination.[10] However, Liberalism's endorsement of similar principles in domestic politics on the question of Home Rule, while increasing its appeal to the religious middle class of the Celtic periphery, could not overcome the antipathy of the Roman Church to the party's educational policy. Moreover, Gladstone's commitment to free trade and opposition to what later became Chamberlain's 'Imperial Preference', while fitting with the party's individualism and market principles, increasingly alienated both capital and labour, who benefited from the cheap food imports and the guaranteed export markets of the Empire.

These dynamics are captured in the results in Figure 4.4. If Conservative support is constant across time, support for Liberalism evidences the making of a realignment of electoral politics in late Victorian Britain. The results show the Liberals consistently gaining support in areas where the Nonconformist Alliance is strong and losing ground in the presence of the Anglican Alliance and the Roman Catholic working class, while failing to gain support from the newer constituencies of the working class and trade unionism. These results stand in direct contradiction to scholars who held that the Liberals gained from the newly enfranchised working class and that Labour's support was 'not socially distinct from that of the Liberal party'.[11] The first of these comments is addressed here, the second below; neither are supported. While Clarke's findings were limited to Lancashire, his findings do not appear to be supported by the best available country-wide data. The results here strongly support the conclusion that, after controlling for the effects of religion, class and franchise, the Liberals did not gain from the newly enfranchised working class. Nor were the Liberals able to win over the trade union movement. As we shall see below, the Labour Party is the prime beneficiary of the expanded working-class franchise and the rising class consciousness among the working class.

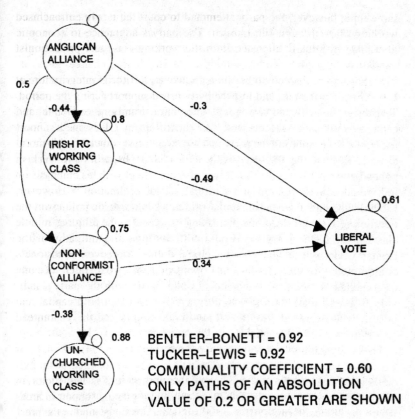

Figure 4.4   VPA model for Liberal vote trend 1885–1910

What the model does suggest is that while Liberalism gains among middle-class Nonconformism outside England, the party was losing support from among the Anglican Alliance and Irish Roman Catholic working class. Strongest losses are evident among the Irish Roman Catholic working class, with secondary losses among the Anglican Alliance. Thus, despite Liberalism's healthy electoral appearance in the last years of the period, the foundations of the party had shifted and it no longer enjoyed the broad-based support necessary for a stable electoral base.

The broad trend so evident in these models marked the shift of Liberalism to the defence of the 'Celtic periphery' in the politics of late Victorian Britain, an explanation examined in more detail in Chapter 6. Here we offer only some preliminary comments. Until 1906 Liberalism appealed to both the middle-class Nonconformist Celtic periphery as well as elements of the middle class in England and, via Lib-Labism, the emerging working class. After 1906, the party found itself increasingly isolated among the peripheral middle classes. These changes may be directly traced to three sources: the consequences of the franchise reforms of 1883–5 which gave vent to peripheral nationalism for the first time in electoral politics, the increasing separation and eventual split of the labour movement from the Liberals; and the Liberal Party's stance on the 'Four Es'. The last two explanations are considered in more detail in Chapters 6 and 7. Commenting on the effects of franchise expansion in Wales, Morgan notes:[12]

> The immediate impetus [for the Liberal ascendancy in Wales], however, lay in the crucial impact of the franchise reform. The Reform Act of 1884, coupled with the redistribution of constituencies in 1885, had a massive effect on Welsh politics. That Act may have been conceived in terms of the 'high politics' of manoeuvring between Gladstone, Salisbury, and other party leaders in London. The Celtic 'fringe', apart from Ireland, may have played only a minor part in their calculations. But the result was to make a new kind of politics in Wales. The enfranchisement of the householder in the counties made Wales something resembling a political democracy for the first time.

The franchise reforms of 1883–5 were therefore an important element in the growth of peripheral nationalism, accounting for the increasing Liberal isolation among the peripheral middle class. The consequences of the reforms for the working class and Labour are more disputed.

In contrast to the Unionists and Conservatives, organisational efforts have little effect on the Liberal vote trend. Although the Birmingham caucus is often represented as progenitor of party organisation, it is important to remember that its originator bolted from the Liberal Party in 1886 with the Liberal Unionists. In the following decade, Liberal organisational efforts fell on hard times, so that in later years Herbert Gladstone could remark that the National Liberal Federation was 'almost useless for any sort of electoral organisation'.[13] Hence the organisational efforts embodied in the Primrose League and trade unionism, which are important for explaining Unionist and Conservative support, offer no additional explained variance. Instead the religious, social and economic factors best explain Liberalism's trends during the period.

The elements accounting for Liberalism's increasing coherence lie with the social factors: the increasing alienation of the Roman Catholic working class and the Anglican Alliance, and the increasing reliance on the Nonconformist Alliance. These results are entirely consistent with several analyses of the Liberal Party's fortunes during the period. More significant is the inability of the Liberals to gain support among the growing working class. Neither the 'unchurched' working class nor the trade union movement show any support for the Liberal trend during the period.

These results make a considerable contribution to the 'Strange Death of Liberal England' question. Beneath the apparent electoral success and stability of the Liberal Party festered signs of Liberalism's decline. Its increasing isolation among its Nonconformist middle-class and rural supporters, and its inability to win support among the growing working class in general and the trade unions in particular, preceded the decline of the Liberals' electoral vitality. The full effects of these forces did not appear until the inter-war period, but received a major impetus from several short run changes discussed in the following chapter.

THE RISE OF LABOUR

Two broad explanations for the rise of Labour dominate the interpretations of the late Victorian period. One emphasises the expansion of the franchise to the working class and their subsequent mobilisation by the Labour Party. This interpretation[14] argues that the franchise reforms of 1883–5 significantly enlarged the working class electorate, with some authors going so far as to state that: 'By 1885 the British electoral system had assumed much the same form it has today.'[15] 'The Franchise Act of 1884 went almost all the way to universal male suffrage.'[16] The conclusion of this interpretation is that 'it was then [1885] that the lower working class first entered the electorate in large numbers'.[17] In this scheme of things the franchise reforms generated a new reservoir of potential working-class voters whose natural party was Labour. Relatively little emphasis is placed on party organisational efforts.[18]

An alternative interpretation emphasises the limitations of the 1883–5 franchise reforms, holding that in fact they did not achieve extensive suffrage for the working class.[19] This school of thought instead emphasises the limited enfranchisement of the working class until the 1918 reforms, and stresses the continued importance of religious and ethnic loyalties in determining the vote. One variant of this argument holds that the limited enfranchisement of the working class and the continued dominance of religion in politics delayed class politics until after the 1918 reforms. A second variant argues that, although the enfranchisement of the working class was limited, the organisational efforts of trade unions favoured class politics. As Matthew, McKibbin and Kay[20] state, the rise of Labour is accounted for by 'an authoritarian mass organisation which drew its strength primarily from non-parliamentary and quasi-political organisations, the trade unions'.

Our results lend a clear preponderance of evidence to the latter interpretation: trade unionism is critical, but is not the only explanation for the rise of Labour. Clear evidence present in Figure 4.5 shows that Labour's support arises from the 'unchurched' working class mediated by trade union organisation, and from the Roman Catholic working class; also that these contributions rise dramatically across time. The level of enfranchisement and turnout provide no additional explanation for Labour's rise between 1885 and 1910. Thus, the social character of Labour is in striking contrast with that of the Liberal Party. While the Liberal Party increasingly comes to rely on the Nonconformist middle class, it is Labour that effectively incorporates the working class through the trade union movement.

These results add another piece to the puzzle of the 'Strange Death of Liberal England'. The Liberal Party's inability to win over the unionised working class is critical to its decline. The working class moves consistently towards the Labour Party, and particularly after 1906. A second contribution to the rise of Labour comes from the Roman Catholic working class, which divides its loyalty between the Conservatives on the school question and Labour on the class question. Regardless of the size of the working class, the shift in working-class politics is well under way prior to the First World War.[21]

THE RISE AND FALL OF LIB-LABISM

The rise and fall of the Lib-Lab alliance presents the other face of the growth of the Labour Party. The success and failure of the alliance illustrates the inability of the Liberal Party and Lib-Labism to channel the growing class divisions and collectivist loyalties in late Victorian Britain exemplified in the trade union movement. Lib-Labism can be traced back at least to 1875.[22] In the previous year the Tory repeal of the Criminal Law Amendment, and its replacement with the Conspiracy and Protection of Property Act of 1875, removed the greatest stumbling block between the Liberals and the labour movement. It was the Liberal-Whig opposition to repealing the Criminal Law Amendment that had kept the two apart. However, far from being grateful to the Tories for the more lenient, although more ominous sounding, Act, the labour movement renewed its alliance with the Liberals for numerous long standing reforms, including expanded suffrage. The period of Lib-Labism which followed was characterised by Labour's limited influence within the Liberal Party, and secured by the former's moderation.

The break-up of the alliance originated from two quite disparate strains. The first involved the rise and fall of Chamberlain who, despite his positions on other issues, favoured municipal socialism, social reforms and progressive taxation (which at the time even exceeded the demands of the labour movement). Chamberlain was important because he represented an alternative to Gladstonian Liberalism with which the trade union movement could empathise. His influence was ended, however, by the question of Empire and his bolting with the Liberal-Unionists to the Conservative-Unionist alliance. Chamberlain's leaving meant Gladstonian Liberalism would face increasing difficulties in understanding, let alone accommodating, the class consciousness and collectivist ideologies developing in the labour movement.

The rise of class consciousness and the economic changes supporting labour militancy presented a second challenge to Lib-Labism. The foundation of the Democratic Federation in 1881 by Hyndman, renamed in 1884 the Social Democratic Federation, attracted the discontented within the Liberal Party. Numerous other groups followed in the succeeding years. Underpinning these new challenges to Liberal dominance were the changing nature of industrial production and the trade unionism to which it gave rise. Accompanying the new industrial order came the New Unionism, whose origins can be traced to the early 1880s. The New Unions emerged from the new mass production industries with their demands for unskilled labour which was often drawn from the most alienated classes of society. Such classes were inherently more sceptical of the state and often rejected state intervention in the labour movement.[23] They were, however, attracted to newer collectivist ideologies. As Duffy[24] comments:

> The unskilled and newly organised workers were less inhibited in their attitude towards the state. They had no privileged position to protect, little bargaining power, and not surprisingly came to draw their inspiration from a new, confident, buoyant Socialism, rather than 'laissez-faire'. Certainly they felt themselves less obligated to the Liberals, with whom ties were tenuous at best.

The franchise expansion of 1884 and the election of 1885 brought larger numbers of Lib-Labs into Parliament. Despite the losses in the 1886 election, the labour movement was emboldened and increasingly talk devel-

oped of an independent electoral party. The Dock Strike of 1889 highlighted the power of the New Unionism and furthered tensions between
the Lib-Labs and Independents. Opposition to Lib-Labism continued to
mount, with such leaders as Hodge and Tillett arguing for more independence from the Liberals and the formation of a Labour Party. By 1893 the
Independent Labour Party (ILP) was debating the 'Fourth Clause' which
would forbid its members from supporting candidates of any other party.
In the 1895 election the ILP put up 28 candidates, some in direct opposition to Lib-Labs. By 1900 the Trade Union Congress Conference proposed
that since 'neither of the two major parties can or will effect these reforms
[necessary for the working class], this Conference is of the opinion that
the only means by which such reforms can be obtained is by direct
working-class representation in the House of Commons'.[25]

Even those unions which continued to resist any electoral involvement
were activated by the Taff Vale judgement of 1901. The decision marked
a judicial offensive against the new union militancy and labour politics.[26]
The judgement galvanised labour into action to reverse the effects of the
decision. In 1903 the Lancashire and Cheshire miners allied to the Labour
Party and they were followed in 1906 by the Miners' Federation, which
required its MPs to sit with Labour. Although Labour allied itself in the
1906 election with the Liberals to repeal Taff Vale, the election also
marked a clear break of Labour from the Liberals.

These changes are picked up by the models in Figures 4.5 and 4.6. The
results show a clear movement of the organised working class and the
Roman Catholic working-class towards Labour, and with a corresponding
decline for the Lib-Labs. Moreover, these shifts correspond to the changes
in the Lib-Lab fortunes discussed above. Labour support becomes increasingly associated with trade unionism; while between the two periods,
1885–95 and 1900–10, Lib-Lab support becomes less predictable in general,
but is more associated with the unorganised industrial working class.

These results support the conclusion that the Lib-Labs never developed
a cohesive base, but achieved their greatest success among the unorganised working class. Across the two periods support for the Lib-Labs shifts
from the unorganised Roman Catholic working class to the unorganised
industrial working class.[27]

SUMMARY

Chapter 3 established the broad religious, social and economic groupings
and political alignments characterising late Victorian Britain. The current

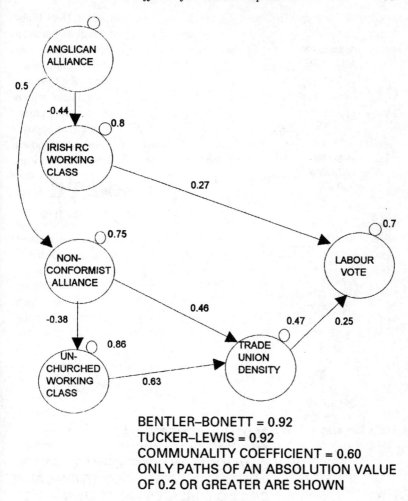

BENTLER–BONETT = 0.92
TUCKER–LEWIS = 0.92
COMMUNALITY COEFFICIENT = 0.60
ONLY PATHS OF AN ABSOLUTION VALUE
OF 0.2 OR GREATER ARE SHOWN

Figure 4.5   VPA model for Labour vote trend 1885–1910

chapter developed statistical models which related these groupings to long run trends in voting. The models support explanations for the parties' long run vote trends. In contrast to previous research on the period this analysis placed emphasis on two factors: the varying relationship between class and religion and the importance of organisational efforts in accounting for long run political alignments. The traditional representation of late Victorian Britain portrays religion as spread equally across all classes. In

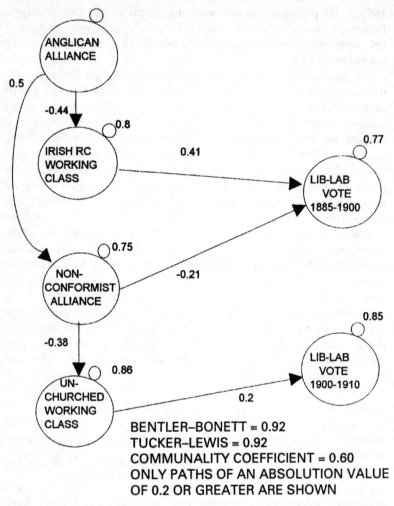

Figure 4.6   VPA model for Lib-Lab vote trends 1885–1900 and 1900–100

contrast, this analysis demonstrates that organised religious involvement was most prevalent among the middle classes and the rural populations. On the other hand, the industrial regions of Britain became repositories for an 'unchurched' working class.

   Second, the analysis emphasised the importance of organisational efforts to mobilise the newly expanded electorate following the reforms of

1883–5. Of particular interest were the efforts of the Conservative's Primrose League and Labour's trade unionism. In both cases, but particularly in the latter, organisational efforts are critical in explaining the long run political trends.

The general pattern of the period is characterised by the Unionist coalition, consisting at its core of the Conservative Party. The coalition gained support from the Anglican Alliance composed of urban and rural voters wrapped in the religious robes of the Church of England. Additional support for the Conservatives developed from the Roman Catholic working class over the religious education question, but this class also shared its support with the inchoate Labour Party. For the Liberals the period marked a major realignment as the party lost support among all groups while it became increasingly dependent on the middle-class Nonconformism of the Celtic periphery.

The emerging Labour Party was clearly the greatest beneficiary of the organisational efforts of trade unions. In addition, Labour gained from the Roman Catholic working class. The rise of Labour was mirrored in the decline of the Lib-Labs. Of great importance was the lack of support given by the working class to the parties most representative of the rising nationalisms found in the Unionist and Liberal opposition. The working class was not drawn into the Home Rule issue nor into the Imperialist debate; rather, the working class clearly demonstrated class voting. Even the Irish working class split more over the issue of religious education than nationalism. While perhaps not conclusive, the strongest available evidence strongly rejects the notion that the working class was seduced by nationalism and imperialism. In subsequent chapters we investigate three additional aspects of this question: Chapter 5 examines the short-run fluctuations around the trend line discussed here, particularly the elections of 1895 and 1900 which are often portrayed as heightened contests over imperialism. Chapter 6 compares the core and peripheral working classes on the nationalist-imperialist question, and Chapter 7 examines the labour aristocracy thesis and its relationship to nationalism and imperialism. Here, however, we can conclude that nationalism and imperialism are most strongly associated with the religious middle classes, not the working class.

These results leave little doubt that both class and religion were major forces in the changing electoral landscape of Britain following the suffrage reforms of 1883–5. Organisational efforts marked attempts to form new links to replace those weakened by the corrosion of Pope's vast chain of being. These new bonds were crucial, particularly for the working class not incorporated into organised religious life.

CONCLUSIONS

This chapter opened with the 'comfortable contemplations' by hopeful representatives of a new electoral politics. Each statement reflected the security of the present as well as the visions for the future. None of these visions were to be realised; however, some fared distinctly better than others. For the Conservative-Unionists, the Church and Empire suffered major retreats in the period from disestablishment and loss of territory, yet the resilience of the Conservatives was remarkable. Their steady strength across the period is accounted for by their ability to hold on to their traditional constituencies.

For the Liberals the electoral returns of the period are deceptive. What would seem to support the optimism expressed in the *Nonconformist and Independence* on the first day of the new year in 1880 concealed an arresting realignment, eventually leading to their 'Strange Death'. As the models clearly show, it was not 'the nature of right to win at last'. Beneath the steady electoral successes of the Liberals were the shifting sands of social change into which were cast the new links for the vast chain of being. Ironically, the turning point appears as the 1906 election, the greatest triumph of the several Liberal electoral successes. The decline of the Liberals is clearly evident in their increasing isolation among the peripheral, Nonconformist middle classes and their failure to win the support of the working class.

Where the Liberals failed to achieve, Labour established itself. Although Labour never came close to winning an election outright, the models clearly show it installing itself among the working class via its trade union strategy. Key to this success was the fact that significant portions of the working class were not incorporated into organised religion, thus making them available to Labour appeals. Of course, Labour changed a great deal during the period, becoming more moderate and eventually dropping much of the language of the Bradford conference, but the foundations of the Labour party are clearly laid in this period.

The rise of Labour contrasts with the decline of the Lib-Labs. Quite clearly the Labour Party captured the working class and trade union base of Lib-Labs with the result that the Lib-Labs finished the period with little and diffused support.

Lastly, the findings clearly demonstrate the importance of both class and religion in late Victorian Britain to any consideration of the Empire question. The middle classes are divided by religion over the territorial integrity of Empire, while the organised working class remains largely outside this debate and is motivated by class politics.

Our discussion here has only focused on the broad historical trends in late Victorian Britain; to understand the shorter-term fluctuations requires a different strategy, and it is to this that we now turn our attention.

5 'Our Best Friends': Short-Run Changes in Issues and Party Alliances

The Duke of Norfolk has been put into the Ministry; Mr Matthews has been made a Peer of the Realm; and the Roman Catholic Bishops in all parts of the country have issued instructions to their flocks that they are to vote for the clerical candidates. The alliance between Romanism and Conservatism is complete.

Methodist Times, 18 July 1895

The political future seems to me – an optimist by profession – most gloomy. I told you that your Education Bill would destroy your own party. It has done so. Our best friends are leaving the party by the scores and hundreds, and they will not come back.

Chamberlain, 1902

It is your habit, when you wish to prevent an offence, to direct your punitive efforts on the person who commits it. But here you wish to prevent a certain number of people from getting drunk – therefore you are asked to prevent four, five and six times as many, who are sober consumers, from having any opportunity of the indulgence and sustenance to which they have a right. Why are you to punish the innocent in order to save the guilty?

Lord Salisbury, 1901

The faint echo of the same movement which has produced massacres in St Petersburg, riots in Vienna and Socialist processions in Berlin ...

Balfour, 1906

Issues in British electoral politics between 1885 and 1910 revolved around numerous questions centred on the four Es – Education, Entertainment, Establishment and Empire – and class. The salience of these issues varied from election to election, representing fluctuations around the long-run trends in electoral politics discussed in the previous chapter. In this chapter we shift our focus to these short-run fluctuations as the parties sought to win over 'our best friends' through appeals to the electorate on the questions of Education, Entertainment and Establishment. The challenge to the Empire is reserved for the following chapter.

We open this chapter with the words of Salisbury, Chamberlain and Balfour. All speak with a deep concern for the future of a political world they had helped to create. This world would change in ways they could not foresee; but contrary to the general tone of pessimism in their remarks, the Conservatives and their Unionist allies would fare much better than the Liberals whose words we heard in the last chapter.

Built on an alliance of the Conservatives and the Liberal-Unionists, the Unionists hoped to paper over important differences on domestic issues by appeals to Empire. The domestic issues of Education, Entertainment and Establishment challenged this accommodation. Salisbury's remark in a debate on the Licensing Act of 1902 highlights the division between the Conservatives and Liberals on social reform, with the Liberal-Unionists feeling some affinity with the Liberals. To Salisbury the growth of social reform challenged the world Conservatism had helped to construct. His position on the temperance question was influenced by both his commitment to individual liberty and responsibility as well as 'our best friends' in the trade. With Salisbury's death in 1903 the Unionist alliance he had worked so hard to secure began to unravel. The Education Act of 1902 divided the Unionist alliance as Chamberlain's remark so clearly demonstrates. Chamberlain held fast to his vision of a grand empire, but feared that this alone could not hold the Unionist alliance together. Balfour, who inherited the party leadership from his father-in-law, sought to contain such divisiveness. However, while the Unionists turned inward over these and other issues, the social forces which earlier seemed to favour them now worked against them. The resurgence of religion in the form of the Nonconformist revival and the increased class conflict aided the Liberals and the small but growing Labour Party. The growing independence of Labour's electoral politics, the surge of the New Unionism and the impact of Taff Vale set in motion forces which found expression in the 1906 election. The election which represented the greatest landslide since 1832 reduced the Unionist representation in Parliament from 400 in 1900 to a mere 157. The Liberals increased from 184 to 400 in the same period, while the Labour Representation Committee returned 30. For the first time since 1885 the Liberals had an absolute majority. Balfour, speaking for the Conservatives, captured the fearful implications of the election.

In the previous chapter we established the broad changes in electoral politics between 1885 and 1910: the reform of the electoral system, the expansion of franchise to the first segments of the emerging industrial working class, the rising religious tensions and the challenge to imperial integrity represented in the 'Irish Problem' which found resonance with ethno-nationalism across the Celtic fringe in Wales and Scotland as well.

In contrast to the interpretation that religion formed the base of political life, Chapter 4 demonstrated that religious life was ensconced in the middle classes and rural areas, but that the burgeoning working classes lacked organised religion, the sole exception being working-class Roman Catholics. The partial opening of the gates to political participation by the industrial working class and the elaboration of party organisational strategies initiated a competitive incorporation of the new citizenry into political life. For the developing working classes, the growth of trade unionism was crucial to their political activation. To illustrate these changes Chapter 4 constructed structural equation models examining the long-run trends. While this technique was appropriate for displaying the broad trends, considerable information was necessarily lost. The present chapter will correct this weakness.

MODELS OF THE STRUCTURE OF CHANGE

The general strategy of this chapter is to account for the electoral dynamics of late Victorian Britain by separating across-time change into two components: sources of continuity linking the several elections across time and sources of change developed in the previous chapter. This chapter examines the dynamics of political change for each party within the political context of the period. The models which illustrate these changes employ the Weiner simplex processes, a statistical modelling technique designed to capture the components of change. In this manner, it is possible to disentangle the across-time continuity of each party's vote from the effects of the socio-economic and organisational variables (see the Appendix II for a discussion of these models).

THE POLITICAL CONTEXT OF SHORT-RUN CHANGE

We expect the models in this chapter to capture the dynamics of short-run change across the dimensions of conflict and the various parties. Since we will gauge the models' predictive success by the changes in the coefficients across time, it is appropriate to recount the major benchmarks of political change during the 1885–1910 period. Again we break these into two broad issues: religion and class. Issues of imperial integrity expressed in the Home Rule debates in general and the Irish question in particular are reserved for the following chapter.

Religious issues: establishment, entertainment and education

Religious issues revolved about three questions represented by the Triad of Es: Establishment, Entertainment and Education. Class focused on the accommodation of the demands of the growing working class embodied in the trade union movement and the Labour Party.

Establishment gained increasing prominence in the elections between 1885 and 1895 and decreased afterwards.[1] Raised anew by the 1870 Education Act, the position of the established Church most significantly divided the Liberals from the Conservatives in the election of 1885. Both sides sought advantages from the expanded franchise and redrawn electoral districts. As Machin[2] comments:

> The voluntaries [in the Liberal camp] were encouraged by the country franchise of 1884 and the creation of more equal constituencies by the Redistribution Act of 1885. The introduction of single member districts as a norm was expected to boost radicalism by ending the practice of running a Whig and a radical in partnership. Conservatives also hoped to gain from redistribution, as this would give more political weight to 'villa toryism' of the urban constituencies, and Salisbury enthusiastically agreed to this change in compensation for franchise extension.

Gladstone, however, clearly recognised the divisiveness of the question for the Liberals and sought vigorously to keep the question out of politics. On the other hand, the Conservatives, realising its disruptive potential, exploited the question to the Liberals' disadvantage. In the election of 1886, dominated by the Home Rule controversy, establishment became entangled in this larger question, which will be taken up in more detail in the subsequent chapter. However, the establishment issue regained momentum and by 1891 it was included in the Newcastle programme on which the Liberals intended to fight the 1892 election. Establishment probably reached its high point in the election of 1895, but continued to be a feature of British politics throughout the period. After 1895 it became increasingly embroiled in the Home Rule controversy.[3]

Entertainment in late Victorian Britain invariably involved the 'social question,' meaning pleasure in general and drink in particular.[4] To the Nonconformists, drink, particularly among the urban working class, represented a dire social problem brought forth by the temptation residing in the public house.[5] For the Liberals, the solution lay in legislation regulating public house hours, local option and taxation of alcohol. Wald and Inglis both[6] trace the Liberal obsession with drink to Puritanism, a heritage which led Sir William Harcourt to remark that 'temperance is the backbone of the Liberal party'. The controversy intensified after 1895 when Harcourt cast about for an issue and landed on the local option question. Gladstone sought to fend off the issue as divisive to the party.

The Conservative position relegated drink to a matter of individual preference, but the party's dependence on financial support from the 'trade' no doubt bolstered this commitment to individual taste.[7] As Halevy[8] remarked,

> The old Tory party, which viewed with an indulgent eye the coarse pleasures that helped the lower classes to endure their poverty cheerfully, had for many years past found it good electioneering tactics to oppose the puritanism of the Radicals on this point, and financially profitable to conclude an alliance with the large breweries which monopolised the drink trade in Great Britain. The alliance undoubtedly contributed to their victory in 1895.

The issue was raised anew by a court decision in 1902 on the renewal of licenses. The decision challenged the 'Parson and Publican' alliance and opened the possibility for the Liberals to alter the drink trade by closer regulation. The Conservatives successfully resisted major changes with the passage of the 1904 Licensing Bill. Nevertheless, in the eyes of the Liberals the matter remained unsettled and increased in intensity reaching its high point in the elections of 1910.[9]

The Education Act of 1870 resulted in two classes of schools: voluntary schools associated with the Church of England and Roman Catholicism, and board or state schools financed by the rates and favoured by the Free Churches. Local boards of education chosen in local elections were given responsibility for administration. From the beginning the issue was highly charged and Nonconformists viewed the electoral reforms of the period as an opportunity to gain control over board schools. These elections often directly pitted the religions against each other. As Keith-Lucas[10] noted:

> The elections were generally fought on a purely party basis; in many districts the Church of England, the Roman Catholics and the Dissenters each put up their candidates, and by their supporters concentrating their votes, all interests were represented, but in most places there were two

parties; one, basically Conservative, known as Church, Denominational, Manchester or Tory Party, and the other which was Liberal in essence, known as the Secularists, Nonconformists, Birmingham or Radical Party.

By 1896 the system was under increasing pressure for reform by the Conservatives who sought to weaken Nonconformist influences over local schools by transferring control to county and municipal councils as well as developing secondary education (also to be administered by the councils). These reforms were presented in the Education Bill of 1901. However, even more galling to the Nonconformists and as a result of Church of England pressure, Clause 8 of the bill also enabled the new councils to provide aid for voluntary schools, a clause which led to John Clifford's famous remark of 'Rome on the rates'. Despite strong Nonconformist condemnation, the bill became the Education Act of 1902.[11] Opposition continued to mount, however, uniting the factions of the Liberal Party and even bringing Labour into opposition. Prosecution of Nonconformists for refusal to pay rates for church schools only raised the profile of the issue. In Wales the Act was so controversial it was credited with spurring the Welsh Evangelical revival of 1904–5 as well as propelling Lloyd George into national prominence.[12] In Britain, in general, the act reinvigorated Nonconformist Liberalism.[13]

Following the Liberal electoral triumph in 1906, the government sought unsuccessfully to alter the 1902 Act. Reform bills were introduced in 1906, 1907 and 1908, but all were unable to find majority support. Every attempt met with frustration from numerous sources; for example, Catholics sided with Conservatives to support the 1902 Act even though they voted with the Liberal Home Rulers. However, no obstacle was more controversial than the strident and highly visible opposition in the House of Lords. The failures of the parties in the Commons to reach a consensus might be distasteful, but at least they represented the will of the people in some sense. The Lords, in contrast, were seen as representing only parochial interests and views. In this way the expanding educational controversy fed the growing constitutional crisis. As Balfour remarked in 1906: 'the resources of the British Constitution were not wholly exhausted. A way must, and would be, found by which the will of the people, expressed through their elected representatives in that House, must be made to prevail.'[14] In this sense the educational issue prepared the ground for the constitutional crisis revolving around Lloyd George's 1909 budget and its resolution of 1911.

Class

The period from 1880 to 1914 was marked by the growth of class divisions in British electoral politics. Major contributors to this were the expansion of the political franchise, the changing nature of industrial organisation, the rise of international competition with resulting pressures on prices and wages, the growth of the New Unionism and the ending of the Lib-Lab alliance followed by the emergence of the Labour Party.

Fox[15] highlights the impact of the 'Great Depression' of the mid-1870s to the mid-1890s as forcing changes in industrial relations underpinning class in Britain. By 1880 Britain had evolved an accommodative system of labour regulation of the craft unions based on a series of *ad hoc* compromises and selective use of state sanctions to make the working class 'respectable'. However, these arrangements increasingly faltered under the rising pressure of international competition, newer technologies and production forms. The responses of state, employers and labour itself heightened class antagonism as each sought to preserve its prerogatives and accommodate change.

The attack on labour by the state took place in the courts where judicial decisions weakened the legislative acts of 1871 and 1875. These acts had sanctioned trade unions, but did not endow them with legal personality. Increasing attempts to impose a legal personality on trade unions after 1895 met with success in the Taff Vale case of 1901 when the House of Lords ruled unions legally liable for their actions. The effect of the Taff Vale decision mobilised labour into political action. By 1903–4 over half the membership of the Trade Union Congress was affiliated to the Labour Representation Committee.[16] In 1909 a second legal decision, the Osborne judgement, challenged the political action of trade unions when the Lords ruled that political action did not conform to the purposes of trade unions as defined under the 1871 and 1875 acts.[17] The 1906 Trade Disputes Act restored legal immunity to the trade unions as well as the freedom to engage in peaceful picketing.[18] The effect, however, was to foment greater strike activity which provoked further employer reaction.[19]

This increasing activity of trade unions led to a counter-response by employers. The attacks were directed not only against the New Unions representing the rapid growth in industrial employment, but against the craft unions as well.[20] Central to the employers' strategy was the argument that unions had so raised wages that British manufacturing was no longer internationally competitive, particularly with Germany. Moreover, the increasing rivalry with Germany in several fields even led to charges of German provocation of labour unrest.[21] Meanwhile, a decline in real wages with the depression of 1908–9 further enhanced labour action.[22]

Central to the growing labour militancy and class conflict was the growth of industrial unionism. The dock strike of 1889 is often cited as the beginning of the New Unionism. The New Unionism represented several major changes in labour organisation and class relations: first, the New Unionism represented a response to the changing nature of British industry in which ever larger firms replaced family capitalist enterprises.[23] Second, the New Unionism represented the organisation of labour by industry rather than by craft.[24] The two developed in tandem: after a slump during the depression of 1903–5, membership in the New Unions increased rapidly.[25] Third, as a consequence there emerged a tripartite stratification of labour: a labour aristocracy consisting of skilled workers in craft unions, organised industrial workers and unorganised general, unskilled labour.[26] We pursue the political implications of this tripartite division in Chapter 7.

Although most scholars agree the 1883–5 electoral reforms did not give full political franchise to the working class, particularly the lower working class, the reforms did provide for greater electoral expression of growing class divisions in the society.[27] Expressions of class were encouraged by several developments: one important element was the politicising of the New Unions with the revival of Socialism in the 1890s. Although founded in 1881 by Hyndman as the Democratic Federation, it was not until 1884 that the Federation added 'Social' to its name.[28] The Social Democratic Federation provided considerable intellectual stimulation for a debate on Socialism as well as political leadership to the New Unionism during the 1890s. By 1893, however, the influence of Socialism was in decline, and, with the founding of the ILP in 1893 at the Bradford conference, most of its adherents were incorporated into the ILP.

While the Socialists were incorporated into the ILP, a growing separateness of Labour from the Liberals was also apparent during the period: the adoption of the 'Fourth Clause', ruling out dual membership in other political associations, also at the Bradford conference of 1893, marked the beginning of a break with the Liberals. In the election of 1895, the 'Fourth Clause' became the official policy of the party.[29] The growing desire for separateness from the Liberals within the Labour movement gained further momentum from the spreading disillusionment of the old unions with *laissez-faire* and the benefits of the Lib-Lab alliance. The legal attack on trade unions with the Taff Vale decision in 1901 crystallised the need for independent political action on Labour's part.[30] Moreover, Labour's success with the Trade Disputes Act of 1906 heartened Labour to seek greater autonomy from the Liberals affirming the separation of 1906. The Osborne judgement of 1909 provided only further evidence of the need for Labour action.

This brief sketch of the short-run changes between 1885 and 1910 would lead us to expect the following changes in the electoral support for the parties: first, the increasing salience of religion, particularly among the growing middle classes, should produce greater polarisation of the religious base of the parties. In particular, we expect the Conservatives to demonstrate rising gains from the Anglican Alliance as the Liberals do likewise from the Nonconformist Alliance. These changes should increase at an increasing rate across time. Previous models demonstrated the splitting of Roman Catholics between the Conservatives and the Liberals over the religious education and Home Rule questions. However, the working-class base of Roman Catholicism and the separation of Labour from the Liberals should permit the greater expression of class voting among the Roman Catholic working class after 1906. Finally, the 'unchurched' working class should find an increasing outlet for class expressions in the Labour Party, again particularly after 1906.

THE UNIONIST COALITION AND THE CONSERVATIVES

Political issues revolving around the three Es of Establishment, Entertainment and Education worked synergistically to coalesce the Conservatives and Liberals into opposing camps and in particular contributed to Liberal ascendancy in Wales.[31] However, these same issues which pitted the Conservatives against the Liberals also divided Liberal-Unionists from the Conservatives within the Coalition, as illustrated above by the *Methodist Times'* commentary as well as by Chamberlain's remark to the Duke of Devonshire on the Conservatives' Education Bill of 1901. What held the Unionist Coalition together was a commitment to imperial integrity and opposition to Home Rule. In the early years of the period, Church establishment figured most heavily, but tended to fade after 1895 to be replaced by Entertainment, Education and Empire. Educational issues continued to influence politics to the end of the period by becoming increasingly embroiled in the constitutional crisis over the House of Lords. Meanwhile, issues of class and Empire continued to heighten throughout the period.

These effects are evident in the models in Figure 5.1. Between 1885 and 1895 both the Anglican Alliance and the Roman Catholic working class show increasing support at an increasing rate for the Conservatives.

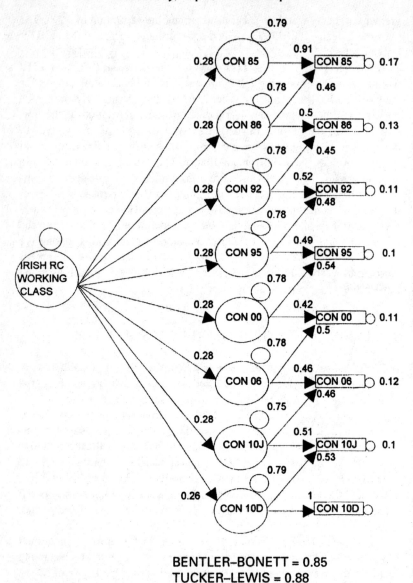

BENTLER–BONETT = 0.85
TUCKER–LEWIS = 0.88
COMMUNALITY COEFFICIENT = 0.70

Figure 5.1   LVPA simplex model of Conservative vote 1885–1910

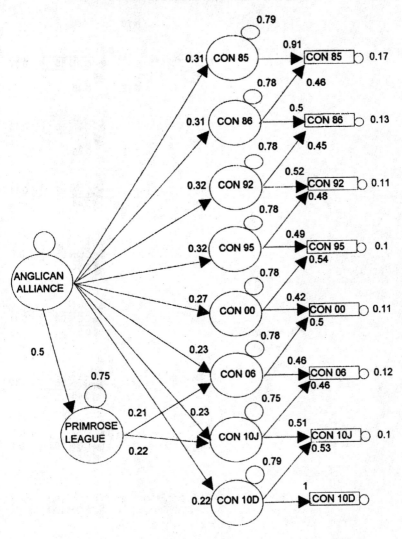

BENTLER–BONETT = 0.85
TUCKER–LEWIS = 0.88
COMMUNALITY COEFFICIENT = 0.70

Figure 5.1 (*cont.*)

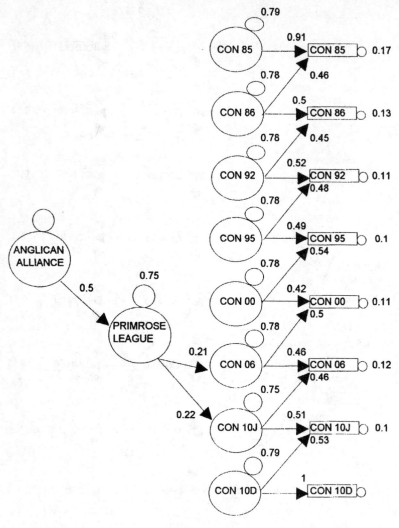

BENTLER–BONETT = 0.85
TUCKER–LEWIS = 0.88
COMMUNALITY COEFFICIENT = 0.70

Figure 5.1 (*cont.*)

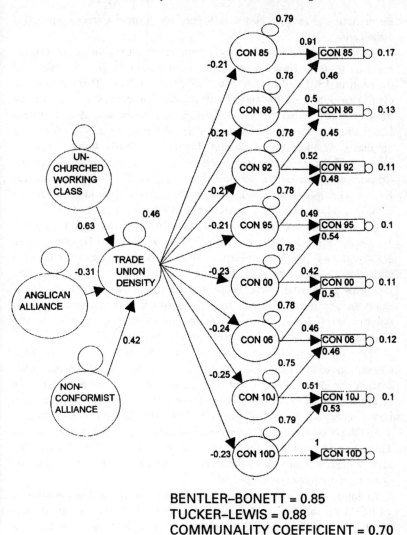

BENTLER–BONETT = 0.85
TUCKER–LEWIS = 0.88
COMMUNALITY COEFFICIENT = 0.70

Figure 5.1 (*cont.*)

After 1895 the rate of increase slows and remains higher for Roman
Catholics than for Anglicans. We have already noted in the previous
chapter that education was the salient issue for Roman Catholics. Figure
5.1 confirms this as well as demonstrating that the salience remains high

throughout the period, and it is higher for Roman Catholics than for Anglicans.

Class issues became increasingly pronounced during the period following the rise of the New Unionism, the formation of the ILP, the Taff Vale decision in 1901 and the Osborne judgement of 1909. These effects are clearly evident with the steady rise of anti-Conservatism as a result of trade unionism across the period. Finally, the effectiveness of the Primrose League for Conservatives increased after 1900 corresponding to the rising emphasis on questions of Empire. Figure 5.1 clearly shows these dynamics. There is a steady movement of trade unionists against the Conservatives across the period. Also in Figure 5.1, it is plain that the Primrose League is more significant to the Conservatives in the latter part of the period, particularly the elections of 1906 and January of 1910.

When we compare these results to those for the Unionists in Figure 5.2, after removing the effects of Conservatism, we find that Unionism more clearly draws the Nonconformist fire. Nonconformist opposition to Unionism increases between 1885 and 1892, declines in 1895 and then increases again after 1900. These periods correspond to the salience of religious and imperial issues in politics which included Establishment debates after 1885, followed by the reassertion of Education and Entertainment as well as the tensions of Empire after 1900.

The effectiveness of organisational efforts are highlighted for both the Conservatives and Unionists. The Primrose League contributes independently to the electoral success of both, particularly after 1906 with the rise of imperialist issues. Similarly trade unionism is a source of opposition to both Conservatism and Unionism. In both cases the opposition increases across the period, but is more pronounced to Conservatism than Unionism. These results confirm again the presence of class voting well before the First World War as well as the abstention of the working class from the growing nationalism of the period.[32]

Attention now focuses on the paths from the social and organisational variables on the left-hand side of Figure 5.1. The simplex process is capable of generating non-linear dynamics since the model specifies that the 'changes are independent, additive and persistent'.[33] Thus, the Conservative Party shows curvilinear, persistent, additive and sizeable gains from the Roman Catholic working class and the organisational efforts of the Primrose League as well as losses resulting from trade union organisational efforts. These changes are occurring at an increasing rate across time. In contrast support from the Anglican Alliance increases but at a decreasing rate after 1895. It is quite clear that there is a steady, increasing and persistent broadening of support for the Conservative Party

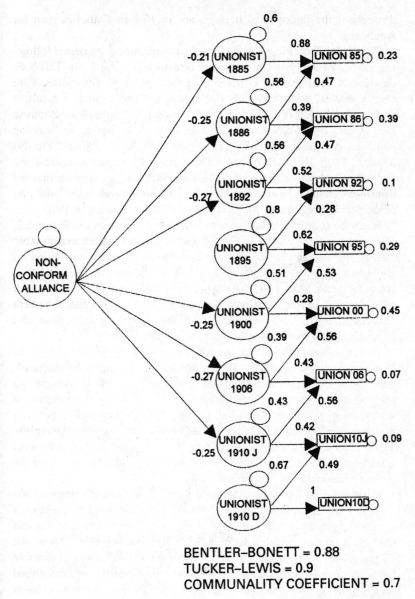

BENTLER–BONETT = 0.88
TUCKER–LEWIS = 0.9
COMMUNALITY COEFFICIENT = 0.7

Figure 5.2   LVPA model of Unionist vote 1885–1910, controlling for Conservatism

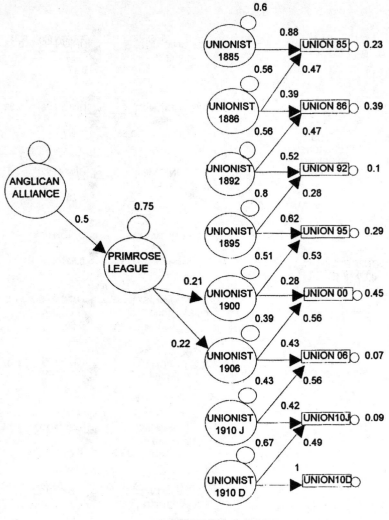

BENTLER–BONETT = 0.88
TUCKER–LEWIS = 0.9
COMMUNALITY COEFFICIENT = 0.7

Figure 5.2   *(cont.)*

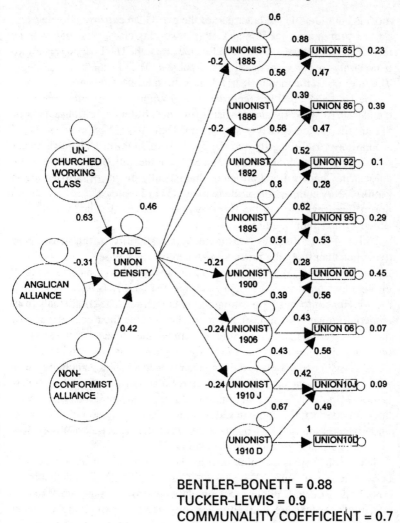

BENTLER–BONETT = 0.88
TUCKER–LEWIS = 0.9
COMMUNALITY COEFFICIENT = 0.7

Figure 5.2   (*cont.*)

across time. The party developed from an early reliance on the Anglican Alliance to increased support from the Roman Catholic working class and also expanded into areas of low trade union density. In contrast to the results in Chapter 4, these results show the shift is not so much towards the party's Anglican Alliance base as suggested by the long term stability models but rather, in the latter part of the period, an expansion to new supporters from among the Roman Catholic working class, areas of low trade unionism and centres of Primrose League strength. The League was established only in 1883 as central to the party's 'Tory Democracy' strategy. The findings in the model clearly demonstrate its effectiveness.

The Unionist Coalition represented a grouping of elements centred on the Conservative Party and consisting of, in addition to the Conservatives, the unofficial Conservatives and Liberal-Unionists. The Unionists rallied around territorial integrity and the symbols of Empire.[34] The differences between the Conservatives and their allies in the Unionist Coalition were evident in Chapter 4 and are more dramatically displayed across time in Figure 5.2. A comparison of the two models in Figures 5.1 and 5.2 shows the differences between the Conservative sources of support and those added by its Unionist allies.[35]

Unionist vote displays considerably less stability in the across-time dynamics than the same process modelled for the Conservative vote over the same period. Whereas the Conservatives show almost a smooth moving average across the eight elections, the Unionists form a lightning rod for Nonconformist opposition during the period. The coefficients from Nonconformism to Unionism are more than double their counterparts for the Conservative Party alone after we remove the impact of Conservatism on Unionism. Moreover, after we control for the influence of Conservatism on Unionism, the Anglican Alliance makes a negligible contribution to Unionism. These dramatic results indicate an growing polarisation of politics among the middle classes along religious and ethnic lines. In contrast, the unorganised working class shows no affinity for the imperialism espoused by Chamberlain, while the organised working class evidences a steadily increasing opposition.

These conclusions are reinforced by those paths of reduced importance between the two figures. Whereas the Conservative Party gained support among the Roman Catholic working class and lost it among trade unionists, these factors are markedly less important in explaining Unionist support. Thus, while the Conservatives manifest the effects of both religion and class, the additional contributions of Unionist coalition partners are principally religious and cultural. These results clearly show that Unionism added a well-defined element to Conservative strengths: the appeal to religious and ethnic differences which enabled the Conservative party to maintain its appeal to the Roman Catholic supporters on the educational question while their Unionist partners opposed Irish Home Rule.

The general pattern across Unionism and Conservatism is quite clear: an increasing polarisation of politics along both religious and class divisions.

Religious issues were particularly salient among middle-class Unionist opponents. The Conservatives show a clear class dimension not present for the Unionists, while the Unionists demonstrate a clear religious and ethnic character significantly less present for the Conservatives. These results enlarge our understanding provided by Wald[36] who concluded that there was no class 'reorientation among social groups between 1885 and 1910'. At least as far as the Conservatives are concerned this is not correct, but firmer conclusions must await the analysis of other parties. However, in this analysis class politics are clearly in evidence for the Conservative Party opposition.

THE LIBERAL PARTY

Changes in the fortunes of the Liberal Party in late Victorian Britain have been the focus of extensive study. Nevertheless, considerable disagreement exists over the late Victorian decline of the Liberals. Much of this debate focuses on the Liberals' relationship to the emerging Labour Party; we will explore this argument in more detail later in this chapter. At this point our focus remains on the Liberals position *vis-à-vis* their principal rival, the Conservatives. Again the Weiner simplex models enable us to examine these dynamics by decomposing change across time. Figure 5.3 presents the results of a model for the Liberals after removing the Conservative vote trend line.

If we did not remove the influence of Conservatism, the model's results would be overdetermined. With the removal of the impact of Conservatism on the Liberals, we can observe the additional effects after controlling for the Conservatism. With these controls, the movement of the parties in opposite directions on the religious dimensions of the period is even more clear. Where the Conservatives are gaining support among the Anglican Alliance in Figure 5.1, the Liberals gain from Nonconformism in Figure 5.3. Where the Conservatives demonstrate gains among Roman Catholic working class, the Liberals show declines.

More interesting, however, are the asymmetrical dynamics: where the Primrose League adds to Conservative strength, the League shows no significant effect on Liberal support. Even more important are the shifts in working-class support. Working class and trade union density are examined in both models in such a way as to illustrate the independent effects of each on the parties. Here the results are quite different for the Liberals and the Conservatives. The Conservatives evidence clear and significant losses among trade unionists, but far less significant losses among the

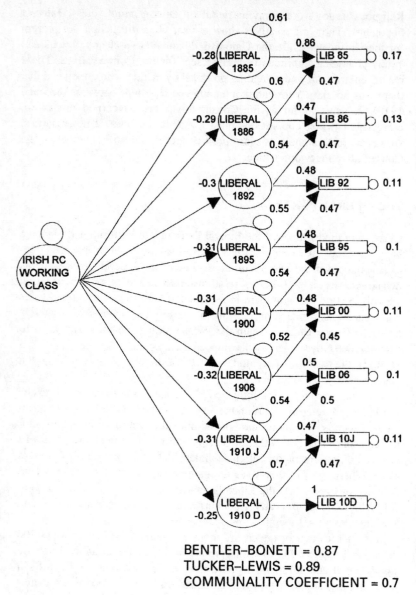

BENTLER–BONETT = 0.87
TUCKER–LEWIS = 0.89
COMMUNALITY COEFFICIENT = 0.7

Figure 5.3   LVPA simplex model of Liberal vote 1885–1910, controlling for Conservatism

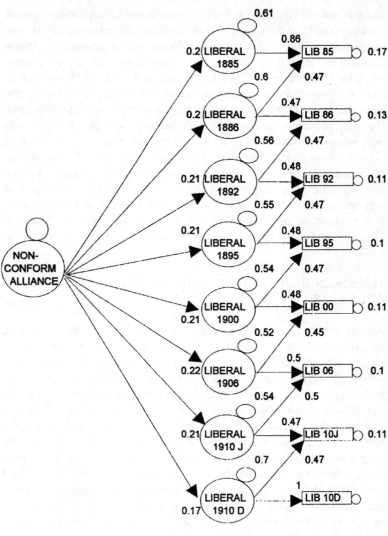

BENTLER–BONETT = 0.87
TUCKER–LEWIS = 0.89
COMMUNALITY COEFFICIENT = 0.7

Figure 5.3 (*cont.*)

unorganised working class and indeed gain from the Irish Roman Catholic working class. For the Liberals there are no significant relationships with organised working class, but major losses appear among the Roman Catholic working class. These results suggest the obvious conclusion: while the Liberals were becoming the party of the Nonconformist middle class, the Conservatives were becoming more diverse by attracting support from the Anglican rural and urban elements, together with the Roman Catholic working class, as well as benefiting from anti-working class expressions. However, these results also beg the question: if the working class is moving away from both the Conservatives and Liberals, and the organised working class is strongly moving against the Conservatives and offering little or no support for the Liberals, where is working-class support moving? The obvious answer is the Labour Party, but the correct answer is not as straightforward as it might appear for it touches upon 'The Strange Death of Liberal England' question.

THE STRANGE DEATH OF THE LIBERAL PARTY AND THE RISE OF LABOUR

Perhaps no other question is as much studied, and as little agreed upon, as the origins and causes of the Liberal decline in late Victorian Britain. At the risk of some precision, the explanations may be characterised as falling into two broad interpretations: the traditionalist and the revisionist. To the traditionalists belongs the interpretation that the flowering of class politics and the new alignment of the parties had to wait until after the First World War when the impact of the war, the growth of the industrial economy, the increased secularisation of society and the effects of the 1918 franchise reform worked their effects on the electorate. One strain of the traditionalist argument emphasises the continued powerful association of Liberalism with Nonconformity, and that only the weakening of religion in the post-war period facilitated the rise of obvious class voting which worked against the Liberals and in favour of Labour. Glaser[37] states this interpretation most strongly:

> The war completed the undermining of the secure world in which Liberalism had performed its work. As has been seen, however, even before 1914 the decline of Nonconformism had as an inevitable consequence the decline of Liberalism. The ebbing of the Nonconformist conscience entailed the gradual loss of the Liberal party's practical

political strength and, more important, the loss of the religious ethos and moral passion which had distinguished English Liberalism in its creative golden age.

A corollary in the traditionalist interpretation places its emphasis on the failure of Liberal Party leadership. This interpretation, most famously offered by George Dangerfield's book, *The Strange Death of Liberal England*,[38] traces the decline of Liberalism to the failure of party leadership to take account of the rising challenge of Labour. Dangerfield cites the election of 1906 as an important, but unnoticed or misread, juncture in the Liberal history. The demise of the Liberals is attributed to an 'accidental convergence of unrelated events'.[39]

In contrast, the revisionist interpretation stresses the importance of the rise of class divisions before the First World War and the salience of growing support for the Labour party. Among the revisionists are Clarke, Pelling and Blewett.[40] Pelling[41] sums up the revisionist interpretation:

> We may conclude, therefore, that the decline of Liberalism was not due to a sordid intrigue [among the political leadership]. Nor was it due ... to the impact of the war upon the Liberal values and upon the unity of the parliamentary Liberal Party. Rather it was the result of long-term social and economic changes which were simultaneously uniting Britain geographically and dividing her inhabitants in terms of class; enabling the population to achieve the full dimensions of political democracy but condemning it to years of bitter strife owing to the forced contraction of the staple industries which had prospered so remarkably in the later Victorian era – an era politically as well as socially distinct from that of the inter-war period.

Pelling's statement is intriguing from a number of perspectives. He not only argues in favour of the revisionist or class interpretation of late Victorian Britain, but he also suggests the unifying effects of class on national politics. Implied in this interpretation is the assumption that class politics will bring forth territorial unity as pre-industrial religious, ethnic and territorial loyalties are effaced and replaced by class divisions. The implications of this proposition are fully explored in subsequent chapters. Here the analysis is limited to a more general postulating of the revisionist interpretation that class emerged clearly and separately before the First World War and functioned independently from declining religious ethos in explaining the death of Liberalism.

Considerable printer's ink has been devoted to disentangling the two interpretations of the period and the decline of the Liberals. Wald[42] summarised the contending interpretations as follows:

The revisionists have challenged [the traditionalist] interpretation directly, insisting that the cleavage shift from religion to class was a separate process from the displacement of the Liberals by Labour as the major anti-Conservative party. As already noted revisionists argue that the social base of voting had already shifted from denomination to class when the Liberals won three consecutive general elections between 1906 and 1910.

After extensive statistical analysis, Wald[43] concludes:

Despite the differences in data quality across the electoral systems, it is clear that the traditional interpretation is accurate in so far as it draws a sharp line between the pre- and post-war cleavage patterns ... The analysis sustains the traditional view of a dramatic alternation of cleavage bases between 1910 and 1918, a movement of the vote from a confessional to a class alignment. That finding leads inescapably to the conclusion that the rise of Labour and the decline of the Liberals are bound up in the same packet with the substitution of class for religion as the major social division underlying the British party system.

Wald's analysis and conclusions flow from the assumption, common to many analyses of the period but challenged in the previous chapter, that religious affiliation was more or less equally spread across all classes. Chapter 3, however, examined this interpretation in considerable detail and concluded that religious incorporation was not equally distributed across class. In general, with the exception of the Roman Catholics, it was the middle classes and not the working classes who found the most solace in religion. Only if it is assumed that religious commitments are equally spread across class can it be argued that the religious decline is necessary for a shift to a class alignment.

Instead the urban working class found itself culturally, religiously and increasingly physically isolated in the large industrial cities during the period. This isolation of the industrial working class became one of its defining characteristics. Such conditions give rise to Disraeli's Two Nations remark in his 1845 novel, *Sybil*, but conditions remained little changed in the late Victorian period. As Jones[44] remarked:

The distinctiveness of a working-class way of life was enormously accentuated. Its separateness and impermeability were now reflected in a dense and inward-looking culture, whose effect was both to emphasise the distance of the working class from the classes above it and to articulate its position with in an apparently permanent social hierarchy.

Under these conditions, any support offered to the Liberals by the working class was a marriage of convenience, not conscience, least of all religious conscience. Therefore, a decline in religious fervour is not necessary for the rise of class politics among the working class; rather, the preconditions for class politics among the working class lie only in their effective mobilisation, something that could be accomplished by the emerging trade union movement and Labour Party. Moreover, increasing religious fervour among the middle class would be entirely compatible with this explanation for if the working classes are unchurched and religiously marginal, and perhaps even hostile, then enhanced religious enthusiasm among the middle class could be unappetising to them at best.

While the unchurched working class may have been open to appeals based on class, the same cannot be said of Roman Catholics from similar backgrounds. Despite the restoration of the Church hierarchy in the 1850, the Catholic Church continued to encounter hard times as evidenced by the continual laments of 'leakage' as middle-class English Catholics drifted from its fold. This situation was dramatically reversed with the massive Irish working-class migrations to London and the industrial cities of the Midlands.[45] More importantly for this analysis, the leakage of the English middle class and the influx of the Irish working class dramatically changed the social character of the Church, necessitating an intensive organisational effort which met with more success than its Protestant counterparts.[46]

The results of Chapter 4 addressed part of the Strange Death question: what was the role of religion in the cause of death? The conclusion was that the decline of Liberalism is not due to the loss of its religious appeal to middle-class Nonconformists who are moving towards Liberalism in increasing numbers. While it is true that the Liberals suffer losses to the Conservatives from among the Roman Catholic working class, this is not due to the waning of religion, but to the triumph of religion over ethnicity: for Irish Roman Catholics, religious education is more important than Home Rule. The traditionalist interpretation appears to be decisively rejected.

If the importance of religion is increasing during the period, does the revisionist interpretation centring on class voting receive support?

Figure 5.4 presents the model addressing this question. In this model the Liberal, Lib-Lab and Labour simplex processes are pitted against each other. The results clearly demonstrate that it is the increasing loss of working-class support channelled to Labour through the trade union movement that lays the foundations for the death of Liberalism. The election of 1906 marks the turning point in Liberalism's fortunes. In that election Labour broke with Lib-Labism and, although formally still allied with the Liberals, ran its own candidates in many contests. The results are clearly evident in the model: the accelerated movement of working-class support to Labour begins in 1900 and increases rapidly in 1906. Moreover, Roman Catholic working-class support shifts from the Lib-Labs to Labour after 1906, leaving the Lib-Labs to gain slightly from unorganised labour and the Nonconformist Alliance. In the meantime, the Liberals show continued gains from the Nonconformist middle class (these results are similar to those in Figure 5.3).

The path coefficients linking the parties display these shifting alliances. All three parties – Liberals, Lib-Labs and Labour – move on different dimensions. From 1885 to 1906 the Liberals and Lib-Labs are becoming more distinct, but begin to become more similar after 1906. Until 1895 Labour has little to distinguish itself from either the Liberals or the Lib-Labs, but after 1900, and particularly after 1906, Labour becomes increasingly distinct from both.

These findings clearly support the revisionist interpretation, but with some important caveats. Class appears conclusively as an important dynamic prior to the First World War and it does play a role in the decline of the Liberals. However, is not the general rise of class that is crucial: it is the enfranchisement and incorporation of the unchurched working class that sets the stage for the death of Liberalism. Thus at the same time that religion is becoming more politically salient among both middle-class Anglicans and Nonconformists, the unchurched working class is coming into its own through the trade union movement and the Labour Party.

The distancing of Labour from the Liberals and the Lib-Labs opened up new possibilities for vote shifts, and among these were the Roman Catholic working class. Previous models demonstrated that the Liberals' religious fervour could alienate Roman Catholics despite the Liberal Party's advocacy of Home Rule. The Lib-Lab alliance attached this same stigma to Labour. The years preceding the 1906 election were marked by considerable rancour within Labour over alliance with other political groupings, including the Liberals, and this growing separateness of Labour was accommodated by the Liberals who accepted a greater number of straight fights between Labour and the Conservatives. Cole[47] noted that

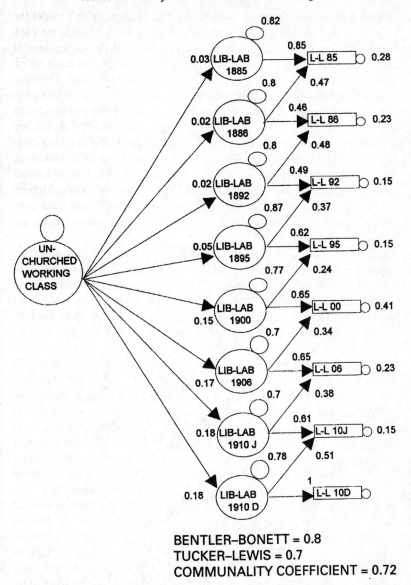

BENTLER–BONETT = 0.8
TUCKER–LEWIS = 0.7
COMMUNALITY COEFFICIENT = 0.72

Figure 5.4   LVPA simplex model of Lib-Lab vote 1885–1910, controlling for Liberal, Labour and non-voters

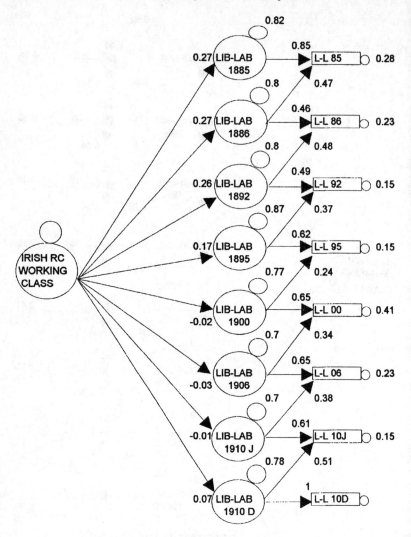

BENTLER–BONETT = 0.8
TUCKER–LEWIS = 0.7
COMMUNALITY COEFFICIENT = 0.72

Figure 5.4   (*cont.*)

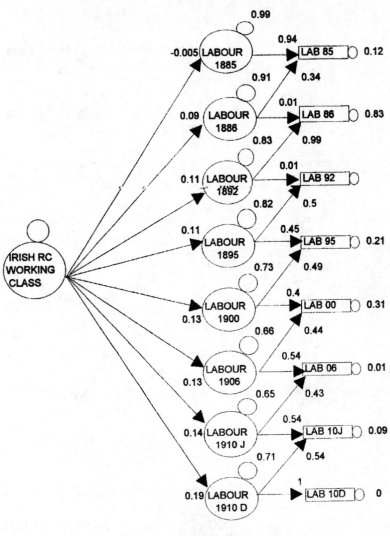

BENTLER–BONETT = 0.8
TUCKER–LEWIS = 0.7
COMMUNALITY COEFFICIENT = **0.72**

Figure 5.4 *(cont.)*

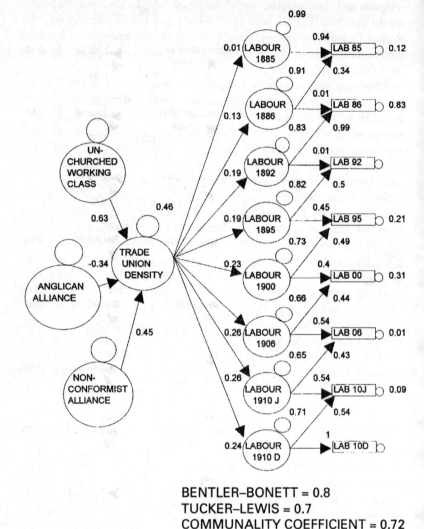

BENTLER–BONETT = 0.8
TUCKER–LEWIS = 0.7
COMMUNALITY COEFFICIENT = 0.72

Figure 5.4   (*cont.*)

precisely these conditions occurred in Lancashire, a area of heavy Irish
Roman Catholic concentrations. Hence, these two conditions – distinctiveness from the Liberals and straight fights with the Conservatives – meant
the Roman Catholic working class could more readily choose between

religious and class appeals. And choose they did. The models demonstrate nicely that before 1906 both the Liberals and Labour were losing the Roman Catholic working-class vote to the Conservatives over the religious education issue, but that after 1906 Labour reversed this trend while the Liberals continued it.

Additional evidence on the changing nature of Liberalism confirms the earlier model's results. It was noted above that Liberalism's success is found to be increasingly associated with low voter turnout rates. Later models make it clear that both the Liberals and the Lib-Labs are increasingly successful in areas of declining voter participation. The most likely interpretation is that both found themselves ensconced in one-party dominant districts typically characterised by lower voter turnout.[48]

The conclusion must be that the revisionist interpretation of the decline of Liberalism and the rise of Labour receives strong and decisive support from this analysis. A decline of religious fervour is not a pre-requisite for the rise of Labour. Indeed the increasing polarisation of politics along religious lines and the middle-class religious revival of the period could co-exist and even abet the rise of class consciousness among the unchurched working class. The models developed in this section provide strong support for this interpretation. The Roman Catholic working class, overwhelmingly of Irish extraction, placed religion above ethnicity as evidenced by their support for the Conservatives. However, following the weakening of Lib-Labism, when the Roman Catholic working class was increasingly offered a class versus religious choice, a significant proportion moved to Labour.

CONCLUSIONS

The aim of this chapter was to define and illustrate short-run changes in electoral alignments between 1885 and 1910. To achieve this goal, Weiner simplex models of change tested several interpretations of the politics of the period. The general findings point to a three-way polarisation of politics: the increasing adherence of the Anglican Alliance to the Conservatives and Unionists, matched by a similar adherence of the Nonconformism to the Liberals. Meanwhile, a growing class division in society enables the expression of class in politics via the rise of Labour. The polarisation is evident in the rates of change found in the Weiner simplex models: all changes grow at increasing rates. One exception exists to this general pattern: internal divisions found within the Roman Catholic working class created by cross-cutting religious and class issues. For the

Roman Catholic working class, the increasing separateness of Labour from the Liberals and Lib-Labs after 1906 opens the possibility for clearer expressions of class, but even then a portion of the Roman Catholic working class continues to place religious schools above class and ethnicity, as evidenced by support for the Conservatives.

These results shed considerable light on the debate between the traditionalist and revisionist interpretations for late Victorian politics in general, and the decline of the Liberal Party in particular. The former emphasises the importance of the religious base of political life and holds that class was of little importance before the First World War in general, and in accounting for the decline of Liberalism in particular. The latter argues the importance of the rise of class to displace religion during the period. The conclusions of this research are that religion and class are less entangled than either interpretation allows. Instead, the findings demonstrate that, while religion was becoming more important for the urban middle class and rural elements, organised religious life was, at best, weak among the urban working class. Consequently, the rise of working-class political cohesion is not dependent on a decline in religious fervour and could even be enhanced by the religious polarisation so evident among supporters of both the major parties.

6 'There are Races, as there are Trees': Challenges to Domestic Empire in Late Victorian Politics

the splitting up of mankind into a multitude of infinitesimal governments, in accordance with their actual differences of dialect or their presumed differences of race, would be to undo the work of civilisation and renounce all the benefits which the slow and painful process of consolidation has procured for mankind ... There are races, as there are trees, which cannot stand erect by themselves, and which, if their growth is not hindered by artificial constraints, are all the healthier for twining round some robuster stem.

Lord Salisbury, 1859

What we require is the administration of public affairs, whether in the executive or the legislature department, in that spirit of the old constitution which held the nation together as a whole, and levelled its united force at the objects of national import, instead of splitting it into a bundle of unfriendly and distrustful fragments.

Lord Salisbury, 1883

Imperialism, sane Imperialism, as distinguished from 'wild cat' Imperialism, is nothing but this – a larger form of patriotism.

Lord Rosebery, 1884

Salisbury's[1] article appeared in the midst of the debate on the franchise expansion and the burgeoning Home Rule controversy of the early 1880s. He and similar thinking Conservatives had long opposed the expansion of democracy and Salisbury himself felt the First Reform Act of 1832 had set England on the course towards mass democracy of which the Second Reform Act of 1867 was merely another step on a self-destructive path. With ever greater concern he followed the development of politics in France and strenuously affirmed his conviction that expanding the franchise was folly, leading inevitably to the confrontation of the propertied aristocracy and unpropertied masses. Schooled in the classical and contemporary debates surrounding the Classical Republican Problem, Salisbury increasingly and alarmingly viewed a growing struggle over property redistribution. In 1862, he wrote:[2] 'The struggle for power in our day lies not between the Crown and people, or between a caste of nobles and a bourgeoisie, but between the classes who have property and the classes who have none'. His fears were further heightened by the tendency of working men to unite in the nascent trade union movement of the 1860s. In 1867 he worried about the potential for unity among the working classes to redistribute property.[3] In Salisbury's mind the historical questions of politics revolving around the Reformation were being displaced by conflicts of class.

However, by the 1870s Salisbury became increasingly aware of a third spectre haunting Europe: the potential to join class questions to the growing intensity of popular nationalisms. The Conservative set-back in the 1880 election distressed Salisbury as it illustrated the worst effects of mass democracy, class antagonism and the potential of ethnic and national conflict to sway the mass electorate. Gladstone's attack on the Conservative government's toleration of the Bulgarian atrocities in 1876, followed by his successful Midlothian campaign and the Conservative defeat in the 1880 election, deeply alarmed Salisbury and other Conservative aristocrats.[4]

The growth of popular democracy, the increasing class tensions and rising spectre of divisive nationalisms within Britain faced the Conservatives with a severe dilemma. How could the party's traditional leadership overcome their disdain for popular electoral politics and prevent the disintegration so feared by Salisbury and others? Salisbury's revulsion at popular electoral democracy and the demands of campaigning were shared by many in the party. Like other Conservatives, he disdained any effort to curry favour among the newly enfranchised and considered others' attempts to do so as a compromise of the principles of good government as well as the Conservative party. Unlike Disraeli he saw little to be gained from wooing the unpropertied masses with social reforms since such efforts created a danger of 'laying down new principles of legislation which, upon other subjects and under a political system where power resided with the greatest number, would some day be used most disadvantageously against them.'[5] The disastrous Conservative defeat of 1880 further discredited the 'Tory Democracy' of Disraeli and reinforced the anti-democratic convictions of Salisbury and Northcote among others. In addition, the death of Disraeli in 1881 removed his weakened voice from the Tory Democracy debate.

DEMOCRACY, SALISBURY AND THE PRIMROSE LEAGUE

Nevertheless, at the same time that Salisbury and old line Conservatives were steadfastly opposing any truck with democracy, the Fourth Party founded the Primrose League. The League was the Conservatives' attempt to educate the expanded electorate to dance in their chains in a period of greater scrutiny of electoral expenditure and threat of imperial disintegration. While membership was open to all, barring only atheists and enemies of the British Empire, the oath made clear the League's purpose:[6]

> I declare, on my honour and faith, that I will devote my best ability to the maintenance of Religion, of the Estates of the Realm, and of the unity of the British Empire under our Sovereign ...

Salisbury's proclamations on 'disintegration' and his reluctant support for the League illustrates the Conservatives' struggle to come to terms with the reforms of 1883–5. Equally important, they also offer some contemporary insights into the forces of mass politics; in spite of Salisbury's vague understanding and reactionary interpretation, his views are crucial to understanding the Conservative response to the 1880s. During this period Salisbury served as Prime Minister three times as well as being Foreign Secretary. His influence on the Conservatives' transition to mass politics was substantial and his reluctant acceptance of the League was crucial to this transformation.

However much Salisbury disdained mass politics, his hyperbolic and reactionary 1883 article correctly identified the three central forces threatening the Empire in late Victorian Britain: democracy, capitalism and nationalism with their attendant consequences for classes, masses and races. This chapter focuses on the interactions among these forces as manifested in the effects of the Third Reform Act, the growing class awareness and the rise of ethno-nationalism which culminated in the Home Rule debates and underpinned the political realignment of the period. Previous chapters described a three-way polarisation of politics: the increasing adherence of the Anglican Alliance to the Conservatives and Unionists, matched by similar adherence of middle-class Nonconformism to the Liberals. Meanwhile, a growing class division in society found expression in the rise of Labour. In previous chapters the analysis of the role of ethnic and regional differences was set aside while we examined broad, country-wide trends in mass politics. We now introduce territorial dimensions into the political analysis as a means of capturing these regional and ethnic dynamics.

THE TERRITORIAL DIMENSIONS OF EMPIRE: CORES AND PERIPHERIES

The forces which Salisbury only vaguely grasped as potentially undercutting the Empire underlay the increasing national fragmentation sweeping across Europe in the late nineteenth century. Salisbury's dread that Europe in general, and Britain in particular, would split 'into a bundle of unfriendly and distrustful fragments' seemed to be borne out by the events of the time. Nationalists, inspired by Mazzini's cry, 'Every nation a state, only one state for the entire nation', found ready mass followings among Europe's mosaic of ethnic populations.[7]

It was, however, the dynamics of democracy, capitalism and nationalism which constituted the origins of the threats to the Empires of Europe. Democracy represented by the expansion of the franchise held dual consequences for Salisbury's fears of 'disintegration': the electoral reforms of 1883–5 made emotional appeals to the mass electorate increasingly effective; and politicians soon discovered the emotive power and charisma of nationalism to move the masses, fragment class movements, and mobilise the citizenry for war. Often national unity was achieved at great cost to ethnic minorities. Capitalism fed this dynamic through uneven geographic diffusion and development and thus, while some regions prospered, others became economic backwaters; where such regions possessed ethnic distinctiveness, the conditions were ripe for challenges to imperial authority.

In an effort to better understand the dynamics of empire, scholars have elaborated the core-periphery analysis.[8] The purpose of the core-periphery paradigm was to wrest comparative political analysis from dependence on the nation-state as the prime unit of analysis. The common thrust of core-periphery analysis argues that nation-states must not be seen as autonomous, monolithic units, but rather as composed of cores and peripheries which themselves are embedded in a world economy consisting of cores and peripheries.

One central concern of the core-periphery paradigm is nation-building, ethnic mobilisation and resistance to nation-building. Two broad theoretical approaches distinguish the analysis of these concerns and agree on the distinguishing features of cores and peripheries: first, a set of attributes distinguishes cores from peripheries; second, exchanges between core and periphery are defined by the goods exchanged and the nature of the exchange relations; third, the pattern of interaction between cores and peripheries.[9] Without exception cores appear as advantaged and peripheries as disadvantaged. First, economic attributes define cores and peripheries: peripheries are poorly developed primary economies, with low technology and high labour-intensive activities, having a lower standard of living and quality of life, lacking in technical capacity and capital goods, and having less diverse economies.

The second feature defining core-periphery relations is exchange patterns: what and how exchanges take place. Most scholars hold that peripheries export low value-added products and import high value-added ones.

While there is agreement on what is exchanged, there is less agreement on how it is exchanged. One interpretation leans towards developmental arguments based on neo-classical economic assumptions and limited assimilation theory. In the long run, core-periphery exchange is to be mutually beneficial: exchange follows comparative advantage, trade partners are rational and obtain the freedom of choice permitted by the market. Inter-personal comparisons of utility are symmetrical and markets are noncumulative, self-correcting mechanisms. An alternative interpretation holds that capitalist cores penetrate pre-capitalist or weak capitalist peripheries to exploit their peoples, to transport surplus value to the core, and to distort and dominate peripheral economies, polities and cultures. Exchange is, therefore, cumulative exploitation, domination, distortion and permanent underdevelopment of the periphery by the core.

The third feature of core-periphery relations is the interaction pattern. Generally core-periphery interaction is portrayed as feudal: interactions among peripheries of the same core are minimal; interaction with other peripheries and other cores is mediated by each periphery's own core.

In sum, most scholars employing the core-periphery metaphor make the following distinctions between cores and peripheries: cores are more economically, politically and socially developed, while peripheries are much less so. Cores export high value-added goods to peripheries and import low value-added goods from peripheries. While cores may interact with other cores, they do not have direct access to other cores' peripheries. Moreover, peripheries are limited to dealing directly with their own core; other interactions are mediated by that core.

Core-periphery analysis provides the conceptual tools to understand the rise and nature of territorial politics in late Victorian Britain. Territorial politics rearranged political divisions in yet another manner in Britain, dividing class from class and religion from religion. It is crucial for understanding the transformation of the Conservatives, the 'Strange Death of the Liberals' and the rise of Labour. Core-periphery research generates explanations for this transformation.

The bulk of this research is summarised in three hypotheses[10] on the relationship of core-periphery location, class and peripheral nationalism:

1. *The developmental hypothesis* holds that the rise of class politics will efface territorial, ethnic and religious identifications which undergird pre-capitalist political life rendering in its extreme class-based politics. The hypothesis builds on nineteenth century social theory, finds more recent expression in the structural-functionalist literature, but has been severely challenged by the resurgence of peripheral nationalism.

2. *The reactive ethnicity hypothesis* states that uneven class development, combined with the continuance of territorial, ethnic and religious identifications, engenders the cultural division of labour in the periphery bringing forth reactive ethnic cleavages. This hypothesis has two variations: the first holds that reactive ethnicity is stronger among the peripheral working class and is a response to uneven development, while the second variant maintains that ethnic nationalism represents a response to modernisation by the middle classes, particularly the intelligentsia.

3. *The ethnic competition hypothesis* states that economic development and inequalities will generate political cohesiveness across classes within ethnic groups as these groups become more aware of their economic subordination to the core.

THE POLITICS OF EMPIRE: CORE AND PERIPHERY IN LATE VICTORIAN BRITAIN

With the core-periphery paradigm the disintegration which so concerned Salisbury becomes much easier to understand and interpret. It provides a theoretical basis for analysing the challenges to Empire which so dominated late Victorian politics. The question obviously arises: did late Victorian Britain possess the salient features of the core-periphery dynamic?

With few exceptions the economic, territorial and cultural divisions correspond to those characteristics required in core-periphery analysis. Core-periphery analysis establishes four features as typical of cores and peripheries: (1) wealth and its sources; (2) cultural strength, homogeneity and integration; (3) the nature of goods produced and exchanged; and (4) the interaction between cores and peripheries.

In examining Britain in this period, it is quite apparent that significant differences in wealth exist between the core and periphery. Despite the presence of important economic centres in the Midlands, Wales and Scotland, Urwin[11] traces differences in industry and wealth across the period and notes that, although there is some convergence by the inter-war period, during the late Victorian Era significant regional differences remain. Moreover, not only are there differences in wealth between the core area of London and Central England and the remainder of the country, but the origins of the wealth differ as well. Rubinstein[12] notes: 'In economic terms, the chief distinction between the London- and provincial-based middle classes was that one was largely capital- and the other largely labour-intensive.' Thus, in terms of both the level of wealth and its origins, the core-periphery distinction holds for late nineteenth-century Britain.

The cultural distinction between Central England and the remainder of the country is, of course, well known and noted by numerous scholars.[13] Whereas Central England is overwhelmingly Anglican and English speaking, the periphery is largely divided among non-established church and chapel with significant non-English speaking areas. Moreover, whereas the core is culturally homogeneous, the periphery is culturally fragmented by religious and linguistic differences. Cultural fragmentation significantly affected the potential alliances across classes in both the core and the periphery. Again, as Rubinstein[14] notes:

The ties between London's middle class and the old society were many and varied. Two of the more important were in religion and in the education secured for its sons. Most London-based businessmen who were not aliens were Anglicans, and few were Protestant dissenters – a quite different profile from their northern counterparts. The Anglicanism of London's business class, together with its wealth, made its members far readier to send its sons to a major public school and Oxbridge than were the manufacturers. Most of the major public schools were located in London and the Home Counties and were of Anglican foundation.

A further feature of core-periphery relations is the nature of the exchange between them. Here again a distinction is evident between Central England and the remainder of the country. According to core-periphery analysis, peripheries are characterised by the export of raw materials and semi-finished goods and labour to the core while cores export higher valued-added goods. Lee[15] identified four regional economies in Britain in 1881: rural, textile manufacture, clothing manufacture and a metropolitan region focused on London and the Home Counties, the latter 'strongly linked to the growth of service industries and to a number of consumer and market oriented manufacturing trades': in other words, a core.

Similarly, labour migrated during the period from lesser developed regions to more developed regions where new employment opportunities were to be found.[16] The result was that population growth came to characterise the more developed regions, particularly the South-East. As a consequence, Urwin[17] notes: 'Population was concentrated in the new industrial regions, and led steadily to an increase in England's share of the British population at the expense of the other regions.'

The combination of regional economic development and population movements held distinct territorial consequences. Lee[18] notes that the general increase in service employment during the period generated distinct regional effects:

> This nationally dominant pattern is most strongly associated at the regional level with the economy of South East England. As was noted above, over half the new jobs in Britain between 1841 and 1911 were in service employment; 20 percent of those service jobs were in London and Middlesex and 40 percent were in the twelve counties of the South East. In other words, for every ten jobs created in the entire country one was in services in London and another was in services in the rest of the South East.

The effects of regional economies, moreover, reinforced disparities in regional wealth. Employment associated with the highest wages was also found in the growing service sector. The consequences for wealth and income generation were 'that larger populations and higher incomes at the national and, of course, regional level, are more internally-generated and less export-orientated than is the case in smaller populations. The South East appears to have become the world's first large-scale consumer economy.'[19] With some exceptions, for example, the Clydeside, value-added is a direct inverse of a function of distance from the core.

A final characteristic of core-periphery relationships is found in the pattern of interaction between them. Cores function as mediators among peripheries; peripheries have little direct contact with each other. The centralisation of political power and administration at Westminster typifies this relationship. Even more characteristic are dendritic patterns of communication and trade.[20] While the construction of the Victorian railway did indeed knit Britain more tightly together than ever before, its dendritic pattern channelled most all communication and commerce through London, greatly restricting inter-periphery contacts.[21]

To pursue the core-periphery analysis further, we must first establish approximate boundaries of core and periphery and then define the differing nature of each. Previous research[22] confirms the judgement of others that the greatest differences exist between Central England and the remainder of the country.[23] In other words, London and the South-East form the most distinctive economic region with the balance of the country more similar to itself than to Central England.

We can test these differences with our data. The test examines the success of the measurement model for the socio-economic LVs used in the previous analysis to reconstruct the observed data in both the core and periphery, defined as Central England and non-Central England. If there are no significant differences between the core and periphery, then the model of socio-economic LVs developed earlier should possess equal predictive powers in both core and periphery. If there are significant differences, then the model should falter in either core or periphery. The results presented in Table 6.1 confirm significant differences between the core and periphery.[24] The Tucker–Lewis goodness-of-fit statistic accounts for the degrees of freedom differences across the models, making comparisons of goodness-of-fit contrast possible.

The statistics show that the model for all of Britain provides the best overall fit to the social factors in both the entire country as well as the periphery, (that is, non-Central England). On the other hand, the country-wide model generates a poor fit for the core (that is, Central England). Examining the best fitting model for the core, we see that it provides the best fit to the data for Central England, but fits the peripheral data less well than the total model. The core model fits the country-wide data poorly, producing several incorrect signed coefficients. In other words, while the model of socio-economic LVs developed for Britain as a whole fits the periphery quite well, it does not fit the core as well. Hence, it is necessary to construct a better model of the socio-economic contours of the core.

Table 6.1   Goodness-of-fit tests for core-periphery differences
(Tucker–Lewis fit statistics)

Model	Data		
	Total	Core	Periphery
Total	0.450	0.167	0.435
Core	0.333*	0.258	0.285

*Some coefficients are incorrectly signed.
Core = Central England = London and Home Counties.
Periphery = Remainder of the country.

Turning our attention to the resulting configuration of social factors generated by the best fitting models in the core and the periphery, we find, as expected, the factors are identical in the periphery and the all-Britain model. In the core, however, a different set of factors appear.

1. *Anglican Alliance*: This factor is similar to that found in the periphery, but obtains higher loadings on both Church Sunday and day school, while developing a lower loading on agricultural employment and middle class.
2. *Nonconformist Working Class*: In contrast to the all-Britain and periphery models, the working class in the core is more incorporated into organised religion. The Nonconformist working class loads highly on chapel attendance and Sunday school attendance as well as manual labourers, and moderately high on industrial and skilled labour. It also loads negatively on the middle class.
3. *Nonconformist Alliance*: This factor is close to its counterpart in the all-Britain and periphery models, loading on middle-class and rural areas with high Welsh born migrant population. In contrast to the all-Britain and periphery models, the factor does not load on chapel or Sunday School attendance, but only on Nonconformist clergy.
4. *Roman Catholic Working Class*: In contrast to its counterpart in the all-Britain and periphery models, this factor, while loading on Catholicism, loads less on the least-skilled Irish born labour, and more on industrial workers incorporated in the Roman Church.
5. *Unchurched Migrant Working Class*: This is a new factor representing the least skilled, non-agricultural general labour, and in the core is heavily recruited from Irish and Scottish, and to a lesser degree Welsh, migrants. These workers are not incorporated into organised religion.

These results demonstrate a different relationship between the working class and religion than is found in the periphery. In the periphery, paralleling the all-Britain results, there appears an unchurched working class not incorporated into organised religion. The only members of working class evidencing religious incorporation are Irish Roman Catholics. In the core, however, there appear to be three working classes: Roman Catholic, Nonconformist and the unchurched. These results suggest that Roman Catholic efforts to reach the working class met with considerable success in both core and periphery, although with different results. In the periphery, the Roman Church accomplished its greatest successes, with Irish migrants among the least skilled. In the core success was greater among industrial workers. In both instances, the Sunday schools and day schools were central to the Church's efforts.[25]

For the Nonconformists, their successes appear mostly among the middle and rural classes in the periphery, but at the core their efforts were successful among middle, rural and working classes. The middle-class and rural adherents receive more ministering, while the working classes enrolled in the Sunday school movement. The importance of the Sunday school movement to both Nonconformist and Catholics should not be underestimated. It emerges as the most important institution for domesticating the working classes in the core.[26] Wickham[27] termed the Sunday schools 'a major working class institution in the nineteenth century, and the source of an indefinable, no doubt slight, but pervasive influence upon the people at large'. Thompson[28] states the accomplishments of the Sunday school movement in incorporating the working classes in England:

> By 1833 the Sunday schools were claiming 1.5 million pupils and by 1851 almost 2.5 million, a figure that represented roughly two thirds of the five to fourteen age group; their popularity continued to increase, as church attendance itself declined, to reach a peak of 6 million pupils in 1906, well over 80 percent of the age group. In other words it was exceptional for the late Victorian child, of whatever social class, not to go to Sunday school.

As Thompson[29] notes, the Sunday school teachings instilled the values of 'orderliness, punctuality, industry, and cleanliness ... the same as those found in the respectable working class home'. The values of Sunday school and the respectable working-class home 'reinforced each other, as mutually supporting strands in the working class culture into which the Sunday schools had been incorporated'. Thompson,[30] terming his own work 'Anglocentric', indicates his comments are most appropriate to England rather than the entire country.

Finally, there exist at the core the least skilled and least religiously incorporated members of the working class: the non-agricultural general labourers, consisting heavily of migrants from the periphery who are not affiliated with organised religion. It was this class that observers like Booth most despaired of as 'outside all religious bodies' and most infected with the social ills of the times.[31]

THE POLITICS OF EMPIRE: CORE AND COUNTER-CORE MASS POLITICS

Core-periphery analysis encourages the testing of interpretations of territorial politics and counter-core movements in late Victorian Britain. In the previous section of this chapter the four arguments central to core-periphery dynamics were briefly reviewed. Now it is possible to examine the developmental, the two reactive ethnicity and the ethnic competition hypotheses in the context of the politics of Empire. In this section we again use Weiner simplex models of the political changes of the period to disentangle these competing interpretations.

The developmental hypothesis forms the null hypothesis since it postulates no differences between core and periphery; instead it holds that the rise of class politics will efface territorial, ethnic and religious differences. Pelling's analysis rests precisely on this interpretation. He states: the rise of Labour and the decline of the Liberals 'was the result of long-term social and economic changes which were simultaneously uniting Britain geographically while dividing her inhabitants in terms of class'.[32] Previous research[33] directly tested the hypothesis and found it lacking. Moreover, secondary evidence cited above offers little support for the developmental argument.

On the other hand, the core-periphery interpretation postulates three possible outcomes for peripheral nationalism: reactive ethnicity on the part of the middle classes, reactive ethnicity on the part of the working classes and ethnic competition where class divisions are subordinated to ethnic identities. To examine these arguments we analyse models of party voting in core and periphery comparing both to the all-Britain model developed in Chapter 4.

Before examining the model's results it may be helpful to describe the various anticipated findings. The developmental hypothesis postulates no core-periphery differences. If the models display increasing polarisation of voting for the parties advocating territorial differences, the Liberals and the Unionists, then these results counter the developmental interpretation.

The reactive ethnicity interpretation offers two possible outcomes: first, heightened peripheral nationalism among the middle class while the working class supports class politics. This would be evidenced by polarisation of the Anglican and Nonconformist middle class between the Unionists and the Liberals while the working class supports Labour. Next, the second reactive ethnicity hypothesis sees heightened peripheral national consciousness among the working class while the middle class supports class politics; this would be underlined by working-class support for the Liberals and middle class support for the Conservatives.

Finally, the ethnic competition reasoning states both middle and working classes will support the peripheral nationalism; this would be indicated by both middle-class and working-class support for the Liberals, with the Unionists, Conservatives and Labour doing poorly in the periphery.

Meanwhile in the core several alternatives are also possible. If the core middle and working classes are flattered by the heights of Empire, they will support the Unionists and the integrity of Empire against the Liberals and Labour. This outcome was a popular contemporary interpretation and one that continues today with distinctions sometimes drawn among different elements of the working class.[34] On the other hand, if religion and class are more salient than imperial grandeur, then Nonconformists will support the Liberals while the working class will go with Labour.

THE POLITICS OF PERIPHERAL DISSENT

The results of the analysis for the periphery model generate no support for the developmental interpretation. Instead of increasing homogeneity of regional electoral politics across the period, increasing differences appear. We see the increasing polarisation of electoral politics between the Unionists and Liberals in the periphery. These results support the interpretation of increasing regional differences across the period as the Anglican and Nonconformist Alliances are more and more drawn towards the parties advocating divergent positions on the central issue of the politics of Empire: Home Rule. For the Liberals in the periphery this meant a growing reliance on their Nonconformist, middle-class and rural support as they became the defenders of the periphery against the core. As Urwin[35] notes, these trends foreshadowed the decline of the Liberals in the inter-war period:

In Scotland and Wales [the Liberal party] was driven back to the rural fringes where it continued to reflect, for a while, more traditional peripheral values and social network politics. The party's decline, in a sense, emphasised more pointedly its historic stance as an 'anti-centre' party: where effective communication (that is, with London) was weaker, a relatively stronger Liberal vote tended to persist in the following decades.

Figures 6.1 and 6.2 present the model for the party vote growth curves in the periphery and core respectively; we will first focus our analysis on peripheral politics. A comparison of the regional differences for the parties shows that the regional electoral polarisation is almost exclusively a phenomenon among the middle class and rural populations in both the country at large as well as in the periphery. The unionised and non-unionised working classes demonstrate no support for either the Unionist or Liberal causes in either model. Instead class politics predominates with both the unionised and non-unionised working class supporting Labour. These results are further confirmed by the shift of support for the Lib-Labs in the periphery between 1885–95 and 1900–10, as shown in Figure 6.1. With the break-up of the Lib-Lab alliance in 1906, both the unionised and non-unionised working class show a marked shift to Labour and away from the Lib-Labs. The 1900–6 Lib-Lab vote trend generates no significant paths from the socio-economic LVs.

Contrasting class differences between the periphery and the all-Britain models in Figures 4.2–6, we find clear evidence to reject the ethnic competition hypothesis as well as the reactive ethnicity interpretation for the working class. While the Anglican and Nonconformist middle classes moved strongly towards the Unionist and Liberal camps, the working class showed no support for either party. Instead the working class exhibited increasing support at an increasing rate for Labour, which after 1906 was mobilised and concentrated by the trade union movement. The development of class voting among the unchurched working class is strong across both core and periphery, but markedly stronger in the periphery.

These findings help to clarify a number of important points related to core-periphery politics. Reactive ethnicity is indisputably a phenomenon of the religious and ethic middle classes and rural workers, but not apparent for the urban working class. The religiously incorporated middle classes display increasing conflict, particularly in the periphery on the question of Empire. The working class, on the other hand, develops increasing similarity across the core-periphery divide.

The situation becomes more complex, however, when the working class is divided by religious differences. So far the analysis has focused on the middle classes where religion, class, ethnicity and imperialism are reinforcing. However, the Roman Catholic working class represents a strata where religion, class and imperial loyalties are in competition. As we witnessed earlier, working-class Roman Catholics were attracted to the Conservatives' policies on religious education, but repulsed by the Conservatives' alliance with the Unionists on the Home Rule question. On the other hand, they found the Liberals' position on Home Rule, in

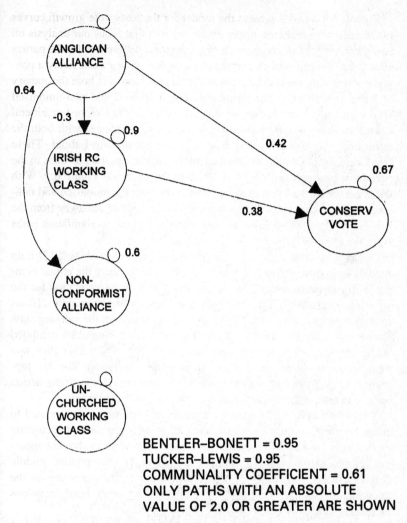

BENTLER–BONETT = 0.95
TUCKER–LEWIS = 0.95
COMMUNALITY COEFFICIENT = 0.61
ONLY PATHS WITH AN ABSOLUTE
VALUE OF 2.0 OR GREATER ARE SHOWN

Figure 6.1   LVPA model of peripheral vote trends 1885–1910 ((a) Conservative Party vote trend

general, and on Ireland, in particular, appealing, but the Liberals' opposition to religious schools offensive. Moreover, both parties', and particularly the Conservatives', stance on class questions was antagonistic to working-class Catholics. The dilemmas were no clearer with respect to Labour. While Labour's solicitations on class were engaging, the party's

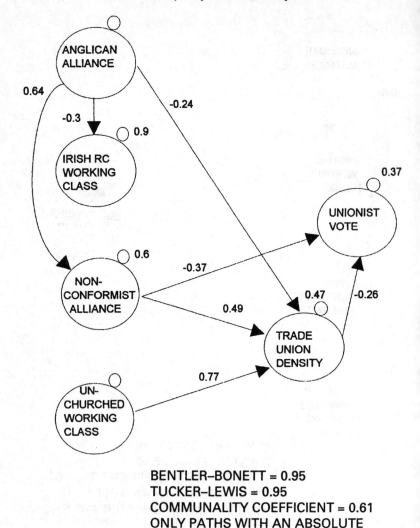

BENTLER–BONETT = 0.95
TUCKER–LEWIS = 0.95
COMMUNALITY COEFFICIENT = 0.61
ONLY PATHS WITH AN ABSOLUTE
VALUE OF 2.0 OR GREATER ARE SHOWN

Figure 6.1   (*cont.*) (b) Unionist vote trend controlling for conservative trend

attitude on religious schools was not. We observed in Chapters 4 and 5 how these dilemmas worked themselves out in the all-Britain model; here we contrast these dynamics with those in the periphery. As in the all-Britain model, working-class Catholics are torn between class, religion

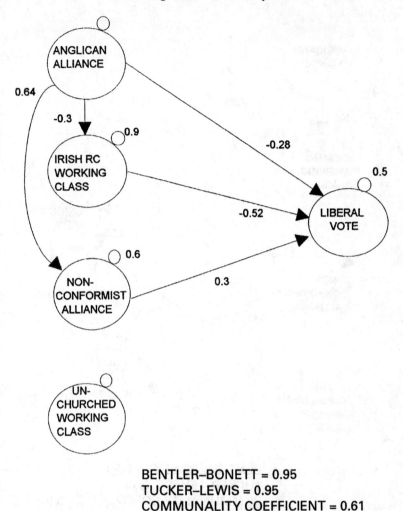

BENTLER–BONETT = 0.95
TUCKER–LEWIS = 0.95
COMMUNALITY COEFFICIENT = 0.61
ONLY PATHS WITH AN ABSOLUTE
VALUE OF 2.0 OR GREATER ARE SHOWN

Figure 6.1 (*cont.*) (c) Liberal vote trend

and empire, seemingly resolving the dilemma by dividing their support
between the party most favourable on religious education but
unfavourable on class (that is, the Conservatives), and the party most
favourable on class and least unfavourable on religion (that is, Labour),

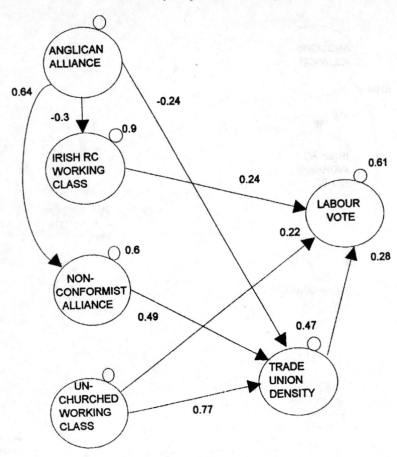

BENTLER–BONETT = 0.95
TUCKER–LEWIS = 0.95
COMMUNALITY COEFFICIENT = 0.61
ONLY PATHS WITH AN ABSOLUTE
VALUE OF 2.0 OR GREATER ARE SHOWN

Figure 6.1   *(cont.)* (d) Labour vote trend

while avoiding the party most unfavourable on empire (that is, the Unionists). In the periphery this dynamic is confirmed: neither in Britain as a whole nor as the periphery does the Roman Catholic working class support the Unionists. In both core and periphery, support is divided

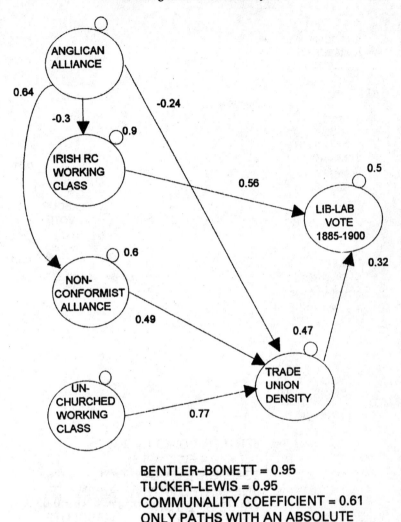

BENTLER–BONETT = 0.95
TUCKER–LEWIS = 0.95
COMMUNALITY COEFFICIENT = 0.61
ONLY PATHS WITH AN ABSOLUTE
VALUE OF 2.0 OR GREATER ARE SHOWN

Figure 6.1   (*cont.*) (e) Lib-Lab vote trend

between the Conservatives and Labour, with support for Conservatives stronger in the periphery and support for Labour stronger in the all-Britain model. The support for the Conservatives increases after 1895 when attention to education issues increased. The election of 1895, in particular,

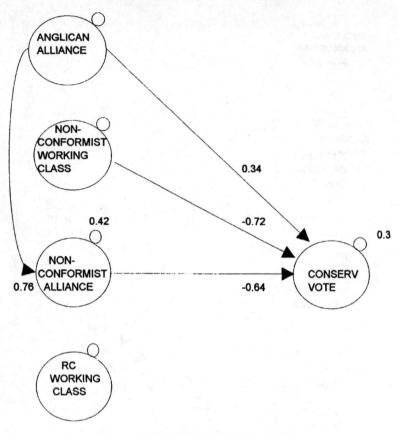

BENTLER–BONETT = 0.89
TUCKER–LEWIS = 0.88
COMMUNALITY COEFFICIENT = 0.66
ONLY PATHS WITH AN ABSOLUTE
VALUE OF 2.0 OR GREATER ARE SHOWN

Figure 6.2   LVPA model of core vote trends 1885–1910 (a) Conservative vote
trend

sharpened the issues on the religious, class and Home Rule questions for
Catholics. The Church issued proclamations for the faithful to support
clerical candidates; our results indicate their apparent success. The Liberal
analysts of the election's results agreed, attributing the losses in the
Scottish constituencies to the Roman Church's action.[36] The technical
results of the models confirm the above interpretations.[37]

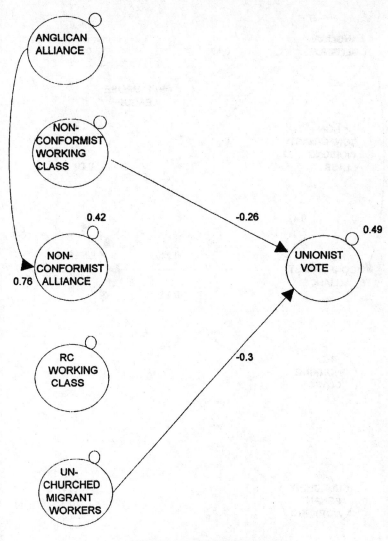

BENTLER–BONETT = 0.89
TUCKER–LEWIS = 0.88
COMMUNALITY COEFFICIENT = 0.66
ONLY PATHS WITH AN ABSOLUTE
VALUE OF 2.0 OR GREATER ARE SHOWN

Figure 6.2   (*cont.*) (b) Unionist vote controlling for Conservative vote trend

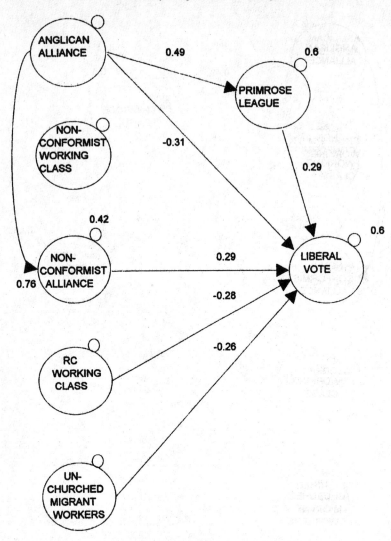

BENTLER–BONETT = 0.89
TUCKER–LEWIS = 0.88
COMMUNALITY COEFFICIENT = 0.66
ONLY PATHS WITH AN ABSOLUTE
VALUE OF 2.0 OR GREATER ARE SHOWN

Figure 6.2   *(cont.)* (c) Liberal vote trend

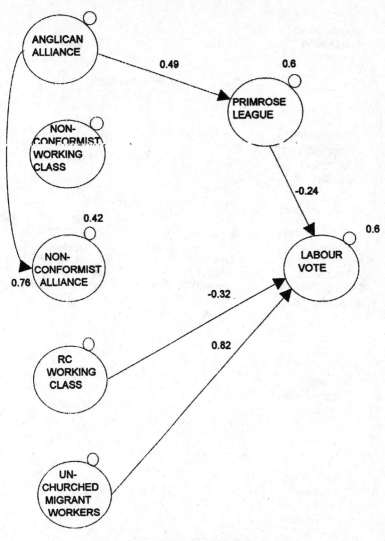

BENTLER–BONETT = 0.89
TUCKER–LEWIS = 0.88
COMMUNALITY COEFFICIENT = 0.66
ONLY PATHS WITH AN ABSOLUTE
VALUE OF 2.0 OR GREATER ARE SHOWN

Figure 6.2 (*cont.*) (d) Labour vote trend

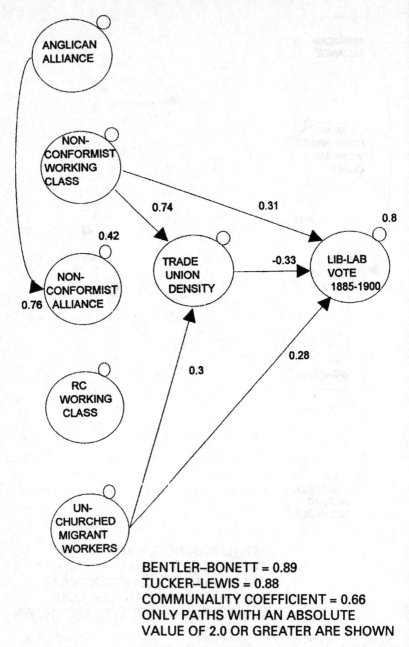

BENTLER–BONETT = 0.89
TUCKER–LEWIS = 0.88
COMMUNALITY COEFFICIENT = 0.66
ONLY PATHS WITH AN ABSOLUTE
VALUE OF 2.0 OR GREATER ARE SHOWN

Figure 6.2   (*cont.*) (e) Lib-Lab vote trend 1885–1900

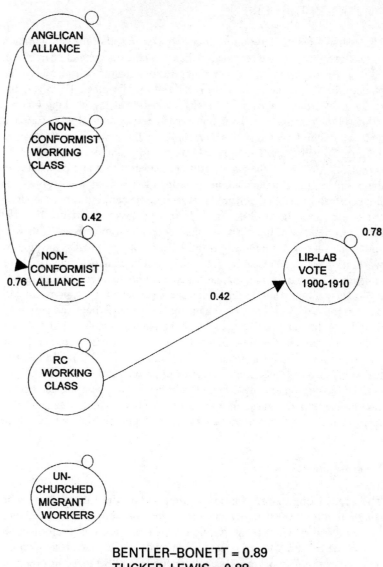

BENTLER–BONETT = 0.89
TUCKER–LEWIS = 0.88
COMMUNALITY COEFFICIENT = 0.66
ONLY PATHS WITH AN ABSOLUTE
VALUE OF 2.0 OR GREATER ARE SHOWN

Figure 6.2   (*cont.*) (f) Lib-Lab vote trend 1900–10

POLITICS IN THE CORE

The distinctive nature of politics in the core is a result of the configuration of its classes. While the Anglican Alliance retains its general character in both core and periphery, the remaining factors change considerably. The Nonconformist Alliance is more rural and middle class. However, the greatest differences appear in the characteristics of the working classes. While in the periphery a distinction existed between the Roman Catholic and unchurched working class, in the core three working classes are evident: Roman Catholics, Nonconformists and unchurched migrants. The composition of these classes also differs between core and periphery. In the periphery the Roman Catholic working class is composed strongly of Irish born and unskilled general labourers; in the core industrial labourers are more important while Irish born are less important. For the Nonconformist working class, manual workers are most important, with additional support from industrial and skilled workers. Finally, the migrant working class draws heavily from the most marginal elements of the working class (that is, migrant, unskilled general labourers).

We have already noted some differences between the religiously incorporated middle classes and rural elements in the all-Britain and periphery models. In the periphery the Anglican and Nonconformist middle classes and rural elements are more divided by questions of Empire than in the country as a whole. These results differ from those in the core. In the core the Anglican and Nonconformist middle class and rural elements are more divided by religion than by Empire. Thus, in the core there is greater cohesion on the imperial question than in the periphery. The evidence for this interpretation exists in the rise of the Liberal Imperialists and the social base of their support.

Liberal Imperialism

The Liberal Imperialists formed a group within the Liberal Party who sought to reform the party by advocating positions long thought anathema to the Liberal creed: state intervention in the economy, social reform, revision of the free trade doctrine, and accommodation to Home Rule within a more general policy of 'progressive' imperialism, all wrapped in a rhetoric of 'national efficiency'.[38] These responses grew out of a concern for the relative decline of Britain in the world economy in general and as a response to the Boer War in particular. The Liberal Imperialists, led by Rosebery, Haldane, Asquith and Grey, advocated a position closer to Conservative-Unionism on the Empire question than the mainstay of the

Liberal Party. Rosebery in particular sought to cast off the Little England image of the Liberals and counter Chamberlain's Liberal-Unionist appeal to the grandeur of Empire. Based on imperial issues alone, by 1905 the Liberal Imperialists accounted for one-third of the party's parliamentary members. In the election of 1906 their number increased again to 96 of 399 Liberal MPs, although their proportion in the party declined.[39]

The images of Empire had a decidedly political aim. Rosebery could wax eloquent, if vaguely, in 1900 on the nature of Empire: 'How marvellous it all is! ... Human, and yet not wholly human, for the most heedless and the most cynical must see the finger of the divine... Do we not hail in this less the energy and fortune of a race than the supreme direction of the Almighty?'[40] In 1901 Rosebery made his famous speech at Chesterfield offering his advice to the Liberal Party. He concluded by stating: 'My last piece of advice to the Party is that it should not disassociate itself, even indirectly, from the new sentiment of Empire which occupies the nation.'[41] Somewhat paradoxically the Liberal Imperialists sought to represent the Empire as consistent with Liberal volunteerism as a deliberate association. In 1901 Grey represented the Empire in these terms: 'The idea of Empire was not an idea of one race domineering over another race. The first thing was the attachment of our self-governing colonies and the splendour of having created them.'[42]

Within this vague and paradoxical thinking the Liberal Imperialists sought both the appeals to the glory of Empire as a symbol of social integration, continuity, stability and patriotism as well as accommodation to Home Rule sentiment by advocating a policy of 'a bit of Home Rule all around', all the while steadfastly denying the establishment of a legislature in Dublin.[43] To this end, they deployed the symbols of Empire in peripheral areas benefiting from the trade with the Empire, notably the industrial areas of Scotland and the Midlands.[44] The results of our analysis, however, show that appeals to Empire by the Liberal Imperialists succeeded in the core, but not in the periphery.

As we noted earlier, peripheral Liberalism successfully appealed to counter-core sentiments on the Home Rule question, placing it in direct opposition to the Unionists and garnering support from the peripheral religious middle class and rural elements. Appeals to the grandeur of Empire and watered-down Home Rule held little charm in the periphery, however. Likewise, appeals to peripheral nationalism did not play well in the core, and here the Liberal Imperialists raised the majesty of Imperial imagery, while downplaying the Liberal positions on questions of education, establishment and entertainment.[45] As Matthew noted, in the election of 1900 the Liberal Imperialists experienced their greatest successes in England

and the contemporary Liberal party analyst, E.T. Cook, argued that: 'To regain ascendancy, liberalism must "attract the rising generation in the great centres of population." Liberal Imperialism, Cook argued, would regain for liberalism' its appeal to the national imagination.'[46] This appeal to patriotism was designed to attract the business and middle classes, who were argued to be 'intensely patriotic', and 'to accept social reform as a patriotic duty, necessary for the strengthening of the empire. [The Liberal Imperialists] believed that effective social reform was possible, while maintaining "the social structure of the nation intact and unbroken".'[47]

These regional differences in Imperialism in general and Liberal Imperialism in particular are supported by a study of voting in the House of Commons during the period. Davis and Huttenback note that:[48]

> Regional differences in imperial attitudes tended to be more marked among Liberals than Conservatives. For members of that former party, when measured against the votes of representatives of the industrial Midlands, those from Ireland, the Southwest and the rural Midlands, and from Scotland and Wales voted less often for imperial legislation, while those from London and the Home Counties voted somewhat more frequently. Among the Conservatives, only those from Ireland appear less and those from London and the home counties more imperialistic than the members from Birmingham and Manchester.

Moreover, the authors note that breaks in the Liberal ranks on imperial issues were most frequent in the Parliaments of 1886–92, 1895–1900 and 1900–6. These results support the interpretation that Imperialism was more in evidence in the core, particularly among Liberals, and that it increased across time at least until 1906. From this evidence we anticipate support for imperialism in the core electorate as well.

Evidence for this interpretation appears in Figure 6.2 which includes the results of a model for Liberal support in the core. Figure 6.2 shows that the usual differences appear among the parties: the Conservatives win support from the Anglican Alliance and opposition from the Nonconformist middle and working classes, with Unionism attracting additional opposition from the Nonconformist working class and unchurched migrants. It is important to note that in the core the Conservatives do not gain support from the Roman Catholic working class, which represents a significant difference from the periphery. Meanwhile, the Liberals receive support from the Nonconformist middle class with opposition from the Anglican Alliance and Roman Catholics.

With some exceptions, these results are consistent with those of the all-Britain model.

In addition, however, the Liberals in the core also win support from the Primrose League, the height of imperialist imagery. This result is not a statistical quirk or error in the data. The result appears in all models in all data sets, and persists in the presence of various control variables. The success of Liberalism in the core is dependent on Liberal Imperialism's appeal to the same symbols put forward by the Primrose League. This interpretation is supported by the fact that while the Anglican Alliance shows a strong affinity to the League, Nonconformism does not. Thus it is not on the basis of religion that the Liberals in the core attracted support in the League's strongholds, but rather on the imperialist, patriotic appeals. Moreover, the membership of the League, which was decidedly middle and lower middle class, would be consistent with support for the Liberals once the divisiveness of Home Rule and domestic issues were downplayed and the integrative images of Empire put forward.

Additional support for this interpretation is found in the across-time analysis of Liberal support in the core. Wiener simplex models of Primrose League support for the Liberals show minimal support until 1900, when a steady climb ensues until 1906 and a slight decline in December of 1910. This pattern parallels the rise of the Liberal Imperialists and their eventual decline noted in the above-cited sources.

Although the Liberal Imperialists existed as a distinct and organised group within the Liberal Party before 1900, the Boer War and its effects on the 1900 'khaki' election gave the Liberal Imperialists the opportunity to advance their cause. The Imperial Liberal Council developed a list of 142 candidates designed 'to be in general agreement with the policy of the council', and placed a representative in each district to distribute literature.[49] These results of our analysis illustrate the effects of these events as well as drawing a even closer relationship between the rise of the Liberal Imperialists and Liberalism's support from the Empire's supporters at the core.

The analysis also confirms that imperialism was most seductive to the middle classes who identified with the institutions of the core. In the periphery appeals to Empire find resonance among the Anglican middle classes and rural elements, but meet resistance among the Nonconformists who favour Home Rule as advanced by the Liberals. In the core, however, religious differences are subordinated to attractions of Empire, with both Anglican and Nonconformist middle classes supporting imperialism. From this perspective the working classes stand in marked contrast.

THE WORKING CLASSES AND EMPIRE

The behaviour of the working classes at the core adds further evidence to working class cohesion across the core-periphery divide. If we again take support for the Unionists and Liberals as the best indicators of imperial or anti-imperialist sympathies, the working classes show little difference across the core-periphery. Working-class support for Unionism is negative to non-existent, while the coefficients for the Liberals are negative. Instead class politics is robust and increasing across time as the working class shifts away from both the Conservatives and Liberals and towards Labour.

While the general picture conforms to increasing class politics among the working classes across core and periphery, differences are evident among these working classes in the across-time analysis. The Nonconformist and unchurched migrant working classes offer the strongest support for the general interpretation. After initially backing the Liberals and opposing the Conservatives in 1885, these working classes clearly shift towards Labour, particularly after 1906. Class politics are strong among the Nonconformist and unchurched working classes, with trade union density adding little to these dynamics. Moreover, the impact of the growing separation of the Lib-Labs from Labour is evident in the shift of both working classes away from the Lib-Labs after 1900. This evidence provides strong confirmation of class triumphing over religious and imperial questions for the working classes.

The exception to these trends is the Roman Catholic working class, a class divided by imperial, religious and class questions. In the core the Roman Catholic working class appears to be divided by regional differences as well in the following manner: in the periphery this class moves towards the Conservatives on the religious education issues and Labour on the class issue, particularly following the Lib-Lab separation in 1906. In the core the situation is different. First, the nature of the class differs: the Roman Catholic working class is more distinctly tied to religious education measures and is drawn from the industrial working class rather than the general unskilled labouring class (as in the periphery). Second, the parties' stance on both the imperial and religious education questions differ from the periphery. As we have seen, the Liberal Imperialists were in ascendancy in the core and arguing against Home Rule for Ireland, as were, of course, the Conservative-Unionists. Moreover, the division of the parties on the education question made it difficult for Roman Catholics to side with the Conservatives on that issue. The Education Act of 1902 had benefited both the Anglicans and Roman Catholics by securing for their religious schools a share of the rates.[50] However, it also raised the ire of the Nonconformists who were returned in larger numbers in the 1906 election.

The ensuing debate at first pitted the Nonconformists and Catholics against Anglicans, but later reversed the alliances with Nonconformists and Anglicans uniting against Catholics.[51] Combined with rising imperial sentiment in both the Liberal and Unionist parties, Roman Catholics with a deep commitment to religious education had few places to turn. One alternative was the Lib-Labs who sided with Labour on the question of Home Rule for Ireland, but who did not favour either secular education as advanced by Labour or nondenominational religious instruction as favoured by the Liberal Nonconformists. The results of the analysis confirm this interpretation. As expected this class shows opposition to the Liberals, but in contrast to its counterpart in the periphery it evidences little movement towards the Conservatives on the religious question or Labour on the class question. Rather the Roman Catholic working class moves towards the Lib-Labs after 1900.

One final note is in order. Considerable attention has been directed to the importance of the expanded franchise and the rise of the Labour Party.[52] The general thesis is that the expansion of the franchise disproportionately advantaged Labour and disadvantaged the Liberals by heightening class issues which displaced the religious issues of the period. Our research paints a more complex picture. For major segments of the working class it was not a question of displacement since they were unincorporated into organised religion. Other elements of the working class were divided over religious and class issues. Only one element of the working class – the Nonconformist working class – fits the case of a major social strata making a decisive shift to Labour from the Liberals. Thus, the rise of Labour and the decline of the Liberals is attributable more to the inability of the Liberals to secure the support of a religiously unincorporated working class than the loss of the Nonconformist working class.[53]

CONCLUSIONS

In 1883 Salisbury published his anonymous and controversial article, 'Disintegration', in the *Quarterly Review*, a highly respected journal of Conservative opinion. In it he painted a picture of a coming dark age during which Britain would be torn by issues of class and empire raised to new prominence by the demagoguery of mass democracy, and in which Britain would be split 'into a bundle of unfriendly and distrustful fragments'. To a remarkable extent Salisbury accurately perceived a future fraught with class and territorial dissent; and particularly in Ireland, his dreads were realised. However, like many Conservative critics of mass politics, Salisbury's worst horrors went unrealised, at least in Britain. Nevertheless, the importance of his views were two-fold: first, Salisbury's fears of 'disintegration' captured the alarm of a major segment of the Conservatives and were important in motivating the adoption of mass organisation by younger Conservatives designed to counter 'disintegration'. Second, his writings, however hyperbolic, suggest a dynamic among democracy, capitalism and empire which more recent scholarship has developed in the form of core-periphery analysis.

This chapter examined the interpretation of late Victorian politics that emphasises the territorial dimension of conflict represented by the core-periphery distinctions. The analysis demonstrated that core-periphery differences capture important distinctions between Central England and the remainder of the country, and that these distinctions are meaningful in discussing the society in the core and the periphery. Next, the analysis explored the differences of mass politics between core and periphery and found these to be significant. The models' results describe a dynamic of rapidly increasing reactive ethnicity among the peripheral middle classes, a phenomenon not encountered among the working classes. In the periphery the ethnic and religious base of political life results in increasing polarisation as Nonconformist urban middle classes and rural components march towards the Liberals while the Anglican middle-class and rural elements stride toward the Unionists. The more firmly ensconced these elements are in organised religious life and ancillary party organisations such as the Primrose League, the more strident their step. In contrast, the peripheral working class, outside organised religious life but united in trade unionism, advances towards Labour.

Meanwhile, in the core, the allures of Empire appeal to both the Anglican and Nonconformist middle classes; while, for the working classes, class politics is more prominent. Anglican middle class and rural elements show greater affiliation to Conservative than Unionist politics, while the Nonconformists are split with middle-class Nonconformists moving towards the Liberal Imperialists and working-class Nonconformists gravitating towards Labour. The exception is the Roman Catholic working class, which finds itself divided by three appeals – class, religious education and Irish Home Rule – and ends by favouring the Lib-Labs in the core.

In a paradox which Salisbury probably would not have appreciated, the forces energised by mass democracy, capitalism and empire realigned late

Victorian politics. However, instead of uniting class against class, or the periphery against the core, as Salisbury so deeply dreaded, the era divided the periphery against the core at the same time as it split the Conservative opposition in the core. The results laid the foundations for both the successful transition of the Conservatives and failed adaptation of the Liberals to mass politics, two processes which opened the way for Labour to emerge as the second party.

7 Philosophers, Porters, Parsons and Parvenus

> the infinite fragmentation of interest and rank into which the division of social labour splits the labourers as well as capitalists and landlords.
>
> Karl Marx, *Capital*, Vol. 3

> What do you say to the elections in the factory districts? Once again the proletariat has discredited itself terribly … Everywhere the proletariat is the tag, rag and bobtail of the official parties, and if any party has gained strength among the new voters, it is the Tories … [I]t can not be denied that the increase in the working-class voters has brought the Tories more than their simple percentage increase; it has improved their relative position … The *parson* has shown unexpected power and so has the cringing to respectability. Not a single working-class candidate has a ghost of a chance, but my Lord Tumnoddy or any *parvenu* snob could have the workers' votes with pleasure.
>
> Friedrich Engels, 1868

> The most repulsive thing here [in Britain] is the bourgeois 'respectability' bred into the bones of the workers. The social division of society into innumerable gradations, each recognised without question, each with its own pride but also its inborn respect for its 'betters' and 'superiors,' is so old and firmly established that the bourgeois still find it pretty easy to get their bait accepted.
>
> Friedrich Engels, 1889

Marx's comments on the 'infinite fragmentation of the interest and rank' by the social division of labour introduces us to one of the major controversies of working-class politics in Victorian Britain: the Labour Aristocracy thesis. The thesis is captured by Engels' laments on the reprehensible politics of the upper ranks of the working class.[1] The Labour Aristocracy controversy revolves around two general propositions on the consequences of industrialisation: first, industrialisation would generate working-class political unity resulting from the proletarianization of labour, or, second, the increasing differentiation of labour would lead to the 'infinite fragmentation of the interest and rank', shattering working-class unity. In its broadest terms the debate also reflects another variation of Pope's vast chain of being: would industrialisation enable the working class to break the great chain replacing it with horizontal class links stronger than Pope's vertical ones, or would industrialisation reaffirm the Pope's vast chain by creating 'innumerable gradations, each recognised without question, each with its own pride but also its inborn respect for its "betters" and "superiors," ... so old and firmly established'?

It is perhaps to their credit that the proponents of the first proposition were so keenly aware of the evidence of the second. The resulting dissonance became a major theoretical problem in the analysis of working-class politics in the Victorian age and continues to the present. We see the controversy in the Engels' remarks. His first comment, from a letter to Marx in 1868, disparages the behaviour of the newly enfranchised workers following the Second Reform Act of 1867 which had expanded suffrage to a small segment only of the better-off working class.[2] His second comment in a letter to Sorge reflects his continued exasperation at persistently similar behaviour of segments of the industrial working class following the Third Reform Act of 1884–5.

Both Marx and Engels perceptively identified the source of this controversy in 'the infinite fragmentation of interest and rank', with the resulting 'social division of society into innumerable gradations'. For Engels and others such gradations militated against Marxist theory which postulated increasing class polarisation as a prerequisite to revolution. For others, like Alfred Marshall, the Victorian economist, such gradations opened the door for the working class to become 'gentlemen' and to gain social respectability for themselves as well as political stability for the country. In this chapter we explore these two contending interpretations, generally termed the Labour Aristocracy Controversy.

THE ORIGINS OF THE LABOUR ARISTOCRACY CONTROVERSY

No analysis of class in late Victorian Britain is complete without a discussion of the labour aristocracy thesis. The thesis became explicit in the mid-Victorian age, but became increasingly contested by Marxist and Non-Marxist observers in the late Victorian period. In a much distilled form, the thesis highlighted two general models of industrial development and their consequences. One interpretation, traced back at least to Adam Smith, emphasised the increasing division of labour as the central feature of industrial society. The division of labour formed the basis for the creation of wealth in the economy as well as engendering ever greater specialisation by workers. If the specialisation of labour generated differences of skills and status, the working class itself would be subject to internal divisions producing differences in political behaviour and militating against proletarianisation and class unity.[3]

Central to this interpretation was the notion that natural differences among individuals are less a consequence of inherent traits and more a result of the division of labour in the market. Adam Smith in *The Wealth of Nations* may have been the first to state the thesis so clearly:

> The difference in the natural talents in different men is, in reality, much less than we are aware of; and the very genius which appears to distinguish men of different professions, when grown up to maturity, is not upon many occasions so much the cause as the effect of the division of labour.[4]

Smith continued, citing his famous example of the philosopher and the street porter who while born 'very much alike', soon 'come to be employed in very different occupations. The difference of talents come then to be taken notice of, and widening by degrees, till at last the vanity of the philosopher is willing to acknowledge scarce any resemblance.'[5]

It is the principle of segmentation by skill and status that is central to the labour aristocracy thesis. Contemporary observers of the Victorian working class often cited such distinctions and their effect was to stratify and fragment the working class, much to the delight of Marshall and the disdain of Engels. Thomas Wright's 1873 study of the working class noted: 'The artisan creed with regard to the labourers is that the latter are an inferior class and that they should be made to know and kept in their place.'[6] Similarly, in 1870 George Potter, trade unionist and radical journalist, remarked: 'The working man belonging to the upper class of his order is a member of the aristocracy of the working classes. He is a man of some culture, is well read in political and social history ... His self-respect is also well developed.'[7]

Reactions to this stratification varied with the ideological perspective. Alfred Marshall in 1873, in his presentation to the Cambridge Reform Club on 'The Future of the Working Classes', could speak of the upward progress and differentiation of the working class who were 'steadily becoming gentlemen'.[8] For Marshall, industrial society meant increasing differentiation based on the division of labour bringing improvement and integration of the working class.

In contrast to this view of the division of labour in industrial society stood Marx and Engels. For an analysis which sought to demonstrate the increasing unity within the working class, engendered by impoverishment and deskilling, the increasing differentiation of labour presented a major challenge. In 1885, Engels updated his previous work, 'The Condition of the Working Class in 1844'.[9] In the revised edition, he cited, among other changes in the industrial landscape, the development of labour 'aristocracy' which lived considerably better than the common labourer. Engels noted:

> They form an aristocracy among the working class; they have succeeded in enforcing for themselves a relatively comfortable position, and they accept it as final. They are model working men ..., and they are very nice people indeed nowadays to deal with, for any sensible capitalist in particular and for the whole capitalist class in general.[10]

For a theorist directly concerned with the political behaviour of the working class, these observations led him to lament the lack of revolutionary fervour among the better-off workers.

This lament became a recurring theme among Marxists, and one which persistently cited the egregious presence of the labour aristocracy, with its moderation and accommodationalism, as obstacles to proletarian revolution. For example, three years later following the election of 1892, Engels afresh grieved the moderation of the British working class, this time for allying themselves with the Liberals.[11] Lenin traced the consequences of 'bourgeois "respectability"' among the working class even further, attributing working-class support for imperialism to the 'aristocracy of labour, i.e., for the minority of skilled and well-paid workers [which] who isolated itself from the mass of the proletariat in close, selfish, craft unions' and whose Liberal sympathies were closer to the capitalists than their fellow workers.[12]

Other contemporary observers of different political views also noted the political differences between the 'labour aristocracy' and the industrial working class. In 1861 Henry Mayhew had noted such differences among the working men of London:

> The artisans are almost to a man red-hot politicians. They are sufficiently educated and thoughtful to have a sense of their importance to the State ... The unskilled labourers are a different class of people. As yet they are as unpolitical as footmen, and instead of entertaining violent democratic opinions, they appear to have no political opinions whatever; or if they do possess any, they rather tend towards the maintenance of 'things as they are' than towards the ascendance of the working people.[13]

THE RECURRENT DEBATE OVER THE LABOUR ARISTOCRACY

Over 100 years later, the existence of a labour aristocracy and its political behaviours continues to occupy historians; the better known essays set the tone for this debate.[14] Pelling sought to sum up the debate and put the question to rest by concluding:

> The concept of the labour aristocracy has had its value in drawing attention to differences within the working class; but if it implies the existence in the late nineteenth and early twentieth century of a labour elite distinctly separated from lower strata and marked by political behaviour of an acquiescent type, then it is a concept that does more harm than good to historical truth ...
>
> The growth of the factory and mining population in the nineteenth century meant the growth of a more homogeneous working class than had existed previously, and in this working class there was no labour aristocracy ... As for politics, it is clear that the Marxist historians have completely got the wrong end of the stick: militancy was much more likely to be found among the better-off than among the poorer workers.[15]

Needless to say, the controversy was not laid to rest by Pelling's benediction. Marxist and other historians continued to develop variations on a theme which emphasised the continued growth of the labour aristocracy as a distinct class and their role in promoting moderation and accommodation. In a case study of the labour aristocracy in Victorian London, Crossick emphasised the accommodationalism of the labour aristocracy and its importance to the peaceful transformation of period: 'The labour aristocracy adopted enough of the dominant ideology of mid-Victorian England to contribute to the stabilisation of society as a whole.'[16] Crossick also noted that by the late Victorian period the position of the labour aristocracy was differentiated further from the working class by the formation of the industrial working class enmeshed in large scale production, the consequent deskilling of labour and the resulting increased labour militancy behind the New Unionism of the 1880s.[17] More further commented on the increasing separation of the labour aristocracy from industrial labour by their isolation in smaller factories and shops.[18] Despite, or perhaps because of, the physical and regional division of labour, Perkin stated that the labour aristocracy continued to widen wage differentials at least until 1890.[19]

In an extensive commentary on the literature and the controversy, Gray reviewed the importance assigned to division of labour among the working classes in general, and to the existence of a 'labour aristocracy' in particular.[20] To the labour aristocracy is attributed a central role in the peaceful transition of Britain to mass democracy in an industrial society. The labour aristocracy is represented as an important transmission belt of bourgeois culture to the working class, as providing political leadership for working-class movements and as underpinning the relatively smooth transition to and stability of capitalist society. Moreover, differentiation within the working class was a major factor militating against working-class unity. Thompson lucidly summarised this interpretation as:

> The respectable workingman became a key mid-Victorian figure, the character on whose good sense hopes of social harmony were based, and whose example of independence and self-respect would inspire a whole class ... They became a privileged, highly paid elite, the labour aristocracy, attached to the established industrial order which nourished their privileges, essentially collaborationist and non-militant. The labour aristocracy was thus detached from the main body of the working class which was left insecure, exploited and leaderless.[21]

More recent scholarship has continued to emphasise these themes in the 'remaking of the working class' in the late Victorian period. Industrial concentration, new labour militancy and trade unionism further differentiated the working class, leading to the creation of a new industrial working class feeding the New Unionism of the 1880s.[22] The changing nature of production, the lingering effects of the 'Great Depression' of the 1870s and the appearance of socialist ideologies also contributed to the rise of labour militancy in the period, but not among the labour aristocracy who remained moderate, accommodationalist and protective of their privileges. However, the new militancy of the unionised working class also left behind an unskilled, general labouring class rarely unionised and forming the lowest paid workers who were the subject of numerous investigations by Booth, Rowntree and others into the social consequences of poverty. Perkin and Belchem note a common, contemporary distinction between the 'respectables' and the 'roughs', with the latter consisting of the least skilled, non-unionised and often migrant workers.[23] Irish migrant workers usually formed the least favoured class.[24]

In contrast to those arguing for a highly segmented working class and the moderating influences of the labour aristocracy were those like

Thompson who, echoing Pelling's earlier criticisms, rejected the thesis in these terms:

> Schematically neat, this view [the labour aristocracy thesis] bears little or no relation to reality: respectable workingmen were far more numerous than just the skilled workers or labour aristocrats; the behaviour of the labour aristocracy was created by the nature of the job, not by employers' strategies; high wages and secure employment were not the preserve of the skilled alone; the skilled were more radical than the unskilled; and the proletarians of the 1890s, however cohesive socially, were conspicuously indifferent to fighting the class war.[25]

THE ON-GOING DEBATE

The continuing debate on the distinctiveness and political disposition of the working class echoes those differences between Smith and Marx referred to earlier. Followers of Smith tend to emphasise the innumerable gradations in a voluntarily generated industrial society. Few sharp distinctions exist across the working class and those that do are ameliorated by economic and technological progress and the emergence of mass culture. Working-class culture is portrayed as generally dependent, weak and devalued by its members who would prefer to become 'gentlemen' in 'respectable society'. Political activity and militancy increase as one goes up the social scale. The lowest reaches of the working class are apathetic and disinterested in politics.[26]

The alternative interpretation generally follows Marx in holding that industrialisation brings worker deskilling and class polarisation through the coercive process of the 'making' of the working class. This resulting social isolation enhances an already robust and valued working class subculture which shields the working class from the predatory actions of capital and the state. In general, political militancy is inversely related to social status, although the caveat sometimes is introduced that the residuum may be resistant political mobilisation.[27]

MEASURING FRAGMENTATIONS OF INTEREST AND RANK

Our investigation can enter this debate by examining support for the several propositions advanced in each interpretation. However, this contribution is limited by our ability to measure some aspects of the problem. It is to this question we now turn.

Considerable attention in the labour aristocracy controversy is devoted to defining and measuring the existence of different segments within the working class. In general four characteristics are highlighted as important in differentiating these segments: skill differentials, trade unionism, wage differentials and social security.[28] This research cannot identify all four characteristics, but is limited to measures of skill and trade unionism. While not ideal, these measures parallel the stress placed on these distinctions by all commentators. Once again Engels set the tone for the discussion with his reference to the 'Great Trade Unions', referring to the skilled craft unions which preceded the New Unionism of the late 1880s. Commenting on the changes in the English working class in his 1885 essay, 'England in 1845 and 1885', Engels described the labour aristocracy as:

[T]he Great Trade Unions. They are the organisations of those trades in which the labour of *grown-up men* predominates, or is alone applicable. Here the competition of neither women and children has so far weakened their organised strength. The engineers, the carpenter and joiners, the bricklayers, are each of them a power, to that extent that, as in the case of the bricklayers and bricklayers' labourers, they can even resist the introduction of machinery.[29]

Engels' observations, however, do not take into account the New Unionism of the late 1880s, which incorporated the emerging industrial workers and distinguished them from the earlier craft unions. Hobsbawm distinguishes three components of the late nineteenth-century trade union movement: 'the "craft" societies with their stable (and restricted) membership; the General Unions, fluctuating, but without any marked upward tendency, yet climbing almost vertically after 1911; and the "industrial" unions, growing steadily from 1900, though faster after 1911'.[30] Data on trade unionism in this study begins in 1888 and hence captures the New Unionism which focused on industrial workers rather than the craft workers.

Our measures identify four types of workers: skilled workers, manual workers, industrial workers and unskilled general labourers as well as trade union density in 1888, 1901 and 1910. From these four measures we identify three working-class segments: labour aristocracy, unionised industrial labour and unskilled, general labour. The labour aristocracy is measured by the presence of skilled workers and manual workers, two types of labour characteristic of smaller manufacturing enterprises which continued as an important element in British industry in the late Victorian period.[31]

The second segment of the working class is the industrial working class measured by industrial workers and trade union density in 1888, 1901 and 1910. The third segment of the working class consists of unskilled, general labourers defined as non-agricultural, general, unskilled labourers with no trade union affiliation.[32] These distinctions are supported by other analyses of the data available for the period.[33] These results strongly support the tripartite segmentation of the working class based on distinctions of skill and unionisation which are captured in the terms labour aristocracy, industrial working class and unskilled general labourers.

Differences in political behaviour are measured by support for the two principal parties – Conservatives and Liberals – as well as for the emerging Labour Party and the Lib-Labs. The Lib-Labs, of course, represented the Liberals' attempt to garner the inchoate working-class vote following the reforms of 1883–5 and exemplify a intermediate position between the Liberals and Labour. Following a split between the Lib-Labs and Labour in 1906, the Lib-Labs gravitated more closely to the Liberals. The result is a rough continuum from the Conservatives, who were least sympathetic to working-class demands, to Labour, which is most sympathetic.

LONG RUN TRENDS IN INTRA-WORKING CLASS POLITICS

The analysis below examines the effects of the three working-class segments on party vote. Before examining the results however, the expected results may clarify the arguments. One version of the labour aristocracy thesis argues for more moderate political behaviour among more skilled workers. This should be demonstrated by labour aristocracy support for the Liberals and Lib-Labs, while industrial workers and unskilled general labourers support Labour and oppose the Conservatives. In addition, some versions of this thesis suggest that the presence of the labour aristocracy itself should moderate the behaviour of other segments of the working class, presumably moving industrial workers and unskilled general labourers toward the Liberals and Lib-Labs and away from Labour.

Some scholars also propose the 'Tory Worker' thesis. Hobsbawm spoke of 'the very substantial mass of "Tory working men" who have always existed in Britain, without affecting, in more than the most fleeting and marginal way, the structure, policy and programme of the Conservative Party, which could not win a single election without them'.[34] Several characteristics distinguish the 'Tory worker' in the literature. While skilled and unionised workers appear in the literature as supporters of the Liberals,

Lib-Labs and Labour, the 'Tory worker' is usually painted as a 'rough', politically indifferent and heavily under the influence of tradition, religion or jingoism whose political leanings vary from Tory to indifference.[35]

The second version of the labour aristocracy thesis holds that a smooth gradient and open hierarchy exists in the working class. It also contains a caveat that, to the extent that such differences do exist, more skilled workers will be more militant and radical, and presumably more likely to support Labour over the Liberals and Lib-Labs. While generally less politically active, industrial workers will differ little from the labour aristocracy. As a corollary, the unskilled general labourers will be politically indifferent at best. We begin with an analysis of the long run trends across the eight elections of the period following the procedures developed in Chapter 4 and using the eight elections between 1885 and December 1910. To ensure that we are mapping intra-working class differences, the model employs control variables for religion (see Figure 7.1).

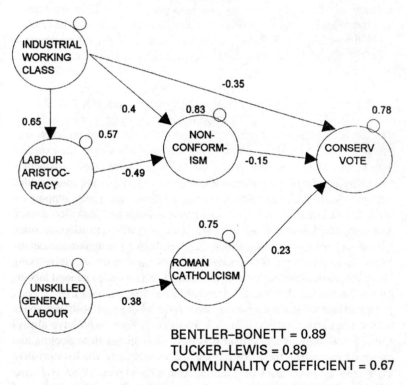

BENTLER–BONETT = 0.89
TUCKER–LEWIS = 0.89
COMMUNALITY COEFFICIENT = 0.67

Figure 7.1   The working class and party vote trends 1885–1910 (a) Conservative vote trend

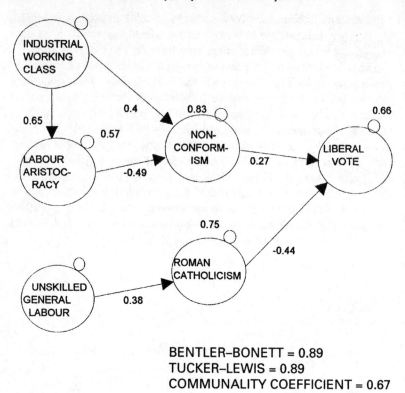

BENTLER–BONETT = 0.89
TUCKER–LEWIS = 0.89
COMMUNALITY COEFFICIENT = 0.67

Figure 7.1   (*cont.*) (b) Liberal vote trend

   The results support the labour aristocracy thesis, but with some important caveats. The labour aristocracy displays more moderate politics than
the industrial, unionised labour. The labour aristocracy is slightly associated with the Lib-Lab trend line after 1906 and displays no support for
Conservatives, Liberals or Labour. Support for the Lib-Labs is decidedly
more moderate after 1906 because the deteriorating relations between the
Lib-Labs and Labour meant the remaining Lib-Labs became increasingly
aligned with the Liberals.[36] Meanwhile, unionised industrial labour
demonstrates strong class voting with forceful support for Labour and
opposition to the Conservatives, and no direct support for the Liberals or
Lib-Labs. Finally, the unskilled general labour shows little class voting
and no support for the Tory worker thesis. These results offer strong
evidence for the presence of differentiation within the working class, and
suggest that this differentiation has decidedly political consequences.

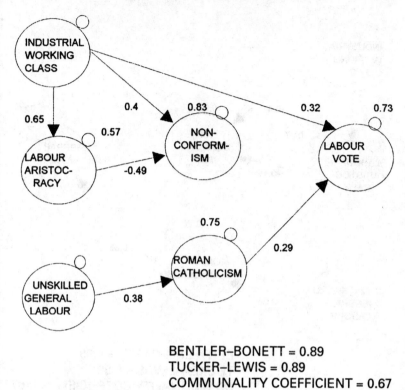

BENTLER–BONETT = 0.89
TUCKER–LEWIS = 0.89
COMMUNALITY COEFFICIENT = 0.67

Figure 7.1 (*cont.*) (c) Labour vote trend

A corollary of the labour aristocracy thesis holds that the labour aristocracy moderated the political behaviour of the working class in general.
Moorhouse summarised this proposition as follows: 'the power and traditions of the labour aristocracy, i.e., the skilled unions, affected later class
formations imbuing these with both the strength and weaknesses (from the
radical point of view) of its modes of organisation and ideological her-
itages'.[37] If true, it should show up in the results in the following manner:
the greater the presence of the labour aristocracy, the more moderate the
politics of other segments of the working class as evidenced by greater
support for the Lib-Labs and lesser support for Labour. No evidence of
this proposition exists in this or any subsequent models. If we control for
the effects of either the labour aristocracy on industrial labour or vice
versa, the coefficients remain the same and stable: the labour aristocracy

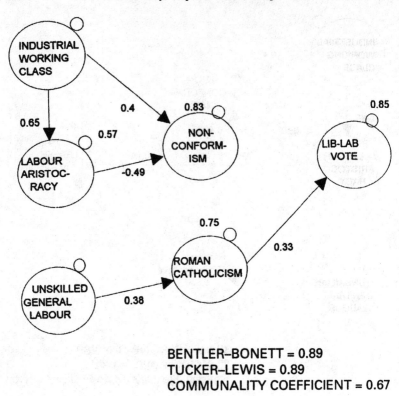

BENTLER–BONETT = 0.89
TUCKER–LEWIS = 0.89
COMMUNALITY COEFFICIENT = 0.67

Figure 7.1   *(cont.)* (d) Lib-Lab vote trend 1885–1900

supports the Lib-Labs, while industrial labour supports the Labour Party and the unskilled general labour are politically indifferent.

Religious incorporation figures in the results in the expected manner, but here serves to highlight class voting. The presence of Nonconformism favours industrial working class support for the Liberals, while its absence improves the lot of Labour. The opposite phenomena works for the Conservatives: Nonconformism reinforces opposition to the Conservatives. Meanwhile, the presence of Roman Catholicism improves Conservative success among unskilled general labourers. This general phenomena has been noted earlier: in the absence of organised religion, the unchurched working class demonstrates class voting; in the presence of organised religion, the working class divides along the traditional religious schisms associated with the parties. In addition, however, when reli-

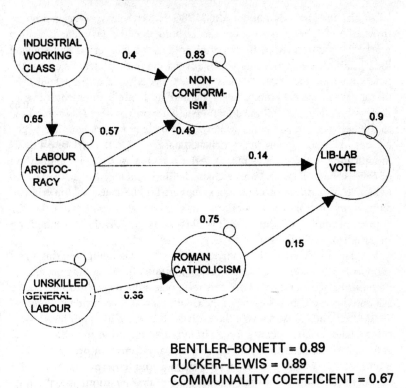

BENTLER–BONETT = 0.89
TUCKER–LEWIS = 0.89
COMMUNALITY COEFFICIENT = 0.67

Figure 7.1   (*cont.*) (e) Lib-Lab vote trend 1900–10

gious influences are removed, class voting is further differentiated by skill level and unionisation.[38]

NATIONALISM, EMPIRE AND THE WORKING CLASS

In Chapters 4 and 5 we have already noted the absence of any relationship between peripheral nationalism or identification with Empire among the working class in general. In Chapter 6 we investigated general working-class electoral behaviour in the core and periphery and affirmed these results. Those findings clearly show that support for imperialism, empire and peripheral nationalism was most prevalent among the religiously incorporated middle classes and, in general, that the working class lent support to the Labour Party with a pronounced shift away from the

Lib-Labs and towards Labour after 1906. Nevertheless, some interpretations of the labour aristocracy thesis hold that the privileged, skilled workers benefited from the imperial policies of the period and showed their gratitude by supporting parties advocating those policies. Perhaps the best known of such statements is Lenin's; his critique of the labour aristocracy was central in the debate.[39] Paralleling Lenin's argument is that of Duffy and others, who argued that unskilled workers were less committed to the existing arrangements which would include imperialism and hence be less likely to support the established parties.[40] On the opposite side of the question is Pelling's inquiry.[41] After a review of the general question of the working class and imperialism, Pelling concluded that 'there is no evidence of a direct or continuous support for the cause of Imperialism among any sections of the working class', and that 'Lenin's view that the "upper stratum" of the working class was politically corrupted by Imperialism is demonstrably false'.[42]

We can directly test these interpretations by examining working class support for the Conservative-Unionist Coalition after removing the effects of both the Conservative vote and religious influences. In doing so we assume that the Unionist wing of the Coalition was more stridently imperialistic than the Conservatives themselves. It is certainly possible to consider Chamberlain as being more strongly committed to imperialism and empire and opposed to Home Rule than many Conservatives. If the elements of the working class were attracted to such rhetoric, we might expect to see support for the Unionist wing of the Coalition.

Figure 7.2 presents the results of the model, which clearly reject any possible interpretation that the labour aristocracy, industrial labour or unskilled general labour gave support to empire and imperialism. These results clearly show that, after controlling for religion, there is no association between the labour aristocracy and unskilled general labour and support for Unionism or Conservatism. Moreover, industrial labour displays strong opposition to both the Conservatism and Unionism. Thus the general findings on the working class in earlier chapters again receive support despite the distinctions within the working class. No segment of the working class evidences support for visions of empire. The technical results of this model, as well as models for other data sets, confirm this interpretation.

THE LABOUR ARISTOCRACY THESIS IN SIMPLEX MODELS

The above models examine the long run trend in class voting within the segmented working class. Such models focus our attention on the continu-

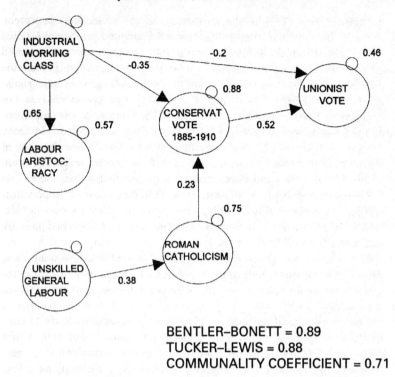

BENTLER–BONETT = 0.89
TUCKER–LEWIS = 0.88
COMMUNALITY COEFFICIENT = 0.71

Figure 7.2   Working class and party vote trends 1885–1910: Unionist vote, controlling for Conservative vote trend

ities across time by drawing out the shared variations across the eight elections between 1885 and December 1910. In doing so, however, the models ignore the short run fluctuations between elections. It might be helpful to think of the situation in the following terms. Change across time is broadly composed of two elements: first, continuities forming across time constancy, and, second, changes representing discontinuous influences; in other words, influences which do not carry over across several observations. In the following section we employ a Weiner simplex model which enables us to distinguish these two general components of change.[43]

The results of the simplex model for the labour aristocracy, industrial labour and unskilled general labour provide clear evidence for the across-time shifts of working class voting in the late Victorian period. The short run components of the trend line confirm the results of the previous model. Again religious control variables remove the effects of organised religion on class voting. The labour aristocracy shows a decided movement towards the Lib-Labs after 1906. Again the labour aristocracy demonstrates no affiliation with the Labour Party even following the split between the Lib-Labs and Labour in 1906. For unionised industrial labour, the results again strongly reinforce the previous findings: industrial labour displays increasing class voting at a growing rate across time as the coefficients become more and more negative towards the Conservatives and more and more positive towards Labour. In this case, however, there is a decided jump in Labour's coefficients after 1900 when the Labour Party began to distance itself from the Lib-Labs, more closely ally itself with the trade unions and more actively seek working class support.[44]

The model decisively illuminates the shifts of the components of the working class across time and clearly displays the differences among the labour aristocracy, the industrial working class and unskilled general labourers. It is evident that the industrial working class develops class voting at an increasing rate during the period, while the labour aristocracy demonstrates greater moderation in politics. Once again, the labour aristocracy shows no moderating effects on other segments of the working class.

The importance of the working class in 'The Strange Death of Liberal England' is even more evident in the model. Chapters 5 and 6 illustrated how the Liberals became more and more dependent on their Nonconformist middle class support, particularly in the periphery. The results presented in this chapter document the failure of Liberals among the working class. The only increase in working-class support for the Liberals appears in the presence of Nonconformism. In other words, the Liberals gain not from working-class politics, but from Nonconformism among the working class. Labour is the clear beneficiary of class politics. These findings lend further support to the revisionist interpretation that the death of the Liberal Party was caused by heightened class consciousness on the part of the working class, not the waning of Nonconformism which, as was demonstrated in Chapters 4 and 5, continually increased Liberal support before the First World War. The strange death of the Liberal Party can be traced to its failure to secure a base among the newly enfranchised industrial working class and unskilled general labour class. Liberal success among the working classes was the result of Nonconformism, not class politics.

The remaining key to the puzzle lies with the Labour Party. Here the shifts in the working-class support become clear: first, the industrial working class moves dramatically towards Labour at an increasing rate, particularly with the elections of 1900 and 1906. Removing the effects of religion, we see that Labour's gains are the direct effect of class politics, not religious influences. Thus, while Labour also gains in the presence of Roman Catholicism, these gains are in addition to class voting. Meanwhile, the Liberals' gain among the working class only in the presence of Nonconformism reaffirms the importance of religion to the Liberals' success among the working class.

In conclusion, these results provide strong support for the labour aristocracy thesis, but also modify it. Clear differences develop among the elements of the working class with the labour aristocracy more moderate than industrial labour. On the other hand, the unskilled general labourers who most closely approximate the proletarians of the 1890s demonstrate no militancy. In sum, the labour aristocracy gravitates to support the Lib-Labs; the industrial working class moves to Labour, while the unskilled general labour is apart from politics. Again, contradicting the labour aristocracy thesis, the labour aristocracy's moderate politics do not produce similar results on other elements of the working class.

CONCLUSION

In this chapter we began with Marx's and Engels' observations on 'the infinite fragmentation of interest and rank' and the resultant 'social division of society into innumerable gradations' which divided the working class and gave rise to the labour aristocracy thesis. The labour aristocracy thesis followed from the increasing division of labour in industrial society and, to the frustration of Marxists and the satisfaction of their critics, militated against working-class unity and encouraged moderation among the working-class in general.

The results of this analysis clearly support the labour aristocracy thesis. Not only do significant differences exist within the working class, but these produce differences in electoral behaviour based on skill and trade unionism. In general, the higher the density of trade unionism and the higher the skill level, the greater the electoral activity. In addition, the higher the skill level, the more moderate the politics. Thus, the labour aristocracy is associated with support for the Lib-Labs, the industrial working class with Labour and the unskilled general labourer with political apathy. Class politics is the central dynamic, with organised religion operating at the margins but in the expected directions.

A corollary of the labour aristocracy thesis, that labour aristocracy's influence moderated working class politics in general, is not supported by the results. While the analysis clearly does not measure all possible influences suggested by the labour aristocracy thesis, it does show that the presence of the labour aristocracy does not increase Lib-Lab support among the other segments of the working class.

Finally, these results parallel those of earlier chapters on the working class and nationalism and Imperialism. Although political differences appear within the working class, these are differences of class politics. In no case do we find any elements of the working class entering into the Home Rule or Imperialist issues of the period.

The impact of industrialisation on the working class was paradoxical: it both created the potential for working-class unity by setting the class apart from the larger society, while at the same time it divided it from within. In the first sense industrialisation did isolate the working class from the issues of nationalism and Imperialism which so divided the middle classes. This was particularly so where the working class was not incorporated into organised religion, the chief rival for working-class loyalties. In the second sense, however, industrialisation also internally divided the working class by organisation and skill which limited its ability to achieve unity. Thus industrialisation broke some links in the vast chain between the larger society and the working class, while at the same time it forged links within and between the working classes and the larger society.

8 'Men Make their own History, but …' 'the Chain is Absolutely Continuous and Unbroken': Continuity and Change in the Transition to Mass Politics

Men make their own history, but they do not make it just as they please; they do not make it under circumstances chosen by themselves, but under circumstances directly encountered, given, and transmitted from the past. The tradition of dead generations weighs like a nightmare on the brain of the living. And just when they seem engaged in revolutionising themselves and things, in creating something that has never existed, precisely in such periods of revolutionary crisis they anxiously conjure up the spirits of the past to their service and borrow from them names, battle cries, and costumes in order to present the new scene of the world in this time-honoured disguise and this borrowed language.

Karl Marx, 1852

At what point, then, in the scale do we first meet the working man? It is an important and hopeful fact that we cannot say where – that the chain is absolutely continuous and unbroken.

Alfred Marshall, 1873

Our journey through late Victorian Britain's transition to mass politics began with the words of its most potent defenders and critics. Three strikingly different views of the future greeted us. While Pope bemoaned the loss of an eighteenth-century society undergirded by principles of harmony, hierarchy and mutual obligation, Marx offered up a vision of equality and freedom under Socialism. Meanwhile, *The Times* warned us of the dangers of mass democracy. Salisbury, in his 1883 article, 'Disintegration', and Lowe in his parliamentary addresses taunted us with the cries of a Hobbesian world of warring factions, while Engels and

Gladstone tempted us with sirens of future paradise. Likewise, each stop on our travels introduced us to contemporaries who offered up their insights and observations as well as their dreads and designs for the future of an age they only vaguely understood, but hoped to mould in their own image. At each weigh station we encountered these contending ideals of the social order, but were also welcomed by the unforeseen consequences of human designs and social forces. Each ideal and every plan was interwoven with paradoxes and unanticipated consequences; history had a way of confounding even its most astute observers. The most ardently stated predictions mischievously avoided encounters with the future.

Marx and Marshall set the tone for our final chapter: despite the most deeply felt dreads and most stridently stated designs, history is as much paradox as progress. As Marx perceptively noted, just when men seem most likely to revolutionise themselves, they grasp at images of the past and, as often as not, recreate the very world they sought to change, leaving only a continuous and unbroken chain in their wake.

Three grand themes guided our journey: democracy, capitalism and empire. Each can be approached on its own, but each is also intertwined with the others. Each created the potential for new unities and identities, while each worked to fragment and splinter the others. Only a society which rejected the principles of equality and the market could embrace the words of Pope and remain underwritten by property and patronage. Democracy had, of course, its proponents as well as its critics. Even leaving aside questions of partisan short run advantage, democracy's proponents recognised, however vaguely, that potential state-power was partly constructed on the organisation and discipline of its citizenry. First attempts to expand the franchise coupled it to conflicting principles of the social order. Traditional notions of mutual obligation and the New Political Economy could not provide a consistent ideological foundation. The New Poor Laws raised a contradiction between the established ideals of hierarchy and mutual obligation and the assumptions of equality and self-reliance. If the presumed advantages of the market were to be realised, then in some fundamental sense individuals must meet on equal terms, acquiring rights of contract in the bargain. But once civil rights to participate in the market were extended, it was increasingly difficult to withhold political rights.

However, classical republican democracy provided little guidance for incorporating an expanded citizenry. The ensuing rampant corruption threatened the solvency of the political class; the costs of managing the multitudes via spectacle became prohibitively expensive. New forms of organisation and politics were necessary to refashion crowds into individuals. Meanwhile, new forms of property dulled Pope's formerly sharp distinctions as a new class sought entry into the political community. Alarms of both probity and bankruptcy drove a debate culminating in the Ballot Act of 1872 which established the principle of the secret ballot whose significance lay in the privatisation and individuation of the only officially recognised political act by the mass of the population. A major link in Pope's vast chain was broken: voting became a matter of private passions and individual interests. As others have noted, however, the secret ballot not only cut the vertical links in the vast chain, but sheared the cross links as well. Between 1883 and 1885 three major legislative acts embodied these logics and moved Britain towards democracy. While mass democracy was most certainly not the outcome, the debate articulated principles that in the future would be put to such service.

Institutional reforms opened both the possibility as well as the necessity of wooing the new electorate. Issues of class, race and religion, ruled out by the old order and kept in the background by limited franchise, could now be moulded to partisan advantage. Political parties responded with new organisational forms and beguiling charms.

Our results show that religion, class and ethnicity all figured prominently in the period and functioned to unite and divide the new electorate along lines that few could have foreseen. Contrary to the traditional interpretation of the period, Britain was not a society divided chiefly by religion. Certainly religion did retain its hold over large sectors of the population, particularly the middle classes and rural elements but, as was evident in our analysis, much of the working class lived beyond the reach of organised religion. Despite some well-known examples in the Welsh valleys, the statistical analysis demonstrates that (with the exception of the Roman Catholics) the urban working class was not well integrated into organised religious life. For the Liberals the existence of the unchurched working class posed a major challenge which they misunderstood and miscalculated. The resulting inability to marry conscience to convenience doomed the party to its 'Strange Death'. In addition, the religious revival of the late nineteenth century, while drawing the party closer to its middle-class supporters, may well have distanced it from the working class. Thus, we find another paradox: the Liberals, who most ardently advanced the cause of suffrage and expected to reap its benefits, were displaced in large part by the very strata upon whom they had placed their hopes. For the Conservatives, on the other hand, religion remained an important foundation, but not the only one, as the party expanded its appeals while retaining its traditional religious and rural constituencies. The gap left by the Liberals opened a route to Labour, initially through the Lib-Lab alliance, but increasingly in their own right. For both the Conservatives and Labour, organisational efforts were crucial in securing a place in the changed electorate.

This three-way polarisation of politics is confirmed by an analysis of issues and short-term movements of the vote across time. Religion and class appear as less interwoven than most interpretations allow. It was not the waning of religion that brought about the Liberals' Strange Death – as a matter of fact, Britain experienced a religious revival during the period – but rather that the party encountered a working class largely outside organised religion which cast a darkening shadow across the Liberals' future, a darkness that reached its fullness following the reforms of 1918.

Territorial dimensions in late Victorian Britain also advanced the fate of the parties. The changing structural bases of political life defined a core and a periphery and brought forth different political and economic fortunes. The Home Rule and Empire questions realigned Victorian politics in yet a different pattern, again to the benefit of Conservatives and Labour, but to the detriment of the Liberals. While class undercut the Liberals in the periphery, empire reduced their effectiveness at the core. In exactly the reverse fashion these issues improved the fortunes of both the Conservatives and Labour. In the Home Rule debates, both the Liberals and the Conservatives 'anxiously conjur[ed] up the spirits of the past to their service and borrow[ed] from them names, battle cries, and costumes in order to present the new scene of the world in this time-honoured disguise and this borrowed language'. But whereas the Liberals' spirits found little appeal outside the peripheral middle class and rural elements, the Conservatives successfully invented tradition. In a paradox which Salisbury, rarely noted for his sense of irony, would not have appreciated, the very forces of democracy, capitalism and nationalism he so adamantly opposed helped to ensure the future of the Conservative Party.

However, religious, class and territorial divisions did not always work to Labour's advantage. The dynamics of capitalism noted by Smith and Marx worked both to unite and divide the labour movement, pulling the working class in opposite directions. Marx was correct in that the working-class experience set the worker apart from the rest of society, giving rise to a distinctive world view. Particularly in the absence of formal religious involvement, this separateness cut the working class off from the 'Four Es' of Establishment, Education, Entertainment and Empire which deeply divided the middle classes by religion and territory. However, industrialisation contained its own internal contradictions. Smith's division of labour was equally as compelling as Marx's proletarianisation. The very industrial division of labour which set the class apart from the larger society also divided it internally by organisation and skill, thus limiting its unity. While industrialisation broke some links in the vast chain between the larger society and the working class, it also forged new links within and between the working classes and the larger society and 'the chain [remained] absolutely continuous and unbroken'. Certainly not 'everyman a gentleman', but neither 'a class-for-itself'.

A chain of paradoxes linked and energised by mass democracy, capitalism and empire realigned late Victorian politics. To the chagrin of Marx and Engels, instead of uniting class against class, or the periphery against the core, as Salisbury feared, history divided the periphery against the core at the same time as it split the Conservative opposition in the core. The results laid the foundations for both the successful transition of the Conservatives and the failed adaptation of the Liberals to mass politics, two processes which opened the way for Labour to emerge as the second party.

DEMOCRATIC TRANSITION: BRITISH EXCEPTIONALISM AND THE EUROPEAN EXPERIENCE

In the study of transitions to mass democracy, Britain is usually portrayed as an outlier. In much of the literature Britain's past sets it apart from the continent. Britain's long and continuous history, its island status, its freedom from foreign invasion, its earlier transition to religious tolerance, its early resolution of the agrarian question, its initial industrialisation, its slow and gradual transition to mass suffrage, its state tradition and its political culture all provide explanations for Britain's successful democratic transition, an outcome usually contrasted with continental failures. Our analysis offers insights on some of these arguments.

In the study of democratic transition, a central comparative explanatory argument relies on class formation and class alliances to account for differing outcomes. From Gerschenkron[1] to Moore[2] and Lipset and Rokkan[3] to more recent works,[4] two points figure prominently in this discussion: the formation of the working class and the potential alliances among the rural elements, capital and labour. One argument focuses attention on the landed elite.[5] This analysis holds that where the landed elite engaged in 'labour-repressive agriculture' and remained strong, while capital depended upon state-sponsored industrialisation and the working class experienced political isolation, the prospects for democracy were dim. Usually Germany and Italy occupy this position. On the other hand, where the agrarian question was resolved early, both capital and the working class were moderate and integrated, and capital was willing to expand the franchise to labour, a transition to democracy was likely. Britain and, to a lesser extent, France are usually examples.

A second argument emphasises crucial alliances among capital, the rural classes and the urban working class.[6] Where capital had gained a dominant position and sought a Lib-Lab alliance with the working class against rural interests, democracy resulted. Where capital allied itself with the rural large or small producers against working-class efforts to organise rural workers, fascism resulted. Britain and, again to a lesser degree, France are prime examples of the first, Italy and Germany of the second.

In both explanations Britain figures as a prominent case of successful democratic transition because of class formation and alliances. Our analysis enters the discussion at several points. First, both arguments highlight the rural sector, the first treating it homogeneously and second emphasising class divisions within it. Our analysis challenges both characterisations: the rural sector in late Victorian Britain is neither homogeneous nor is it solely divided by questions of class. Rather the rural sector was fragmented by questions of class, religion and territory, generating a division of rural areas between the Conservatives and Liberals. Over time these divisions widened as the Liberals became increasingly dependent on middle-class and rural elements in the periphery while the Conservatives cemented a similar coalition in the core. What defeated a potential alliance between capital and agriculture was less the latter's size or internal class antagonisms but more its fragmentation over issues of religion and empire.

Next, both arguments advance the proposition that where capital was confident enough to invite labour into the political community, and more so to seek out an alliance, the transition to democracy was successful. This appears as a partial explanation in Britain. While the Liberals favoured franchise expansion, the Conservatives were deeply divided and many regretted their decisions in 1832 and 1867 and attributed their defeat in 1880 to a failure to foresee Disraeli's miscalculation. Only as a matter of necessity, and after the fact, did the party elaborate the mechanisms to woo the expanded electorate and then only over the resistance of much of the leadership. On the other hand, the Liberals envisioned the franchise as a matter of both conscience and convenience and sought out the Lib-Lab alliance as part of a larger coalition including rural, Nonconformist and peripheral groups. The coalition proved too unwieldy, however, and eventually Liberals gravitated to their middle-class and rural Celtic fringe. Our results show the Lib-Lab alliance endured until the election of 1906, when Labour set its own course. During the alliance the Liberals pacified and domesticated Labour leadership with offices and promises and no doubt guided Labour on to a more moderate track. The invitation to and the incorporation of the working classes rested as much on miscalculation and compulsion as precognition.

Of equal importance, however, were internal divisions within the working class. Both Adam Smith and Cardinal Vaughan exercised their influences on working-class unity. Smith's division of labour and its progeny, the labour aristocracy, fractured the working class. In our analysis the labour aristocracy appeared as more moderate than the 'New Unionism' after 1889. However, prior to the break-up of Lib-Labism in 1906 and the movement of the labour aristocracy to the Liberal fold, the labour aristocracy's moderating influence within the Labour Party lessened. In addition, the new militancy of labour brought forth a counterattack by capital, further undercutting Lib-Labism and provoking Labour directly into electoral politics. Thus the working class was less homogeneous, while the outcome was more conjunctional, than the above arguments suggest.

Religion produced a second division within the working class. While our analysis demonstrated that much of the working class remained outside organised religion, two important segments existed within it: the Roman Catholic and Nonconformist, particularly Welsh, working classes. In both cases religion excited enough sentiment to propel these working-class elements in opposite directions (to the Conservative and Liberal parties respectively).

Class arguments falter in treating their units of analysis, nation-states and classes, as homogeneous, giving the analysis a mechanical and deterministic rather than a fluid and conjunctional logic. Our analysis highlighted religious and territorial dimensions in late Victorian politics which conditioned these outcomes.

THE NEW INSTITUTIONALISM AND THE STUDY OF DEMOCRATIC TRANSITION

Our analysis of democratic transition in late Victorian Britain has been pursued within what has recently become known as the 'new Institutionalism'. Broadly conceived, the new Institutionalism brings context and history back into the study of politics.[7] Institutions are broadly defined as historically conditioned, organised constraints on behaviour. The study of institutions reintroduces notions of appropriateness and obligatory action back into the study of political life. Our analysis lies in this tradition.

The new Institutionalism, which draws upon a long history in the study of society and politics, takes issue with recent approaches to the study of politics which subordinate the polity to other logics: contextualism, reductionalism, utilitarianism, instrumentalism and functionalism. Instead, political institutions were given pride of place in political analysis:[8]

> [P]olitical actors are driven by institutional duties and roles as well as, or instead of, by calculated self-interest; politics is organised around the construction and interpretation of meaning as well as, or instead of, the making of choices; routines, rules, and forms evolve through history-dependent processes that do not reliably and quickly research unique equilibria; the institutions of politics are not simple echoes of social forces; and the polity is something different from, or more than, an arena of competition among rival interests.

Although the new Institutionalists differ over questions of emphasis and method, several general points define the new Institutionalism as found in the comparative analysis of democracy. Each of these is aptly illustrated in our examination of Britain's transition to mass democracy.

First, institutions are organised constraints on behaviour and exist in material, normative and coercive forms. Individuals live in a context and understanding this context is important. Victorian mass politics reflected the influences of material and normative as well as coercive institutions. When we examined both middle- and working-class behaviour, we saw class interests manifested in electoral behaviour but mitigated by normative commitments to religion and nationalism. Often this worked against class unity, sometimes to the detriment of the middle classes, sometimes the working classes. Coercive institutions were probably most in evidence in our discussion of electoral reforms which transformed elections from public spectacles to private acts, dramatically altering the nature of political life and opening politics to new forces.

Second, the new Institutionalism generally accepts some degree of autonomy for the material, normative and coercive institutional forms. In Victorian Britain, the political sphere was not subordinate to the economic, and neither were normative interests mere reflections of economic interests. Both the Conservatives and the Liberals were driven by ideals of a social order, and neither the former's success nor the latter's failure was due to design.

The limits of language illustrate this imperfect correspondence among the forms. Even while the period's most astute observers and strategists vied to understand these forces, each hoping to capture these energies for their own designs, they possessed only a limited language for a new social order. The language of the period only partially captured the consequences of reform. Where Gladstone spoke of the integrative effects of democracy and capitalism, Salisbury emphasised their disintegrative consequences. Where Marx and Engels forecast the unifying effects of proletarianisation on the working class and expressed their frustrations about the potential divisiveness of religion and empire on class, Marshall saw a continuous chain. All of them lacked a language adequate to the task.[9]

The new institutions they devised and built in law, economy, society and polity reflected both their passions and their interests as well as the limited options offered by historical circumstances. The sense of appropriateness varied enormously. Salisbury and the Conservatives simply could not envision a world not based on hierarchy, harmony and mutual obligation, while Gladstone and the Liberals held unbridled optimism in their cause. Responses and designs, as well as successes and failures, were informed by the past. The Primrose League was most certainly the Conservatives' conjuring up of past spirits which proved more successful than the Liberals' appeals to Nonconformist conscience.

Third, the sequencing of events and phases are important to avoid the fallacy of the 'efficiency of history'. This was apparent when we examined how the challenges of democracy, capitalism and empire were addressed. The sequencing of decisions, the *ad hoc* accommodations of interest and principle, the attempts to marry conscience and convenience; all were crucial to the institutional forms. Faced with the general problem of managing the multitudes and disciplining the citizenry, political elites sought reforms of property rights, labour markets and electoral procedures that inadvertently corroded the traditional social fabric and opened possibilities for more dramatic change. The electoral reforms of 1883–5 represented the culmination of a long string of *ad hoc* compromises and poorly understood potentials.

Fourth, institutions tend to reproduce themselves across time. The contrast of the Conservative and Liberal Parties illustrate both outcomes. Therefore, the question of how institutions adapt to change is crucial. In a great historical irony, which Marx would have appreciated, the Conservatives adapted more successfully to mass politics than the Liberals by resurrecting the past rather than promising the future.

Fifth, the new Institutionalism embraces the doctrine of unanticipated consequences. Historical actors do not always know their 'true' interests and do not always act in a 'rational-efficient' manner; instead, they make mistakes; they miscalculate. Actions cannot be read backwards as 'revealed preferences'. Examples abound in our analysis, from Marx's statement that universal suffrage ensured the victory for Socialism to Gladstone's remarks on the same for the Liberals.

Sixth, all institutions make a difference in the flow of history, but are also influenced by history. Not only were the electoral reforms of 1883–5 reflective of the ideas embodied in the New Political Economy, but they facilitated the expression of issues which divided and reformed political alliances for the next 25 years. Probably only under conditions of the secret ballot, controlled campaign expenditures and redistribution of seats could issues of class and nationalism have taken the form they did in Victorian Britain.

Next, formal institutions receive renewed emphasis in the new Institutionalism. Formal institutions channelled politics in late Victorian Britain in particular ways and opened up possibilities closed to other societies. The electoral laws favoured Lib-Labism, which was crucial to class politics during the period.

Finally, the new Institutionalism sees the nation-state not as an autonomous, monolithic unit of analysis, but rather as consisting of shifting internal elements within a wider context. Nation-states consist of historically constructed cores and peripheries, but relations among these are subject to change by the forces of capitalism, democracy and empire. As we saw, Victorian Britain divided along regional, religious and class lines which realigned politics in yet a different configuration.

As the world seemingly experiences the decomposition of the twentieth-century's great empires and many hope to cast the seeds of democracy and capitalism in the expectation of reaping a sweet harvest, we turned our eyes to the past. For this is not the first time the world has sought to secure democracy's dulcet fruit. Democratic transition in the late nineteenth and first half of the twentieth centuries was similarly conceived in the crucible of nation- and state-building marked by the extension of political citizenship, the construction of national consciousness and the transition to market capitalism.

Our journey through Victorian Britain alerted us to both the richness and rules as well as the progress and paradoxes of history. We encountered a society struggling to construct new ordering principles capable of accommodating the contending forces of capitalism, democracy and empire, but with little sense of the shape or magnitude of the challenges. Yet once in place these institutions significantly influenced the future. As we have seen in so many ways, the newly devised institutions evolved quite differently from the best formulated plans.

Victorian Britain evolved the foundations of a temporary equilibrium among democracy, capitalism and empire which forged new links while educating the new orders to dance in their chains.

When you have thus formed the chain of ideas in the heads of your citizens, you will then be able to pride yourselves on guiding them and being their masters. A stupid despot can constrain his slaves with iron chains; but a true politician binds them even more strongly by the chain of their own ideas; it is at the stable point of reason that he secures the end of the chain; this link is all the stronger in that we do not know of what it is made and we believe it to be our own work; despair and time eat away the bonds of iron and steel, but they are powerless against the habitual union of ideas, they can only tighten it still more; and on the soft fibres of the brain is founded the base of the soundest of Empires. (J.M. Servin, 1767)

The strongest is never strong enough to always be master, unless he transforms force into right and obedience into duty. (Rousseau, 1762)

Appendix I
Units of Analysis, Data Description and Sources

UNITS OF ANALYSIS

The units of analysis are surrogate units constructed from electoral constituencies and census areas based on the 1891 social census and the 1851 religious census. The procedure generated 115 surrogate constituencies, consisting of 50 borough units and 65 county remainders. Wald states that 'borough constituencies were treated as coterminous with local government areas (urban authorities of 50 000 or more) when the population disparity between the two areas did not exceed 5 percent'.[1] Wald's data are available through the Inter-University Consortium for Political and Social Research at the University of Michigan.

Primrose League membership and organisational data are coded into Wald's surrogate constituencies.

Table A.I.1 Data means, standard deviation and cases

Variable	Description	Cases	Mean	Standard deviation
ANG91	Anglican clergy per capitum, 1891	115	0.0008	0.0006
ANGMAX	Maximum Anglican church attendance per capitum, 1851	107	0.1169	0.0502
CEDSPCT	Anglican day school attendance per capita, 1851	97	0.0395	0.0153
CESSPCT	Anglican Sunday School attendance per capita, 1851	97	0.0498	0.0228
NON91	Nonconformist clergy per capita, 1891	115	0.0005	0.0004
NONMAX	Maximum Nonconformist church attendance per capita, 1851	107	0.1529	0.0825
NONDSPCT	Nonconformist day school attendance per capita, 1851	97	0.0111	0.0080
NONSSPCT	Nonconformist Sunday School attendance per capita, 1851	97	0.0842	0.0714

Table A.I.1 Continued

Variable	Description	Cases	Mean	Standard deviation
RC91	Roman Catholic clergy per capita, 1891	115	0.00008	0.00006
RCMAX	Maximum Roman Catholic church attendance per capita, 1851	107	0.0141	0.0180
RCDSPCT	Roman Catholic day school attendance per capita, 1851	97	0.0030	0.0052
RCSSPCT	Roman Catholic Sunday School attendance per capita, 1851	97	0.0035	0.0076
CL251	Proportion of economically active males in Class 2 of the 1951 grading scheme for 1891	115	0.1480	0.0777
SKILL[a]	Proportion of economically active males in skilled work by Registrar General's 1911 scheme	115	0.2127	0.0753
MANLAB	Proportion of economically active males in manual labour, 1891	115	0.7629	0.0652
INDLAB	Proportion of economically active males in industry and mining, 1891, (excludes managerial and non-factory)	115	0.4393	0.1665
TUD88[b]	Trade Union Density, 1888	115	0.0454	0.0202
TUD01	Same, 1901	115	0.0918	0.0495
TUD10	Same, 1910	115	0.0922	0.0540
GENLAB	Proportion of economically active males in unskilled, general labour, 1891	115	0.1482	0.0373
AGR91	Proportion of economically active males in agriculture according to 1951 Registrar General's scheme	115	0.1481	0.1663
WPOP91	Proportion of Welsh born population, 1891	109	0.1248	0.3209
SPOP91	Proportion of Scottish born population, 1891	109	0.0131	0.0150
IPOP91	Proportion of Irish born population, 1891	109	0.0189	0.0219
HABPOP	Primrose League Habitations per capita, 1892	110	0.0001	0.0001
MEMPOP	Primrose League members per capita, 1892	97	0.0283	0.0260
NONV85	Proportion non-voters in electorate, 1885	113	0.1586	0.2022

Table A.I.1 Continued

Variable	Description	Cases	Mean	Standard deviation
NONV86	Same, 1886	96	0.3302	0.2662
NONV92	Same, 1892	109	0.2090	0.2183
NONV95	Same, 1895	102	0.2526	0.2958
NONV00	Same, 1900	92	0.3380	0.3042
NONV06	Same, 1906	112	0.1640	0.2580
NONV10J	Same, January 1910	115	0.1056	0.2203
NONV10D	Same, December 1910	103	0.2432	0.2848
CON85	Conservative Party percentage of vote, 1885	113	0.4538	0.0936
CON86	Same, 1886	96	0.3669	0.2100
CON92	Same, 1892	109	0.3820	0.1891
CON95	Same, 1895	102	0.4330	0.1453
CON00	Same, 1900	92	0.4435	0.1478
CON06	Same, 1906	112	0.3575	0.1414
CON10J	Same, January 1910	115	0.4056	0.1430
CON10D	Same, December 1910	103	0.4381	0.1042
UNION85[c]	Unionist percentage of vote, 1885	115	0.4511	0.1046
UNION86	Same, 1886	115	0.4584	0.1768
UNION92	Same, 1892	115	0.4884	0.0965
UNION95	Same, 1895	115	0.4811	0.1306
UNION00	Same, 1900	115	0.4515	0.1842
UNION06	Same, 1906	115	0.4203	0.0943
UNION10D	Same, December 1910	115	0.4664	0.0984
UNION10J	Same, January 1910	115	0.4464	0.1352
LIB85[d]	Liberal Party percentage of vote, 1885	113	0.5313	0.1011
LIB86	Same, 1886	96	0.4702	0.0987
LIB92	Same, 1892	109	0.4825	0.1128
LIB95	Same, 1895	102	0.4449	0.1343
LIB00	Same, 1900	92	0.4372	0.1269
LIB06	Same, 1906	112	0.4445	0.1937
LIB10J	Same, January 1910	115	0.4173	0.1842
LIB10D	Same, December 1910	103	0.4163	0.1738
LAB85[e]	Labour percentage of vote, 1885	113	0.0002	0.0019
LAB86	Same, 1886	96	0.00003	0.00004
LAB92	Same, 1892	109	0.0083	0.0355
LAB95	Same, 1895	102	0.0208	0.0596
LAB00	Same, 1900	92	0.0161	0.0586
LAB06	Same, 1906	112	0.0504	0.1132
LAB10J	Same, January 1910	115	0.0584	0.1142
LAB10D	Same, December 1910	103	0.0487	0.1095
LLAB85[f]	'Lib-Lab' percentage of vote, 1885	113	0.0098	0.0338
LLAB86	Same, 1886	96	0.0154	0.0543

Table A.I.1 Continued

Variable	Description	Cases	Mean	Standard deviation
LLAB92	Same, 1892	109	0.0153	0.0573
LLAB95	Same, 1895	102	0.0304	0.0828
LLAB00	Same, 1900	92	0.0300	0.0819
LLAB06	Same, 1906	112	0.0775	0.1796
LLAB10J	Same, January 1910	115	0.0574	0.1556
LLAB10D	Same, December 1910	103	0.0581	0.1513
FRAN91[g]	Proportion males 21+ years on electoral registrar, 1891	115	0.6725	0.1425

Notes:

[a]Skilled work coding uses the Registrar General's occupational coding for 1911.

[b]Trade union density is calculated by applying the 'national density proportion' of unionisation applied to major occupational sectors: transportation, printing, building, textiles, wood, clothing mining and metals.[2]

[c]Unionist vote is the sum of Conservatives, Liberal Unionist and Independent Conservatives.

[d]Liberal vote includes Liberals and Independent Liberals.

[e]Labour vote includes candidates affiliated with Labour (LRC, Labour Representation Commitee ILP, Social Democratic Federation).

[f]Lib-Lab is coded if a candidate is sponsored by the Liberals and a Labour organisation.

[g]Enfranchisement is a estimate of the male population aged 21+ from the Census of 1891 who were on the electoral registrar in 1892. Estimate is calculated by Electorate in 1892 divided by 0.67 times the male population of 1891.

SOURCES

Primrose League data are from M. Pugh, *The Tories and the People, 1880–1935* (Oxford: Basil Blackwell, 1985).

All other data are from Wald, *Crosses on the Ballot*. The data file and matching scheme is available from the Inter-University Consortium for Political and Social Research.

Appendix II
Analytical Techniques

LATENT VARIABLE PATH ANALYSIS

In recent years social science analysis has benefited from the development of data analytic techniques which mark a significant advancement over most commonly used forms of regression and factor analysis as well as earlier forms of path analysis. These newer structural equation modelling algorithms generally have several common features: the specification of directed relationships among a set of variables and a series of goodness-of-fit statistics to evaluate the explanatory power of model by comparing the researcher's specifications to the data. More recent innovations incorporate the principles of factor analysis and other data reduction techniques into a class of models called Latent Variable Path Analysis (LVPA). These models formulate theoretical or latent variables (LVs) from observed or manifest variables (MVs).

The advantages over more common data analytic techniques are several. Allowing the researcher to specify relationships among the variables not only permits, but demands, a more refined theoretical statement. Theoretically justified relationships must be postulated between MVs and LVs as well as between LVs. This procedure reduces two forms of spurious explanation: mere chance and unspecified variance which appears to explain the dependent variables but of which the researcher may be unaware. In LVPA additional advantages are present. Like factor analysis or canonical correlation, these techniques allow for data reduction without which the usual regression techniques would be overwhelmed. However, unlike factor analysis or canonical correlation, LVPA models permit the researcher to specify independent and dependent variables. The researcher thus obtains the advantages of both data reduction and path analysis.

A further advantage accrues to LVPA techniques: the more accurate representation of the processes under investigation. Since observed variables only rarely are isomorphic to the theoretical constructs of interest to the researcher, models which include only observed variables (typically regression analysis as well as path analysis without LVs), incorporate measurement error into the model. Therefore, conclusions about a MV model are biased and unreliable. In contrast, LVPA modelling techniques can separate error from theoretically meaningful effects.[1] LVPA models have obvious advantages, particularly in cross-group comparison where the researcher can confidently construct theoretically similar latent variables from group specific MVs.

A number of algorithms exist for LVPA. The first estimation algorithm employed Maximum Likelihood (ML) estimation methods as seen in LISREL techniques.[2] Other estimation techniques have been developed by Bentler and

Weeks employing generalised least squares (GLS).[3] These techniques achieve the advantages stated above, but at the cost of rigorous theoretical and statistical assumptions. Since LISREL primarily tests the model specified by the researcher's starting values against the co-variance matrix, it is parameter-oriented; however, the level of theoretical knowledge necessary to achieve consistent starting values is rarely available in social science research. Second, LISREL assumes both linearity and multi-normality, assumptions difficult to meet with most social science data.

THE STATISTICAL ALGORITHM: LATENT VARIABLE PARTIAL LEAST SQUARES

The basic method

Latent Variable Partial Least Squares (LVPLS) as a basic method was first developed by Herman Wold and later extended by Jan-Bernd Lohmoeller. Wold termed the method 'soft modelling', indicating that it was most appropriate under conditions where theoretical knowledge is scarce and stringent distributional assumptions cannot be met. This basic method has been extended by Lohmoeller and others. The following discussion draws upon Lohmoeller.[4]

Model specification

Variables.   The model consists of MVs and LVs linked by a series of linear equations. MVs are directly observed indicators of the phenomenon in question and are partitioned into non-overlapping blocks y_{kj}, $k_j = 1 \ldots$ Kj. each block being indicative of one LV, N_j, $j = 1 \ldots J$.

Inner model.   The LVs, constructed from the MVs, constitute the inner model and are linked by one of more linear equations. The basic method requires the LVs to form a recursive path or causal chain:

$$\eta_j = \beta_{j0} + \sum_i \beta_{ji}\eta_i + V_j \tag{1}$$

where B_{ji} is a path coefficient, v_j is an inner residual variable, and the index i ranges over the predictors of N_j. The predictor specification is taken to be,

$$E\left(\eta_j / \forall \eta_i\right) = \beta_{j0} + \sum_i \beta_{ji}\eta_i \tag{2}$$

that is, each LV is taken to be a linear function of its predictors N_i and there is assumed to be no linear relationship between the predictors and the residual,

$$cov(\eta i; v_j) = 0 \tag{3}$$

Outer model. Each MV y_{kj} is assumed to be a linear function of its LV N_j and its outer residual e_{kj},

$$y_{kj} = \pi k_j 0 + \pi k_j \eta_j + \varepsilon_{kj} \qquad (4)$$

where P_{kj} is a loading or path coefficient. The outer relations are also subject to predictor specification,

$$E\,(y_{kj}/\eta_j) = \pi k_j 0 + \pi k_j \eta_j \qquad (5)$$

which implies that the outer residuals E_{kj} are uncorrelated with the LV of the same block,

$$cov(\varepsilon_{kj}; \eta_j) = 0 \qquad (6)$$

Estimated model. The estimated model replaces the theoretical constants B_{ji}, P_{kj} and the theoretical variables N_j, V_j, E_{kj} are replaced with their estimates, termed b_{ji}, p_{kj}, Y_j, u_j, e_{kj}.

Weight relations. The LVs are estimated by weighted aggregates of their indicators,

$$Y_j = \sum_{kj} w_{kj} y_{kj} \qquad (7)$$

where w_{kj} is a weight coefficient. These weights are estimated by least squares techniques. The algorithm offers two methods of estimating the parameters; the one used in this analysis is the regression mode where the instrument $\bar{y}_j$ is regressed on the MVs:

$$\tilde{Y}_j = \sum_{kj} \tilde{W}_{kj} Y_{kj} + \tilde{d}_j \qquad (8)$$

The weights w_{kj} in equation 7 are rescaled parameters of the provisional weights w_{kj} from equation 8, and ensure that the LV in equation 7 has unit variance.

The PLS algorithm

The procedure for estimating the unknown parameters proceeds through three stages. The first two stages treat the MVs and LVs as deviations from their means, while in the third stage the LV means and location parameters are estimated.

The first stage

In the first stage the outer approximation of the LV weights is estimated by multiple regression using Y_j as an instrumental variable. Constraints are enforced to ensure that var(Y_j) = 1. The process proceeds through successive iteration cycles until the estimated weights converge and cease to change.

The second stage.

After estimation of the LV weights in Stage One, the loadings and path coefficients are estimated by ordinary least squares (OLS).

The third stage

In the third stage the location parameters of the MVs and LVs are estimated:

$$m_{kj} = \sum_n \bar{y}_{kjn} \tag{9}$$

$$n_j \equiv \sum_n \bar{Y}_{jn} = \sum_{kj} w_{kj} m_{kj} \tag{10}$$

$$p_{kj}0 = m_{kj} - p_{kj} n_j \tag{11}$$

$$b_{j0} = l_j - \sum_i b_{ji} l_i \tag{12}$$

An applied example

In this section we take an example from the concerns of this project to illustrate the application of LVPLS. Because the purpose is to illustrate the technique and not test hypotheses, not all relevant variables are included in the model. Instead, we limit ourselves to a relatively simple model. The models presented in the text are logical extensions of the one presented here.

One abiding concern of scholars of late Victorian politics is the rise of class voting and the importance of class and trade unionism in accounting for this rise. While much of this book discusses this concern in great detail, the logic of the statistical models parallel the following simplified representation.

Figure AII.1 presents a general representation of the problem. We begin with three theoretical variables: working class, trade unionism and class voting. In the parlance of LVPA these are LVs since they cannot be observed directly, but some manifestations of the LVs are found in several MVs.

The data used in this study provides us with a variety of observable measures of these three LVs. For capturing the working class LV, the observable measures of industrial workers, manual workers and skilled workers are available. To capture trade unionism we possess measures of trade union density in 1888, 1901 and 1910. Finally to measure the incidence of class voting we can turn to party vote for the several parties in the period.

Several previous analyses employed measures of the Unionist vote on the assumption that opposition to Unionism captured working-class voting.[5] This

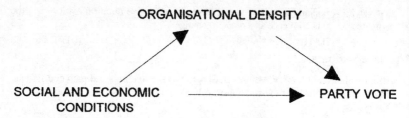

Figure AII.1   A simple conceptual model of class voting

measure is faulty on two grounds: first, the Unionist vote is at best only a negative measure of working-class voting and, second, the Unionist vote conflates this negative measure with territorial and ethnic politics. In the model below and in the text, a vote for the Labour Party is held to be a better measure of class voting by the working class. Third, past analyses did not employ across-time analysis of the voting trends, instead analysing each election separately and drawing inferences from changing coefficients. In time-series analysis when observations contain a time-dependent process, such interpretations can lead to bias. In the model below, we generate a trend line in a simplex model from the across-time observations.[6]

Figure AII.2 illustrates the links between the MVs and the LVs. The MVs are assigned to the LVs according to both theoretical and statistical criteria. In Figure AII.2 we follow the conventions of LVPA analysis and represent LVs as circles and MVs as rectangles. We have assigned several MVs to each LV. Theoretically it would seem obvious that the MVs correspond to the LVs in Figure AII.2. We will measure working class by three observed variables: the presence in the economically actively populations of industrial workers, manual workers and skilled workers. A similar logic determines the other assignments of MVs to their LVs.

However, we should also statistically test these assumptions since it is possible that additional MVs might also be appropriate. For example, we have a measure of non-agricultural general labour which could be a measure of the working-class LV. But, when we do a factor analysis to measure the statistical inter-relationship among the four measures, non-agricultural general labour evidences little statistical association with the other measures. Wald concludes that non-agricultural general labour is thus not a good measure of class and drops the variable from his analysis.[7] However, this result also begs a series of interesting questions which are explored more fully in Chapter 7. In this example, however, we drop this MV from the model.

In Figure AII.2 the arrows are directed outward from the LVs to the MVs indicating our assumption that we consider the LV to be reflective of the underlying MVs. Statistically, then, each LV is a common factor (*sensu* Spearman, Thurstone) of the MVs and the LV is meant to generate the covariance of the MVs. The resulting factor scores also provide starting values for the LVPLS model. The arrows linking the LVs are the hypotheses we will test. Therefore, each arrow indicates an equation linking MV to LV or LV to LV. Where there are no arrows, we have hypothesised the relationship at zero.

Table AII.1 presents the correlation matrix providing the input data for the model. The matrix is partitioned into three blocks corresponding to the three LVs.

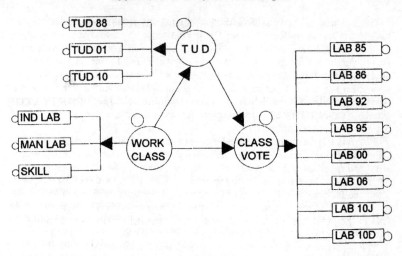

Figure AII.2   Measurement model of class voting

Table AII.1   Manifest variable co-variance matrix

Working class manifest variables
Man Lab 100
Ind Lab   62 100
Skill   9   27 100

Trade union density manifest variables
TUD 88 52 83   12 100
TUD 01 48 73   −5   95 100
TUD 10 49 73 −10   94   99 100

Class voting manifest variables

Lab	85	2	9	1	6	5	6	100						
Lab	86	−21	−8	−16	−2	−2	−2	.	100					
Lab	92	−3	11	10	4	−1	−2	−2	−2	100				
Lab	95	25	34	−2	20	12	18	−4	−5	24	100			
Lab	00	19	28	−5	16	10	15	−3	−8	37	91	100		
Lab	06	29	40	4	37	31	32	−4	6	25	25	14	100	
Lab	10	43	50	1	53	52	51	8	−3	23	21	15	81	100
Lab	10	40	46	.	47	47	47	−4	4	29	23	18	80	94	100

The first block contains our three MVs for working class; the second, the three MVs for trade union density, while the third block contains the eight measures of class voting consisting of the Labour Party vote across the eight elections between 1885 and 1910.

Of particular interest are the dynamics of class voting which we seek to capture by support for the nascent Labour Party. One sense of these dynamics is represented in Figure AII.3 which graphs the mean and standard deviation of the Labour Party vote (in percentage terms) across the eight elections for the observed units of analysis. The figures show that Labour Party vote increases across the period from almost zero to about 5 per cent of the electorate. Meanwhile, the standard deviation suggests that these increases are not spatially uniform, but demonstrate considerable deviation from the mean across territory. It is these dynamics of growth that we will seek to capture.

The next step is to apply the model defined in Figure AII.2 to the data matrix in Table AII.1. In effect we are hypothesising that the only significant relationships are those specified in Figure AII.2 and that all others are fixed at zero. The algorithm then fits these constraints to the data in Table AII.1. How well our hypothesised model fits the data matrix is a statistical measure of the validity of our hypotheses. The results come in three parts: the outer model, (that is, the fit of the LVs to the MVs); the inner model (that is, the explained relationships among the LVs); and the overall fit of the model to the original data.

The results of the outer model, – the parameters linking the MVs and the LVs – are presented in Table AII.2. Numerical entries indicate the parameter estimates

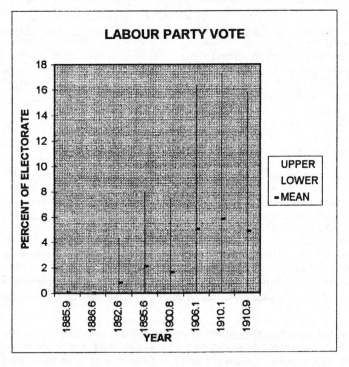

Figure AII.3   Growth of the Labour Party vote 1885–1910

Table A.II.2 Latent variable loading pattern

	Working class	TUD	Class vote
Manual Labour	86		
Industrial Lab	93		
Skilled Worker	22		
TUD 88		98	
TUD 01		99	
TUD 10		99	
Lab Vote 85			3
Lab Vote 86			−8
Lab Vote 92			36
Lab Vote 95			55
Lab Vote 00			48
Lab Vote 06			85
Lab Vote 10J			91
Lab Vote 10D			91

while no entries are those parameters set to zero. Immediately we see several features of the model. First, the loadings for the working-class LV are strong for industrial workers and manual workers, but weaker for skilled workers. This suggests that in more refined models we should test this relationship further, (a exercise carried out in Chapter 7 when we investigate the labour aristocracy thesis). The loadings for trade union density (TUD) are very strong, indicating a powerful measure with high reliability.

Our class voting LV presents an across-time trend line which shows a sharp upward movement to the right and is of particular interest in our efforts to map the dynamics of change. The class voting LV may be termed a latent growth curve for class voting. The LV introduces a common factor in which the factor scores describe the growth curve.[8] When graphed across time in Figure AII.4, the long term shape of the growth curve is clear.

The curve brings together several components which we disaggregate at various stages of the analysis. First, the class voting latent growth curve possesses a variance which we seek to explain with the LVPA models. Second, the growth curve conflates two sources of variance not initially distinguished here: variance which is constant from one observation to the next and that which changes from one observation to the next. In a parallel to time-series regression analysis, it thus includes both the constant term and the change coefficient. In Chapter 5 we focus on short run changes and desegregate these two sources of variance using Weiner simplex models of change.

Table AII.3 presents the parameters for the inner or path model (the parameters of the equations linking the LVs). The results of the model indicate that controlling for the level of TUD, the rise of class voting is attributable more to the presence of TUD than working class, and these relationships strengthen markedly over time. These results indicate that there is little evidence of working-class voting until the

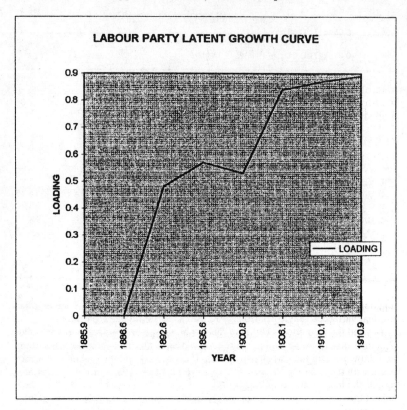

Figure AII.4   Labour Party latent growth curve 1885–1910

Table AII.3 LVPA path coefficients

	Working class	*TUD*	*Class vote*
Working class	100		
TUD	73	100	
Class vote	44	15	100

election of 1892, but that these relationships increase rapidly thereafter, particularly with election of 1906, but level off near the end of the period.

Figure AII.5 presents the model in graphic form where the parameter values are assigned to the relevant paths and loadings. The figure follows conventional LVPA

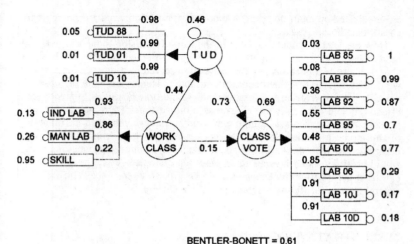

BENTLER-BONETT = 0.61

Figure AII.5   LVPA model of class vote 1885–1910

notation: circles represent LVs; rectangles, MVs; smaller circles on LVs or MVs, residual variances; single headed arrows, paths or causal relationships.

Beyond the theoretical validity of the model, we are also interested in the statistical measures of fit. Several measures are available, all of which address the question: how much of the variance in the data is accounted for by the model? We may begin with the outer model, sometimes called the measurement model, since it represents the measurements of the LVs found in the MVs. The size of the outer residuals of the manifest variables help us to determine the fit of the outer model. These are indicated by the smaller circles attached to the rectangles representing the MVs. Other indices of fit for the inner model include the mean outer residual variance and the communalities.[9]

The fit of the inner or path model is best understood by examining the explained variance of LVs. The model accounts for 31 per cent of the variance in the class voting LV growth curve. The residual unexplained variances are indicated by value associated with the smaller circles attached to the LV circles.

The third measure of the model is its reliability or its probability of recreating the original data matrix. Here numerous statistical measures are available, all of which derive from the question: how well does the model recreate the original data matrix? Two of the most commonly used reliability statistics are the Bentler-Bonett and Tucker–Lewis fit statistics.[10] Both may be thought of as the ratio of the fit of the null model to the fitted model, with a better fit indicated as the statistics approximate 1.0. The Tucker–Lewis statistic has the advantage of controlling for the degrees of freedom and hence is better for comparing across models with varying degrees of freedom (in other words, how much better fit is achieved with additional parameters). The Bentler-Bonett fit statistic for this model is 0.61, indicating a moderately high level of fit to the data. Maximum likelihood fit functions may be computed for LVPLS models, but these indices are predicated on multi-normal distributional assumptions, and are not appropriate for data in this research.

How are LVPA models superior to the usual regression models? First, such models begin with the assumption that a single observed variable is a less reliable measure of a phenomenon than several observed measures. In other words, we do not assume that the theoretical variable is isomorphic with the observed variable plus an error term. Moreover, where multiple measures exist, we more effectively and efficiently use all available information. Therefore, if this logic is accepted and we possess multiple measures, we have enhanced the reliability of the model's results. Second, the construction of LVs from multiple MVs permits us to incorporate into a single model dynamic representations which would be difficult to achieve with ordinary regression analysis. For example, we can treat across-time dynamics as a single growth curve, or as consisting of several trends of differing lengths as we do in Chapter 5.

MISSING DATA PROCEDURES

Missing data problems exist in the data. A difficulty arises because if missing data are excluded for all eight elections, the resulting number of cases reduces the representativeness of the remaining observations. To overcome this limitation the following strategy is used: first, the models are tested with estimated missing values (this technique is described below); second, the resulting models are tested on the following: a sub-set of four elections is chosen across the time period and the model tested on these observations with listwise deletion of cases. Next, this same model is tested on the alternative four elections, again with listwise deletion of cases. Next, each of these models is then tested using all known data on all observations: that is, pairwise deletion of cases. Finally, the resulting estimates of the trend line from all these reconstructions are compared with both listwise and pairwise case deletion of cases. For each step the appropriate goodness-of-fit statistic is computed. Moreover, the models are tested for their coefficient stability.

Reconstruction of missing data

Hertel reviews several techniques for dealing with missing data.[11] Listwise deletion is the most conservative since only complete data are employed, avoiding the problem of computing statistics on varying numbers of cases for each variable. On the other hand, reducing the number of cases below 85 per cent raises the question of how representative the remaining cases are to the full data set. An alternative is to include all observations on a pairwise basis, a technique that possesses precisely the opposite problems and advantages. A third technique employs regression analysis to estimate missing values. This method has the advantage of maximum use of known information, but assumes linearity of the variables.

This research employs all three techniques. If the differences among the models are small, then the results can be accepted with some considerable reliability. After computing the identical models on the three data sets – listwise, pairwise and estimated missing values – three statistics are compared: first, the redundancy coefficient for each model measures the proportion of the variance of the manifest or observed variables reproduced by the LVs indirectly connected to them. When applied across data sets this measures how effectively the model developed on one data set reproduces or predicts the observed data matrix of the other data sets. Second, the root mean squares of the co-variances of the residuals of the observed variables and the LVs measures how successfully the model reduces the residuals and thus incorporates the maximum available observed data into the model.[12] The cross data set comparison then measures how successfully the model developed on one data set can incorporate the information of the observed data in the other data sets. Third, the unweighted least squares fit function is the proportion of the variance in the observed data matrix reproduced (predicted) by the total model.[13] The statistic is defined as unity minus the ratio of root mean square of the observed data matrix minus the predicted variance over the root mean square of the observed matrix.

MODEL TESTING PROCEDURES

The models are estimated under several different assumptions. The first approximation assumes that the exogenous LVs are not correlated; thus the algorithm seeks to minimise the residual co-variances among the exogenous LVs. Since some of these residuals remain at moderate levels (>0.4), the model is re-estimated designating these residual paths as directed relationships. The fit indices do not change and the inclusion of additional paths enhances the coefficients of previously included paths as well as improving the ability of the model to reconstruct the observed correlation matrix successfully. The additional paths also add theoretical interest to the models' findings.

MODELS OF CHANGE PROCESSES

All change processes involve two general components: first, the lingering effects of an event at one point in time on subsequent observations of similar events at later time points. This process is endogenous to the observed events and is referred to as serial auto-correlation: that is, the observations display a specified temporal ordering, and interest is focused on the effects of earlier events on subsequent events of a similar character. In this analysis the eight elections between 1885 and 1910 form precisely such a sequence of events. The second component of time series observations is formed by changes in subsequent observations not due to the effects of previous observations, but attributable to other causal factors. In an effort to describe the broad trends in late Victorian politics, Chapter 4 did not distinguish between these two components. Chapter 5 specified both the endogenous and exogenous sources of change in the series.

Numerous techniques exist for the analysis of change differing according to the assumption made about the lingering effects of change across time.[14] One such approach defines these phenomenon as simplex processes:[15]

> A simplex, in the manner that Guttman[16] developed the concept, is a pattern among correlation coefficients. The concept can be of particular interest to those studying development because the simplex pattern can be found when, in repeated measurements of a set of organisms, there is both some stability and some instability in the data. These are precisely the conditions that prevail for many of the variables that developmental researchers study. Hence ideas about the simplex patterns can be regarded as prototypes for development, as such.

Central to modelling the simplex process are the assumptions made about the stability dimension in the process. In turn, stability in the across-time data is defined as the result of the lingering effects of an event at one time on subsequent occurrences of the phenomenon. If the lingering effects are assumed to affect only the immediate subsequent observation of the phenomena, the model is termed an auto-regressive or a Markov Simplex model.[17] These techniques are extensively explored in econometric analysis where they are termed lagged-exogenous variable models because the exogenous variable is lagged by one observation on the right-hand side of the equation. The assumption underpinning these models is highly restrictive, assuming, as it does, that all residual effects of the first event cease to exist after the second observation.

The unreality of these models has led researchers to explore more complex models in which the lingering effects are postulated to extend over several subsequent observations. In such models, effects are hypothesised to decay across time with the strength of the coefficients indicating the rate of decay. Such models are termed difference components or Weiner Simplex models because they incorporate the contribution of the effects of each previous observation into the analysis of the subsequent observations. The computational requirements for these models are well suited to the techniques employed here (that is, structural equation models with LVs, where LVs constitute the difference components) or a Weiner simplex process of the vote across time.

Several advantages accrue to the application of structural equation techniques to Weiner simplex models of change.[18] Whereas simpler models of change must assume that change processes are additive and linear, it is probably rare that change follows such simple dynamics. On the other hand, Weiner simplex models permit the specification of several change components which, in combination, introduce non-linearity and hence the possibility that changes are occurring at differential rates. As McArdle and Aber comment on the Weiner simplex model:[19]

> This model leads to a non-linear structure of the covariances ..., where each covariance [of the latent variable] is a sum of the common or overlapping variance components [of the latent variable]. In this model we presume the observations ... reflect the build-up or decay of several additive components [of the

latent variable]. The impact to each component, and the scale of the developmental process, is given by the variance term [of the latent variable].

To determine the precise nature of the change process is an empirical problem solved by the application of several different models of change to the observations. In other words, the Weiner simplex process is a general class of models in which change effects are postulated to linger across several observations, but the exact length of this lingering effect is determined empirically. The most extensive of the Weiner simplex models extend the lingering effects across all observations in the series, but shorter durations are possible. McArdle and Aber term the postulated decay after two observations as a moving average model.[20]

In the application of these models to the task at hand, several limitations must be kept in mind. First, the missing data problem presents the difficulties discussed previously and is dealt with in the same manner: Weiner simplex models are tested on various data sets: reconstructed missing data, only known data for all eight elections, for paired comparisons of four elections and for all data.

A second limitation is found in the Weiner simplex models themselves. In analysis of Weiner simplex models, Joereskog notes they are scale dependent.[21] For this reason all variables are standardised in the models. A second problem arises in the time interval between the measurements, in this case elections. In the application of Weiner simplex models to historical data where intervals between the measurement points are pre-determined and irregular, scalar difficulties result in the models. While it is not required that measurement intervals are equal, interpretation of coefficients are more straightforward when they are equal. For example, four years transpired between the elections of 1906 and 1910, but less than one year between the two elections of 1910. An equal value of a coefficient to the two elections would indicate greater change in the latter than in the former.

ECOLOGICAL ANALYSIS AND INFERENCE

Ecological analysis involves inferring individual or group behaviour from aggregate data. Since the publication of Robinson's article, aggregate data analysis has been plagued by the 'ecological fallacy', despite the fact that much of this criticism is no longer warranted.[22] Since Robinson's article, the nature and aggregation bias is better understood and the conditions under which it occurs severely delimited. Aggregation bias exists if the individuals are grouped into the units of analysis according to either the independent or dependent variables. If only the former is present, the correlation between the areal measures will be higher than the individual measures, but the regression coefficients (the intercept and slope) will not be affected and the aggregate data can be used to estimate individual relations. Grouping individuals by the independent variables thus inflates the correlations, but the regression coefficients remain unbiased. In this analysis:

it is reasonable that the selection by the independent variable is far more important than the selection by the dependent variable. Voting is perhaps the most common subject of aggregate-data studies; with few exceptions ..., it is seems likely that people's residences are determined by the same factors which determine their politics rather than their politics directly.[23]

The key to inferring individual behaviour from aggregate data is a well defined theory and hypotheses about how individuals behave. In other words, the problem is one of unmeasured relevant variables and proper model specification.[24]

Notes

1 'ONE STEP BROKEN, THE GREAT SCALE'S DESTROY'D'

1. A.O. Lovejoy, *The Great Chain of Being: A Study of the History of an Idea* (Cambridge, MA: Harvard University Press, 1936).
2. G. Watson, *The English Ideology: Studies in the Language of Victorian Politics* (London: Allen Lane, 1973), 175ff.
3. H. Perkin, *The Origins of Modern British Society, 1780–1880* (London: Routledge & Kegan Paul, 1969), 39.
4. Ibid, 42.
5. A. Briggs, 'Middle-Class Consciousness in English Politics, 1780–1846', *Past and Present*, 9 (April 1956), 65.
6. P. Corrigan, 'Feudal Relics or Capitalist Monument? Notes on the Sociology of Unfree Labour', *Sociology*, 11, 3 (September 1977), 454. By one calculation domestic servants constituted 4.5 per cent of the total population in 1881 and 34 per cent of all females employed in 1891 (ibid, 438).
7. M. Girouard, *The Victorian Country House* (New Haven, CT: Yale University Press, 1979), 4–5.
8. R. Bendix, *Nation-Building and Citizenship* (New York: Doubleday, 1964), 40.
9. A. Briggs, 'The Language of "Class" in Early Nineteenth-Century England', in A. Briggs and J. Saville (eds), *Essays in Labour History* (London: Macmillan, 1960), 46.
10. P.H. Lindert and J.G. Williamson, 'Reinterpreting Britain's Social Tables, 1688–1913', *Explorations in Economic History*, 20 (January 1983), 96.
11. C.H. Lee, 'Regional Growth and Structural Change in Victorian Britain', *Economic History Review*, 34, 3 (August 1981), 438–52.
12. G. Watson, *The English Ideology*, 174–97; see also G. Himmelfarb, *The Idea of Poverty: England in the Early Industrial Age* (London: Faber & Faber, 1984), 288–304.
13. A.J. Taylor, *Laissez-faire and State Intervention in Nineteenth-century Britain* (London: Macmillan, 1972); J. Lively and J. Rees (eds), *Utilitarian Logic and Politics* (Oxford: Clarendon Press, 1978); A.O. Hirschman, *The Passions and the Interests: Political Arguments for Capitalism Before its Triumph* (Princeton, NJ: Princeton University Press, 1977); A.O. Hirschman, 'Rival Views of Market Society', in A.O. Hirschman, *Rival Views of Market Society and Other Recent Essays* (New York: Viking, 1986), 105–41.
14. Watson, *The English Ideology*, 182–3.
15. Perkin, *The Origins of Modern British Society*, 26.
16. Watson, *The English Ideology*, 155ff; A. Briggs, 'The Language of "Mass" and "Masses" in Nineteenth-Century England', in D. Martin and D. Rubinstein (eds), *Ideology and the Labour Movement* (London: Croom Helm, 1979), 62–83.

17. Perkin, *The Origins of Modern British Society*, 210–11.
18. Watson, *The English Ideology*, 158.
19. T. Carlyle, 'Past and Present', in E. Jay and R. Jay (eds), *Critics of Capitalism: Victorian Reactions to 'Political Economy'* (Cambridge: Cambridge University Press, 1986), 63.
20. Ibid, 74–5.
21. J.S. Mill, 'Principles of Political Economy with some of their Applications to Social Philosophy', in Jay and Jay, *Critics of Capitalism*, 130.
22. Watson, *The English Ideology*, 182.
23. P. Smith, *Lord Salisbury on Politics* (Cambridge: Cambridge University Press, 1972), 257–8.
24. Ibid, 258.
25. T.H. Marshall, *Class, Citizenship and Social Development* (Garden City: Doubleday, 1964), xi.
26. Perkin, *The Origins of Modern British Society*, 34.
27. Ibid, 35.
28. W.D. Rubinstein, 'The Victorian Middle Classes: Wealth, Occupation, and Geography', *Economic Historical Review*, second series, 30, 4 (November 1977), 612, 620–21; H. McLeod, 'Religion', in J. Langton and R.J. Morris (eds), *Atlas of Industrialising Britain, 1780–1914* (London: Methuen Hume, 1986), 212–17; J.R. Hume and M. Oglethorpe, 'Engineering,' *ibid*, 136–9.
29. L. Colley, 'Whose Nation? Class and National Consciousness in Britain, 1750–1830', *Past and Present*, 113 (November 1986), 97–117.
30. H. Kearney, *The British Isles: A History of Four Nations* (New York: Cambridge, 1989), 152.
31. H. Trevor-Roper, 'The Invention of Tradition: The Highland Tradition of Scotland', in E. Hobsbawm and T. Ranger (eds), *The Invention of Tradition* (Cambridge: Cambridge University Press, 1983), 26; C. Harvie, 'Scott and the Image of Scotland,' in R. Samuel (ed.), *Patriotism: The Making and Unmaking of the British National Identity. Volume II: Minorities and Outsiders* (London: Routledge, 1989), 173–92.
32. P. Morgan, 'From Death to a View: The Hunt for the Welsh Past in the Romantic Period', in Hobsbawm and Ranger (eds), *The Invention of Tradition*, 43–100; K.O. Morgan, *Wales in British Politics, 1868–1922* (Cardiff: University of Wales Press, 1980), 6ff.
33. P. Morgan, 'From Death to a View,' 53–4.
34. D. Duff (ed.), *Queen Victoria's Highland Journals* (Exeter: Webb & Bower, 1980), 147–8.
35. D.J.V. Jones, 'The Rebecca Riots, 1839–1844', in A. Charlesworth (ed.), *An Atlas of Rural Protest in Britain, 1548–1900* (Philadelphia: University of Pennsylvania, 1983), 165–71; P. Morgan, 'From Death to a View,' 92ff.
36. T. Williams, 'The Anglicisation of South Wales', in Samuel (ed.), *Patriotism: The Making and Unmaking of the British National Identity*, vol. II, 193–206.
37. K.O. Morgan, *Wales in British Politics*, 13.
38. Kearney, *The British Isles*, 160.
39. Ibid, 173.

40. D. Cannadine, 'The Context, Performance and Meaning of Ritual: The British Monarchy and the "Invention of Tradition", *c.* 1820–1977', in Hobsbawm and Ranger (eds), *The Invention of Tradition*, 101–64.
41. M. Foucault, *Discipline and Punish* (New York: Pantheon Books, 1977), 216.
42. H.L. Dreyfus and P. Rabinow, *Michael Foucault: Beyond Structuralism and Hermeneutics* (Chicago: University of Chicago Press, 1982), 136.
43. C. Seymour, *Electoral Reform in England and Wales: The Development and Operation of the Parliamentary Franchise, 1832–1885* (New Haven, CT: Yale University Press, 1915), 466.
44. Foucault, *Discipline and Punish*, 170.
45. Ibid, 219ff.
46. Ibid, 195–228.
47. A. Smith, *An Inquiry into the Nature and Causes of the Wealth of Nations* (New York: The Modern Library, 1937), 4.
48. W.G. Hoskins, *The Making of the English Landscape* (London: Hodder & Stoughton, 1957), 169.
49. Briggs, 'Middle-Class Consciousness in English Politics', 70–1.
50. Kearney, *The British Isles*, 175; K.O. Morgan, *Rebirth of a Nation: Wales, 1880–1980* (New York: Oxford University Press, 1981), 10–14.

2 DEBATES ON EXPANDING THE POLITY

1. C. O'Leary, *The Elimination of Corrupt Practices in British Elections, 1868–1911* (Oxford: Clarendon Press, 1962), 179; D.E. Butler, *The Electoral System in Britain Since 1918* (Westport, CT: Greenwood Press, 1986), 1.
2. W.C. Lubenow, *The Politics of Government Growth: Early Victorian Attitudes Toward State Intervention, 1833–1848* (Hamden, CT: Archon Books, 1971), 177.
3. T.H. Marshall, *Class, Citizenship and Social Development* (Garden City: Doubleday, 1964), 87.
4. K. Polanyi, *The Great Transformation* (Boston, MA: Beacon Press, 1957), 86ff; P. Dunkley, *The Crisis of the Old Poor Law in England, 1795–1834* (New York: Garland Publishing, 1982); A.J. Taylor, *Laissez-faire and State Intervention in Nineteenth-century Britain* (London: Macmillan, 1972), 44; P. Anderson, *Lineages of the Absolutist State* (London: New Left Book, 1974); D. Fraser, 'The English Poor Law and the Origins of the British Welfare State', in W.J. Mommsen (ed.), *The Emergence of the Welfare State in Britain and Germany, 1850–1950* (London: Croom Helm, 1981), 9–31.
5. M.E. Rose, *The Relief of Poverty, 1834–1914* (London: Macmillan, 1972), 8.
6. P. Dunkley, *The Crisis of the Old Poor Law*, 88–9; G.V. Rimingler, *Welfare Policy and Industrialisation in Europe, America, and Russia* (New York: Wiley, 1971), 38–44.
7. Lubenow, *The Politics of Government Growth*, 30–69.

8. Marshall, *Class, Citizenship and Social Development*, 80–1; Rose, *The Relief of Poverty*, 34–52.
9. Marshall, Class, *Citizenship and Social Development*, 80.
10. Taylor, *Laissez-faire and State Intervention*, 44.
11. Fraser, 'The English Poor Law and the Origins of the British Welfare State', 9–15.
12. Rose, *The Relief of Poverty*, 39; Fraser, 'The English Poor Law and the Origins of the British Welfare State', 10–11.
13. A.J.P. Taylor, *Essays in English History* (Harmondsworth, Middlesex: Penguin, 1976), 71–2.
14. Marshall, *Class, Citizenship and Social Development*, 88.
15. T. Carlyle, 'Past and Present', in E. Jay and R. Jay (eds), *Critics of Capitalism: Victorian Reactions to 'Political Economy'* (Cambridge: Cambridge University Press, 1986), 63.
16. Lubenow, *The Politics of Government Growth*, 180.
17. J. Mill, 'Essay on Government', in J. Lively and J. Rees, (eds), *Utilitarian Logic and Politics* (Oxford: Clarendon Press, 1978), 34–41; A.O. Hirschman, *The Passions and the Interests: Political Arguments for Capitalism Before its Triumph* (Princeton, NJ: Princeton University Press, 1977), 56–66; R.G. Urquhart, 'The Autonomy of Commerce in Eighteenth Century British Political Economy', Unpublished Ph.D. Dissertation, New School for Social Research, New York, 1988.
18. A. Briggs, 'The Language of "Class" in Early Nineteenth-Century England', in A. Briggs and J. Saville (eds), *Essays in Labour History* (London: Macmillan, 1960), 62–3; R. Bendix, *Nation-Building and Citizenship* (New York: Doubleday, 1964), 62–3.
19. Bendix, *Nation Building and Citizenship*, 62.
20. Ibid, 72.
21. N. Gash, *Politics in the Age of Peel* (Hassocks, Sussex: Harvester Press, 1977), 7–8.
22. Gash, *Politics in the Age of Peel*, 24ff; C. Seymour, *Electoral Reform in England and Wales: The Development and Operation of the Parliamentary Franchise, 1832–1885* (New Haven, CT: Yale University Press, 1915), 9ff.
23. Gash, *Politics in the Age of Peel*, 26; Seymour, *Electoral Reform in England and Wales*, 75–7.
24. E. Porritt, 'Barriers Against Democracy in the British Electoral System', *Political Science Quarterly*, 26, 1 (March 1911), 17.
25. Gash, *Politics in the Age of Peel*, 139.
26. Gash, *Politics in the Age of Peel*, 137ff; H.J. Hanham, *Elections and Party Management* (London: Longman, Green, 1959).
27. Seymour, *Electoral Reform in England and Wales*, 198ff.
28. Ibid, 384ff.
29. Gash, *Politics in the Age of Peel*, 153.
30. M. Cowling, *1867: Disraeli, Gladstone and the Revolution: The Passing of the Second Reform Bill* (Cambridge: Cambridge University Press, 1967), 53.
31. Seymour, *Electoral Reform in England and Wales*, 245.
32. Cowling, *1867: Disraeli, Gladstone and the Revolution*, 59–60.
33. Seymour, *Electoral Reform in England and Wales*, 329–30.

34. Seymour, *Electoral Reform in England and Wales*, 258; Cowling, *1867: Disraeli, Gladstone and the Revolution*, 217ff.
35. Hanham, *Elections and Party Management*, xii.
36. P. Smith, *Disraelian Conservatism and Social Reform* (London: Routledge & Kegan Paul, 1967), 95.
37. O'Leary, *Elimination of Corrupt Practices*, 28.
38. Ibid, 56–7.
39. Seymour, *Electoral Reform in England and Wales*, 429.
40. Ibid, 428.
41. Ibid, 72–3.
42. Ibid, 428.
43. S. Rokkan, 'Mass Suffrage, Secret Voting and Political Participation', *European Journal of Sociology*, 2 (1961), 132–52.
44. O'Leary, *The Elimination of Corrupt Practices*, 86.
45. Seymour, *Electoral Reform in England and Wales*, 432.
46. J.B. Conacher (ed.), *The Emergence of British Parliamentary Democracy in the Nineteenth Century* (New York: Wiley, 1971), 131.
47. W.B. Gwyn, *Democracy and the Cost of Politics in Britain* (London: University of London, The Athlone Press, 1962), 52.
48. Hanham, *Elections and Party Management*, 253–6.
49. Gwyn, *Democracy and the Cost of Politics*, 52.
50. A. Briggs, 'The Language of "Mass" and "Masses" in Nineteenth-Century England', in D. Martin and D. Rubinstein (eds), *Ideology and the Labour Movement* (London: Croom Helm, 1979), 71.
51. O'Leary, *The Elimination of Corrupt Practices*, 165.
52. Ibid, 175–6.
53. Hanham, *Elections and Party Management*, 251.
54. Seymour, *Electoral Reform in England and Wales*, 447.
55. Gwyn, *Democracy and the Cost of Politics*, 55.
56. Seymour, *Electoral Reform in England and Wales*, 447ff; Hanham, *Elections and Party Management*, 281ff.
57. Seymour, *Electoral Reform in England and Wales*, 448; R.C.O. Matthews, C.F. Feinstein and J.C. Odling-Smee, *British Economic Development, 1856–1973* (Stanford, CA: Stanford University Press, 1982), 167; Gwyn, *Democracy and the Cost of Politics*, 247.
58. W.A. Hayes, *The Background and Passage of the Third Reform* Act (New York: Garland Publishing, 1982), 85.
59. H. Pelling, *Popular Politics and Society in Late Victorian Britain* (London: Macmillan, 1968), 1–18.
60. N. Blewett, 'The Franchise in the United Kingdom, 1885–1918', *Past and Present*, 32 (December 1965), 31.
61. Blewett, 'The Franchise in the United Kingdom, 1885–1918', 32; D. Butler and J. Cornford, 'United Kingdom', in S. Rokkan and J. Meyrait (eds), *International Guide to Electoral Statistics* (Paris: Mountonord, 1969), 333–4; G.A. Jones, 'Further Thoughts on Franchise, 1885–1918', *Past and Present*, 34 (July 1966), 134–8; H.C.G. Matthew, R.I. McKibben and J.A. Kay, 'The Franchise Factor and the Rise of the Labour Party', *The English Historical Review*, 91, 361 (1976); Seymour, *Electoral Reform in England and Wales*, 415–518.

62. Blewett, 'The Franchise in the United Kingdom, 1885–1918', 34.
63. Seymour, *Electoral Reform in England and Wales*, 109, 361–80.
64. Ibid, 380.
65. Ibid.
66. Hayes, *The Background and Passage of the Third Reform Act*, 253.
67. Ibid, 254ff; M.E.J. Chadwick, 'The Role of Redistribution in the Making of the Third Reform Act', *The Historical Journal*, 19, 3 (1976), 665–83; Porritt, 'Barriers Against Democracy'.
68. Chadwick, 'The Role of Redistribution', 683.
69. J. Cornford, 'The Transformation of the Conservatism in the late nineteenth century; *Victorian Studies*, 7 (1963), 66.
70. Ibid, 58.
71. Seymour, *Electoral Reform in England and Wales*, 505.
72. Smith, *Disraelian Conservatism and Social Reform*, 316–17.
73. Hayes, *The Background and Passage of the Third Reform Act*, 114.
74. Conacher, *The Emergence of British Parliamentary Democracy*, 137.
75. For a description of how the Cecils controlled both the land and its population under siege of the 1867 reforms and the secret ballot of 1872, see W.G. Hoskins, *The Making of the English Landscape* (London: Hodder & Stoughton, 1957), 223–4.
76. D. Cannadine, 'The Context, Performance and Meaning of Ritual: The British Monarchy and the "Invention of Tradition", *c.* 1820–1977', in E. Hobsbawm and T. Ranger (eds), *The Invention of Tradition* (Cambridge: Cambridge University Press, 1983), 101–64.
77. R. Taylor, *Lord Salisbury* (London: Allen Lane, 1975), 73–90.
78. A.J. Lee, 'Conservatism, Traditionalism and the British Working Class, 1880–1918', in D.E. Martin and D. Rubinstein (eds), *Ideology and the Labour Movement* (London: Croom Helm, 1979), 84–102.
79. Smith, *Disraelian Conservatism and Social Reform*, 217.
80. G. Watson, *The English Ideology: Studies in the Language of Victorian Politics* (London: Allen Lane, 1973), 191.
81. Smith, *Disraelian Conservatism and Social Reform*, 265.
82. M. Pugh, *The Tories and the People, 1880–1935* (Oxford: Basil Blackwell, 1985), 24.
83. Ibid, 141.
84. M. Ostrogorski, *Democracy and the Organisation of Political Parties*, two volumes (New York: Macmillan, 1902), I: 535ff.
85. J.H. Robb, *The Primrose League, 1883–1906* (New York: Columbia University Press, 1942), 87.
86. H. Trevor-Roper, 'The Invention of Tradition: The Highland Tradition of Scotland', in Hobsbawm and Ranger (eds), *The Invention of Tradition*, 15–42; P. Morgan, 'From Death to a View: The Hunt for the Welsh Past in the Romantic Period', ibid, 43–100.
87. Hayes, The Background and Passage of the Third Reform Act, 49; J.P.D. Dunbabin, 'The "Revolt of the Field": The Agricultural Labourers' Movement in the 1870s', *Past and Present*, 26 (November 1963), 92.
88. Smith, *Disraelian Conservatism and Social Reform*, 270.
89. A. Jones, *The Politics of Reform, 1884* (Cambridge: Cambridge University Press, 1972), 20.

90. Smith, *Disraelian Conservatism and Social Reform*, 300.
91. Ibid, 274–7.
92. Hayes, *The Background and Passage of the Third Reform Act*, 44.
93. Ibid, 52.
94. Salisbury, Lord (unsigned), 'Disintegration: Speeches of the Right Hon. W.E. Forester, M.P., at Devonport and Stonehouse', *The Quarterly Review*, 156, 312 (1883), 574.
95. Ibid, 588, 593–4.
96. Smith, *Disraelian Conservatism and Social Reform*, 316–18.
97. Ibid, 316.
98. Ostrogorski, *Democracy and the Organisation of Political Parties*, I: 266.
99. Smith, *Disraelian Conservatism and Social Reform*, 316, 271ff; J. Cornford, 'The Adoption of Mass Organisation by the British Conservative Party', in E. Allardt and Y. Luttussen, (eds), Cleaveges, Ideologies and party systems (Helsinki; Transaction of the Westsemark Society, 1964), 400–24; E.J. Feuchtwanger, *Disraeli, Democracy and the Tory Party* (Oxford: Clarendon Press, 1968), 132–66.
100. Hayes, *The Background and Passage of the Third Reform Act*, 122.
101. Ibid, 47.
102. Ibid, 69–76.
103. Seymour, *Electoral Reform in England and Wales*, 466.
104. A.C. Pigou, *Memorials to Alfred Marshall* (New York: Augustus M. Kelley, 1966), 102.
105. Ibid, 105.
106. N. McCord, 'Some Difficulties of Parliamentary Reform', *The Historical Journal*, 10, 4 (1967), 388.
107. A. Jones, *The Politics of Reform*, 21.
108. G.D.H. Cole, *British Working Class Politics, 1832–1914* (London: Routledge & Kegan Paul, 1950), 72–6.
109. H.A. Clegg, A. Fox and A.F. Thompson, *A History of British Trade Unions since 1889*, Volume I: *1889–1910* (Oxford: Oxford University Press, 1964), 1–54; W.H. Maehl, 'The Northeastern Miners' Struggle for the Franchise, 1872–74', *International Review of Social History*, 20, 2 (1975), 198–219.
110. Dunbabin, 'The "Revolt of the Field"', 90.
111. T. Tholfsen, 'The Origins of the Birmingham Caucus', *The Historical Journal*, 2, 2 (1959), 161–84.
112. A. Jones, *The Politics of Reform*, 29ff.

3 CLASSES, MASSES AND RACES IN LATE VICTORIAN POLITICS

1. Lord Salisbury (unsigned), 'Disintegration: Speeches of the Right Hon. W.E. Forester, M.P., at Devonport and Stonehouse', *The Quarterly Review*, 156, 312 (1883), 588.
2. H.J. Hanham, *Elections and Party Management* (London: Longman, Green, 1959), 212ff.

3. K.D. Wald, *Crosses on the Ballot: Patterns of British Voter Alignment Since 1885* (Princeton, NJ: Princeton University Press, 1983).

4. G. Dangerfield, *The Strange Death of Liberal England*, Reprint (London: MacGibbon & Kee, 1935).

5. H. Pelling, *Popular Politics and Society in Late Victorian Britain* (London: Macmillan, 1968), 120.

6. P.F. Clarke, 'Liberals, Labour and the Franchise', *The English Historical Review*, 92, 364 (1977): 582–9.

7. J.F. Glaser, 'English Nonconformity and the Decline of Liberalism', *American Historical Review*, 63, 2 (January 1958), 352–63.

8. R.T. Mackenzie and A. Silver, 'The Delicate Experiment: Industrialism, Conservatism and Working-Class Tories in England', in S.M. Lipset and S. Rokkan (eds), *Party Systems and Voter Alignments: Cross-National Perspectives* (New York: Free Press, 1967), 115–25; H.F. Moorhouse, 'The Political Incorporation of the British Working Class: An Interpretation', *Sociology*, 7, 3 (September 1973), 341–59.

9. C. Chamberlain, 'The Growth of Support for the Labour Party in Britain', *British Journal of Sociology*, 24, 4 (December 1973), 474–89.

10. Wald, *Crosses on the Ballot*.

11. M. Langan and B. Schwarz (eds), *Crises in the British State, 1880–1930* (London: Hutchinson, 1985).

12. For example, see E. Halevy, *Imperialism and the Rise of Labour* (New York: Barnes & Noble, 1961), 139–61; Wald, *Crosses on the Ballot*, 53–65.

13. G.I.T. Machin, *Politics and the Churches in Great Britain, 1869–1921* (Oxford: Clarendon Press, 1987), 141–8.

14. I. Blumer–Thomas, *The Growth of the British Party System*, two volumes (New York: Humanities Press, 1965), I: 161.

15. In 1891 Catholics numbered 1 of 21 in the population in England, and in Scotland, 1 of 12: see Halevy, *Imperialism and the Rise of Labour*, 186.

16. Blumer–Thomas, *The Growth of the British Party System*, 160ff; also see, Machin, *Politics and the Churches in Great Britain*, 284–6.

17. B. Harrison, 'Pubs', in H.J. Dyos and M. Wolff (eds), *The Victorian City: Images and Realities* (London: Routledge & Kegan Paul, 1976), 161–90; B. Harrison, *Peaceable Kingdom: Stability and Change in Modern British Politics* (Oxford: Clarendon Press, 1982), 123–56.

18. Blumer–Thomas, *The Growth of the British Party System*, I: 165.

19. M. Hechter, *Internal Colonialism: The Celtic Fringe in British National Development, 1536–1966* (Berkeley, CA: University of California Press, 1975); S. Rokkan and D. Urwin (eds), *The Politics of Territorial Identity: Studies in European Regionalism* (Beverly Hills, CA: Sage 1982); E.S. Wellhofer, 'To "Educate Their Volition to Dance in Their Chains": Enfranchisement and Realignment in Britain, 1885–1950, Part I: The Decay of the Old Order', *Comparative Political Studies*, 17, 1 (April 1984), 3–33.

20. D. Urwin, 'Towards a Nationalisation of British Politics?: The Party System, 1885–1940,' in O. Buesch (ed.), *Waehlerbewegung in der Europaeschen Geschichte* (Berlin: Colloquium Verlag, 1980), 225–58.

21. E.J. Hobsbawm, *Nations and Nationalism since 1780: Programme, Myth and Reality* (Cambridge: Cambridge University Press, 1990), 102.

22. H. Trevor-Roper, 'The Invention of Tradition: The Highland Tradition of Scotland' in E. Hobsbawm and T. Ranger (eds), *The Invention of Tradition* (Cambridge: Cambridge University Press, 1983), 15.

23. P. Morgan, 'From Death to a View: The Hunt for the Welsh Past in the Romantic Period', in Hobsbawm and Ranger (eds), *The Invention of Tradition*, 43–100.

24. K.O. Morgan, *Rebirth of a Nation: Wales, 1880–1980* (New York: Oxford University Press, 1981), 4.

25. T. Garvin, 'Decolonisation, Nationalisation, and Electoral Politics in Ireland, 1832–1945', in Buesch (ed.), *Waehlerbewegung*, 260–1.

26. J.P.D. Dunbabin, *Rural Discontent in Nineteenth Century Britain* (New York: Holmes & Meier, 1974); see also, J.P.D. Dunbabin, 'Agricultural Trade Unionism in England, 1872–94', in A. Charlesworth (ed.), *An Atlas of Rural Protest in Britain, 1548–1900* (Philadelphia: University of Pennsylvania Press, 1983), 171–3; J.P.D. Dunbabin, 'The Welsh Tithe War, 1886–95', Ibid, 177–9.

27. J. Hunter, 'The Highland Land War, 1881–1896,' in Charlesworth, (ed.), *An Atlas of Rural Protest in Britain*, 179–82; see also, J. Hunter, 'The Making of the Crofting Community', unpublished Ph.D. Dissertation, University of Edinburgh, 1976.

28. Hechter, *Internal Colonialism*.

29. Urwin, 'Towards a Nationalisation of British Politics?'.

30. Urwin, 'Towards a Nationalisation of British Politics?'; D. Urwin, 'Territorial Structures and Political Development in the United Kingdom', in Rokkan and Urwin (eds), *The Politics of Territorial Identity*, 19–74; E.S. Wellhofer, '"Two Nations": Class and Periphery in Late Victorian Britain, 1885–1910', *American Political Science Review* 79, 4 (December 1985), 977–93.

31. E.R. Wickham, *Church and People in an Industrial City* (London: Lutterworth Press, 1957); K.S. Inglis, *Churches and the Working Classes in Victorian England* (London: Routledge & Kegan Paul, 1963); Pelling, *Popular Politics and Society*, 19–36; see also P.F. Clarke, *Lancashire and the New Liberalism* (Cambridge: Cambridge University Press, 1971), 268ff.

32. F. Engels, *The Condition of the Working Class in England* (Oxford: Basil Blackwell, 1971), 141.

33. Inglis, *Churches and the Working Classes*, 334. Pelling similarly concludes 'the English worker had little cause to feel that church or chapel attendance was of any particular value to himself for purposes of social identification'. Pelling, *Popular Politics*, 35–6.

34. Wickham, *Church and People*, 158.

35. Pelling, *Popular Politics*, 35–6.

36. Inglis, *Churches and the Working Classes*, 63–4.

37. Pelling, *Popular Politics*, 22.

38. Also see, Wickham, *Church and People*, 158, 215–16; Halevy, *Imperialism and the Rise of Labour*, 168–9; H. Perkin, *The Origins of Modern British Society, 1780–1880* (London: Routledge & Kegan Paul, 1969), 340ff; H. Perkin, *The Rise of Professional Society: England Since 1880* (London: Routledge, 1989), 80, 100, 107, 114.

39. Pelling, *Popular Politics*, 26, 34–5; Clarke, *Lancashire and the New Liberalism*, 242ff; R. Jefferies, *Hodge and His Masters* (Stroud: Alan Sutton, 1992), 126–7.

40. Pelling, *Popular Politics*, 29.

41. K. Marx and F. Engels, *On Britain* (Moscow: Foreign Languages Publishing House, 1953), 506. Over 100 years later, Hunt described the mutual antagonism between the Irish and the native workers in similar terms. See E.H. Hunt, *British Labour History, 1815–1914* (Atlantic Highlands, NJ: Humanities Press), 167.

42. Halevy, *Imperialism and the Rise of Labour*, 186.

43. Hunt, *British Labour History*, 170.

44. M. Foucault, *Discipline and Punish* (New York: Pantheon Books, 1977), 212.

45. F.M.L. Thompson, *The Rise of Respectable Society: A Social History of Victorian Britain, 1830–1900* (Cambridge, MA: Harvard University Press), 141.

46. Perkin, *The Origins of Modern British Society*, 202.

47. E.J. Hobsbawm, *Primitive Rebels: Studies in Archaic Forms of Social Movements in the 19th and 20th Centuries* (New York: Frederick A. Praeger, 1963); S. Mews, 'The General and the Bishops: Alternative Responses to Decrhistianisation'' in T.R. Gourvish and A. O'Day (eds), *Later Victorian Britain, 1867–1900* (New York: St. Martin's Press, 1988), 209–28; Inglis, *Churches and the Working Classes*, 335.

48. From 1841 to 1911, while clothing and textile employment increased by 1.5 million, mining increased by one million and manufacturing and engineering industries and transport each by about the same. In 1850 there were 200 000 coal miners, by 1880, 500 000 and by 1911 about 1.5 million. Transport employment doubled between 1840 and 1851 and doubled again by 1881. These employment figures were matched by marked increased in heavy industry production. Iron production increased by 240 per cent between 1850 and 1880, steel production by 2800 per cent: and coal production by 200 per cent: E.J. Hobsbawm, *Industry and Empire* (New York: Pantheon Books, 1968), 94–5; C.H. Lee, 'Regional Growth and Structural Change in Victorian Britain', *Economic History Review*, 34, 3 (August 1981), 444; P. Deane and W.A. Cole, *British Economic Growth, 1688–1959* (Cambridge: Cambridge University Press, 1962), 182–240; R.C.O. Matthews, C.F. Feinstein and J.C. Odling–Smee, *British Economic Development, 1856–1973* (Stanford, CA: Stanford University Press, 1982), 228–9.

49. Lee, 'Regional Growth', 444; Deane and Cole, *British Economic Growth*, 142.

50. Charlesworth, *An Atlas of Rural Protest in Britain*, 164–83.

51. Hunt, *British Labour History, 1815–1914*, 144–88; Perkin, The Rise of Professional Society, 62ff.

52. D. Cannadine, *The Decline and Fall of the British Aristocracy* (New Haven, CT: Yale University Press, 1990), 88–181.

53. Chamberlain, 'The Growth of Support for the Labour Party', 482. In the 1870s the average number of workers per factory in iron shipbuilding was 570, 291 in jute manufacture; 177 in cotton manufacture; and 83 in pottery, Ibid, 483–4.

54. L. Hannah, *The Rise of the Corporate Economy: The British Experience* (Baltimore, MD: Johns Hopkins University Press, 1976), 23–4, 211; Lee, 'Regional Growth', 444; Deane and Cole, *British Economic Growth*, 182–240.
55. Foucault, *Discipline and Punish*, 135ff.
56. E.J. Hobsbawm, 'Custom, Wages and Work-load in Nineteenth Century Industry', in A. Briggs and J. Saville (eds), *Essays in Labour History* (London: Macmillan, 1960), 136–7.
57. Hannah, *The Rise of the Corporate Economy*, 23, 211.
58. D.H. Aldcroft, 'British Industry and Foreign Competition, 1875–1914', in D.H. Aldcroft (ed.), *The Development of British Industry and Foreign Competition* (Toronto: University of Toronto Press, 1968), 11–36; Deane and Cole, *British Economic Growth*, 225.
59. R. Davidson, *Whitehall and the Labour Problem in Late-Victorian and Edwardian Britain* (London: Croom Helm, 1985), 42.
60. C.H. Lee, *The British Economy Since 1700: A Macroeconomic Perspective* (Cambridge: Cambridge University Press, 1986).
61. Marx and Engels, *On Britain*, 30–1.
62. P.H. Lindert and J.G. Williamson, 'Reinterpreting Britain's Social Tables, 1688–1913', *Explorations in Economic History*, 20 (January 1983), 96, 98.
63. For example, Hobsbawm, *Industry and Empire*, 135.
64. Ibid, 137.
65. For example, G. Himmelfarb, *Poverty and Compassion: The Moral Imagination of the Late Victorians* (New York: Knopf, 1991), 21–30; for a critique of this interpretation, see H. Perkin, 'Interfere! Don't Interfere!', *The Times Literary Supplement* 22 November 1991, 25.
66. Davidson, *Whitehall and the Labour Problem*, 269.
67. Perkin, *The Origins of Modern British Society*, 414.
68. C. Booth, *Life and Labour of the People of London* (London: Macmillan, 1902); B.S. Rowntree, *Poverty: A Study of Town Life* (London: Macmillan, 1910); R. Griffen, *Essays in Finance: Second Series* (London: G. Bell, 1890); L. Levi, *Wages and Earnings of the Working Classes* (London: J. Murray, 1885).
69. A.L. Bowley, *Wages in the United Kingdom in the Nineteenth Century* (Cambridge: Cambridge University Press, 1900); A.L. Bowley, *Wages and Income in the United Kingdom since 1860* (Cambridge: Cambridge University Press, 1937).
70. Bowley, *Wages in the United Kingdom*, 126.
71. Perkin, *The Origins of Modern British Society*, 414–16.
72. H. Pelling, *The Origins of the Labour Party* (Oxford: Clarendon Press, 1965), 7–8; Hobsbawm, *Industry and Empire*, 135; Himmelfarb, *Poverty and Compassion*, 69.
73. Bowley, *Wages and Income in the United Kingdom*, 32–3.
74. I. Gazeley, 'The Cost of Living for Urban Workers in Late Victorian and Edwardian Britain', *Economic History Review*, Second Series, 52, 2 (1989), 216.
75. Hobsbawm, *Industry and Empire*, 134ff; R. Gray, *The Aristocracy of Labour in Nineteenth-Century Britain, c. 1850–1914* (London: Macmillan, 1981), 30–5; A. Fox, *History and Heritage: The Social Origins of the British Industrial Relations System* (London: Allen & Unwin, 1985), 176–9.

76. M. Langan, 'Reorganising the Labour Market: Unemployment, the State and the Labour Movement, 1880–1914', in M. Langan and B. Schwarz (eds), *Crises in the British State, 1880–1930* (London: Hutchinson, 1985), 106; G.D.H. Cole, *British Working Class Politics, 1832–1914* (London: Routledge & Kegan Paul, 1950), 77–97; M.J. Cullen, 'The 1887 Survey of the London Working Class', *International Review of Social History*, 20, 1 (1975), 48–60; J.M. Cousins and R.L. Davis, '"Working Class Incorporation" – A Historical Approach with Reference to the Mining Communities of S.E. Northumberland, 1840–1890', in F. Parkin (ed.), *The Social Analysis of Class Structure* (New York: Methuen, 1974), 275–98.

77. T.W. Hutchison, *A Review of Economic Doctrines, 1870–1929* (Oxford: Clarendon Press, 1953), 410.

78. S.L. Levy, *Industrial Efficiency and Social Economy by Nassau W. Senior*, two volumes (New York: Henry Holt 1928), II: 287.

79. B.B. Gilbert, *The Evolution of National Health Insurance in Great Britain: The Origins of the Welfare State* (London: Michael Joseph, 1966), 25.

80. Langan, 'Reorganising the Labour Market', 110; Himmelfarb, *Poverty and Compassion*, 46–47.

81. E.J. Hobsbawm, *Labouring Men: Studies in the History of Labour* (New York: Basic Books, 1964), 272–315; E.J. Hobsbawm, *Workers: Worlds of Labour* (New York: Pantheon Books, 1984), 227–72; see also, Pelling, *Popular Politics*, 37–61; Perkin, *The Origins of Modern British Society*, 231, 394ff; Gray, *The Aristocracy of Labour*; Himmelfarb, *Poverty and Compassion*, 37.

82. For a full description of the data see Appendix I. Several measures of religious incorporation and activity, as well as class distinctions, are available. For each of the three major religious groupings – Church of England, Nonconformism and Roman Catholicism – there are four measures of religious activity: (1) clergy per capitum provides an indicator of the religious ministering to the population, (2) maximum number of persons attending the best attended service per capitum indicates general popular religious activity, (3) number of persons attending Sunday school per capitum and (4) church day school per capitum capture the churches' ministrations to the religious, social and educational needs of the population.

Over 350 occupational categories in the 1891 census grasp the rudiments of the class system. Using the 1891 census in conjunction with the 1911 census categories permitted the construction of class distinctions. 'The Registrar General graded the occupational categories of 1911 on a scale intended to measure skill level, occupational prestige, income, life-chances, and other manifestations of inequality' (Wald, *Crosses on the Ballot*, 124–6; see also, J.A. Banks, 'The Social Structure of Nineteenth Century England as Seen Through the Census', in R. Lawton (eds), *The Census and the Social Structure* (London: Frank Cass, 1978), 179–223; W.A. Armstrong, 'The Uses of Information About Occupation', in E.A. Wrigley (eds.), *Nineteenth Century Society* (Cambridge: Cambridge University Press, 1972), 191–310. Wald grouped the 1891 data into six categories distinguished by these characteristics: (1) Class II occupations, consisting largely of commercial, non-production workers, (2) skilled manual workers, (3) manual labourers, (4) industrial labour, (5) non–agricultural general unskilled labour, (6) agricultural labour.

Ethnicity is indicated by the birth region of the residents: Welsh born, Scottish born and Irish born. This is a weak measure of ethnicity, but does capture those units with more ethnically homogeneous populations.

83. The resulting factors form latent variables for the final model in the concluding section of this chapter. Latent variables are similar to factors in that both are theoretical constructs which can be observed only indirectly through the co-variance of the observed or manifest variables. For example, we cannot observe religiosity directly, but we can observe religious manifestations in the form of various behaviours: for example, church attendance, church school attendance and Sunday school attendance. We would expect that these measures would demonstrate co-variance, that is, they would increase or decrease together. We would conclude that if they co-vary, we are observing different facets of the theoretical phenomenon of religiosity we seek to measure, and the higher the coefficients, the more the strongly present the phenomenon. Latent variables, therefore, should display both theoretical and statistical coherence. For a fuller discussion of the analytic technique and its application to the current data and problems, see Appendix II.

84. The measurement model provides strong confirmation for the four configurations discussed above. The communality coefficient, measuring the coherence of the LVs, is 0.62. The residual co-variances of the MVs as well as the residual co-variances of the MVs to the LVs are all below the value of the directed relationships between the MVs and the LVs. The co-variances among the LVs are low indicating strong support for the proposition that we are measuring four independent socio-economic configurations. However, these LV co-variances are strong enough that prudence dictates we control for their inter-relationships in the models developed at later points in the analysis.

85. C. O'Leary, *The Elimination of Corrupt Practices in British Elections, 1868–1911* (Oxford: Clarendon Press, 1962), 182; C. Seymour, *Electoral Reform in England and Wales: The Development and Operation of the Parliamentary Franchise, 1832–1885* (New Haven, CT: Yale University Press, 1915). 484.

86. N. Blewett, 'The Franchise in the United Kingdom, 1885–1918', *Past and Present*, 32 (December 1965), 30–3.

87. G.S.R.K. Clark, *An Expanding Society: Britain, 1830–1900* (Cambridge: Cambridge University Press, 1967), 38.

88. Blewett, 'The Franchise in the United Kingdom, 1885–1918', 31ff; J.P.D. Dunbabin, 'Electoral Reforms and their Outcome in the United Kingdom, 1865–1900', in T.R. Gourvish and A. O'Day (eds) *Later Victorian Britain, 1867–1900* (New York: St. Martin's Press, 1988), 102–3; H.C.G. Matthew, R.I. McKibbin and J.A. Kay, 'The Franchise Factor in the Rise of the Labour Party', *The English Historical Review*, 91, 361 (October 1976), 726–33.

89. D.E. Butler, *The Electoral System in Britain Since 1918* (Westport, C N: Greenwood Press, 1986), 5.

90. Urwin, 'Towards a Nationalisation of British Politics?', 234.

91. Blewett, 'The Franchise in the United Kingdom, 1885–1918', 27–56; G.A. Jones, 'Further Thoughts on Franchise, 1885–1918', *Past and Present*, 34

(July 1966), 134–8; Matthew, McKibbin and Kay, 'The Franchise Factor in the Rise of the Labour Party', 723–52; Perkin, *The Rise of Professional Society*, 40–61.

92. Dunbabin, 'Electoral Reforms and their Outcome', 114–17.
93. Matthew, McKibbin and Kay, 'The Franchise Factor in the Rise of the Labour Party', 742.
94. J. Cornford, 'The Transformation of the Conservative Party in the Late Nineteenth Century', *Victorian Studies*, 7 (September, 1963), 35–66; J.H. Robb, *The Primrose League, 1883–1906* (New York: Columbia University Press, 1942), 9–40; M. Pugh, *The Tories and the People, 1880–1935* (Oxford: Basil Blackwell, 1985), 11–15.
95. R.R. James, *The British Revolution: British Politics, 1880–1939* (London: Hamish Hamilton, 1976), 52–3.
96. Pugh, *The Tories and the People*, 13.
97. P. Smith, *Lord Salisbury on Politics* (Cambridge: Cambridge University Press, 1972), 30.
98. James, *The British Revolution*, 101; see also J. Cornford, 'The Adoption of Mass Organisation by the British Conservative Party,' in E. Allardt and Y. Luttussen (eds), *Cleavages, Ideologies and Party Systems* (Helsinki: Transactions of the Westermark Society, 1964), 400–24.
99. Pugh, *The Tories and the People*, 213.
100. Robb, *The Primrose League*, 148.
101. O'Leary, *The Elimination of Corrupt Practices*, 195.
102. Dunbabin, 'Electoral Reforms and their Outcome', 117; see also, M. Pugh, *The Making of Modern British Politics, 1867–1939* (New York: St. Martin's Press, 1982), 51.
103. P. Thane, 'Late Victorian Women', in Gourvish and O'Day (eds), *Later Victorian Society*, 206; see also, Pugh, *The Making of Modern British Politics*, 52–3.
104. Pugh, *The Tories and the People*, 27.
105. Ibid, 145–8. His findings show 19 per cent businessmen and manufacturers, 18 per cent shopkeepers, 18 per cent skilled manual workers, and 19 per cent semi-skilled manual workers.
106. Ibid, 216–51. Pugh's data on number of Habitations and members per constituency have been merged with Wald's data to generate two measures of the League's organisational density: Habitations and members per capitum. See Appendix I for a description of the data.
107. Cole, *British Working Class Politics*, 138–87; Moorhouse, 'The Political Incorporation of the British Working Class', 341–59.
108. Chamberlain, 'The Growth of Support for the Labour Party', 481ff.
109. Cole, *British Working Class Politics*, 126–37; Fox, *History and Heritage*, 221ff. By 1892 aggregate union membership had reached 1.5 million or about 10.6 per cent of the potential union membership, defined as 'all employees, whether employed or unemployed, who are legally permitted to unionise', G.S. Bain and R. Price, *Profiles of Union Growth* (Oxford: Basil Blackwell, 1980), 8. By 1911, the close of the period under investigation, membership had risen to 2.6 million or 14.6 per cent of the potential union membership or an increase of 66 per cent. Industry differences, however, were substantial: coal mining was 60 per cent unionised in 1892 increasing to 74 per cent in 1911. Other mining and quarrying operations rose from 18 per cent to 23 per cent. Textiles increased from 24 per cent

to 48 per cent in the same period. Railway unionisation grew from 10 per cent to 17 per cent. Printing and publishing union membership rose from 28 per cent to 36 per cent. However, agricultural unionism (which had reached its height in the 1870s) declined from 3.6 per cent in 1892 to 0.7 per cent in 1911. Metals and engineering also declined from 32 per cent to 29 per cent even while potential union members increased by 43 per cent: Bain and Price, *Profiles of Union Growth*, 37–78.

110. H.A. Clegg, A. Fox and A.F. Thompson, *A History of British Trade Unions since 1889*, Volume I: *1889–1910* (Oxford: Oxford University Press, 1964), 87–96; H. Pelling, A History of British Trade Unionism, 89–120; Hunt, *British Labour History*, 304–15.
111. Pelling, *A History of British Trade Unionism*, 90.
112. Wald provides measurements of trade union density at three time-points: 1888, 1901 and 1910. His figures measure the 'national density (the number of organised workers as a proportion of the workforce)' in metal manufacturing, mining, textiles, building, transportation, clothing, printing and wood working in each constituency,

> producing a measure of the workforce likely to be exposed to union influence. This is by no means a direct estimate of union strength because there were undoubtedly significant regional variations in organisation among certain trades. The figure represented instead an estimate of the concentration of those trades with the greatest nation-wide propensity for union organisation. (Wald, *Crosses on the Ballot*, 126)

113. A.L. Lowell, 'Oscillations in Politics', *The Annuals*, 12 (July 1898), 70–1.
114. Principal component factor loadings represent the best fitting linear combinations of the observed variables. Thus, the loadings are measures of association between the observed or manifest variables of the eight elections to the common variance across the elections. The loadings represent the best fit of the manifest or observed variables, but are not entirely determined by them. When the observed variables occur at multiple time points, the result is a linear composite of predictors across time or the trend line for the observed variables.
   The latent growth curve coefficients include the two components of change: that which is constant from one observation to another, and that which changes from one observation to another. In a parallel to regression analysis, the curve represents both constant term and the coefficient. At this point we treat them as singular, but in later chapters we can disaggregate them into difference component models. For a fuller treatment of the technical elements and references, see Appendix II.

4 THE EFFECTS OF FRANCHISE EXPANSION ON SOCIAL-PARTISAN ALIGNMENTS

1. H. Perkin, *The Origins of Modern British Society, 1780–1880* (London: Routledge & Kegan Paul, 1969), 340ff.

232   *Notes*

2. The evaluation of the resulting models depends on their meeting two general criteria: the substantive interpretation of the model's results, and the statistical reliability of the model's parameters. Substantive evaluation of the models rests on the generation of solutions consistent with a wide variety of evidence or, if inconsistent, their ability to support other plausible interpretations. Additional evidence is readily available from other historical and social science research, as well as contemporary accounts of the period. In addition, the models should facilitate the disentanglement of contending interpretations of the dynamics as well as be consistent with historical interpretations. See Appendix II for a discussion of goodness-of-fit measures.

3. E. Halevy, *Imperialism and the Rise of Labour* (New York: Barnes Noble, 1961), 165.

4. K.O. Morgan, *Wales in British Politics, 1868–1922* (Cardiff: University of Wales Press, 1980), 44–5.

5. Halevy, *Imperialism and the Rise of Labour*, 188–9.

6. H.C.G. Matthew, R.I. McKibbin and J.A. Kay, 'The Franchise Factor in the Rise of the Labour Party', *The English Historical Review*, 91, 361 (October 1976), 731–2.

7. D. Urwin, 'Territorial Structures and Political Development in the United Kingdom', in S. Rokkan and D. Urwin (eds), *The Politics of Territorial Identity* (Beverly Hills, CA: Sage, 1982), 40–6.

8. For similar results in Lancashire, see Matthew, McKibbin and Kay, 'The Franchise Factor in the Rise of the Labour Party', 750–2.

9. See for example, A. Fox, *History and Heritage: The Social Origins of the British Industrial Relations System* (London: Allen & Unwin, 1985), 174–220; M. Pugh, *The Making of Modern British Politics, 1867–1939* (New York: St. Martin's Press, 1982), 22–39; E.H. Hunt, *British Labour History, 1815–1914* (Atlantic Highlands, NJ: Humanities Press, 1981), 315ff; S. Hall and B. Schwarz, 'State and Society, 1880–1930', in M. Langan and B. Schwartz (eds), *Crises in the British State, 1880–1930* (London: Hutchinson, 1985), 7–32; H. Perkin, *The Rise of Professional Society: England Since 1880* (London: Routledge, 1989), 40–52, 139–41.

10. W.A. Hayes, *The Background and Passage of the Third Reform Act* (New York: Garland Publishing, 1982); Pugh, *The Making of Modern British Politics*, 23–39.

11. For example, see P.F. Clarke, 'Liberals, Labour and the Franchise', *The English Historical Review*, 92, 364 (1977), 584.

12. K.O. Morgan, *Rebirth of a Nation: Wales, 1880–1980* (New York, Oxford University Press, 1981), 27.

13. Matthew, McKibbin and Kay, 'The Franchise Factor in the Rise of the Labour Party', 747.

14. Clarke, 'Liberals, Labour and the Franchise', 582–9; C. Chamberlain, 'The Growth of Support for the Labour Party in Britain', *British Journal of Sociology*, 24, 4 (December 1973), 474–89; H. Pelling, *Popular Politics and Society in Late Victorian Britain* (London: Macmillan, 1968), 47.

15. C. O'Leary, *The Elimination of Corrupt Practices in British Elections, 1868–1911* (Oxford: Clarendon Press, 1962), 179.

16. D. Butler, *The Electoral System in Britain Since 1918* (Westport, CT: Greenwood Press, 1986), 5.

17. G.W. Cox, *The Efficient Secret: The Cabinet and the Development of Political Parties in Victorian England* (Cambridge: Cambridge University Press, 1987), 105.
18. Ibid, 106ff.
19. N. Blewett, 'The Franchise in the United Kingdom, 1885–1918', *Past and Present*, 32 (December 1965), 27–56; Matthew, McKibbin and Kay, 'The Franchise Factor in the Rise of the Labour Party', 723–52; G.A. Jones, 'Further Thoughts on Franchise, 1885–1918', *Past and Present*, 34 (July 1966); 134–8; H.F. Moorhouse, 'The Political Incorporation of the British Working Class: An Interpretation', *Sociology*, 7, 3 (September 1973), 341–59.
20. Matthew, McKibbin and Kay, 'The Franchise Factor in the Rise of the Labour Party', 747.
21. In Chapter 7 we investigate differences with the working class by skill and trade union organisation, sometimes called the Labour Aristocracy thesis. Here, however, the MV loadings show two dramatic increases between 1886 and 1892 and between 1900 and 1906. The first marks the rise of the New Unionism which stimulated labour organisation and class militancy. The latter marked the break-up of the Lib-Lab alliance and Labour offering its own candidates in elections. Both periods are generally seen as heightening the expression of class conflict in electoral politics.
22. G.D.H. Cole, *British Working Class Politics, 1832–1914* (London: Routledge & Kegan Paul, 1950), 72ff; Hunt, *British Labour History*, 270ff.
23. Pelling, *Popular Politics*, 4–5.
24. A.E.P. Duffy, 'New Unionism in Britain, 1889–1890: A Reappraisal', *The Economic History Review*, 14 (1961/1962), 319.
25. Cole, *British Working Class Politics*, 154.
26. Fox, *History and Heritage*, 179–83.
27. Examining the technical results in the model, we see these conclusions clearly reflected in the trend lines and shift in the directed paths in the model for both Labour and the Lib-Labs. As we noted above, the trend line for Labour increases rapidly between 1886 and 1892 and again between 1900 and 1906 (periods corresponding to its efforts establish independence from the Liberals). After 1906 the slope flattens, but the coefficients are very strong, indicating high and increasing coherence in the Labour vote. The strongest predictors of the trend line are trade unionism and the Roman Catholic working class.
    If we compare Labour and the Lib-Labs, we see almost the mirror image. The trend line for the Lib-Labs breaks into two segments having little association with each other, the first from 1885 to 1895 and the second from 1900 to 1910. The earlier trend line peaks in 1892 and then declines to almost zero in 1900; the second increases rapidly from 1900 to 1906 and then levels off for the remainder of the period. Clearly a major shift has occurred in the character of the Lib-Lab vote across these periods. However, we have limited success in predicting these trends, being able to account for only 23 per cent and 15 per cent of the variance in the trend lines. For the earlier trend line the best predictors are the Roman Catholic working class and weak Nonconformism. Trade union density generates only a weak path (0.1 for the 1885–95 period and 0.02 for the 1900–10 period). The model

generates no strong predictors for the later trend line, but several changes
are significant. The Roman Catholic working class, the Nonconformist
Alliance and trade unionism lose their predictive power; while the
coefficient for the 'unchurched' and unorganised working class increases
substantially, becoming the most powerful predictor.

5   SHORT-RUN CHANGES IN ISSUES AND PARTY ALLIANCES

1. E. Halevy, *The Rule of Democracy* (New York: Peter Smith, 1952), 441;
    A. Simon, 'Church Disestablishment as a Factor in the General Election of
    1885', *Historical Journal*, 18 (December 1975), 791–820.
2. G.I.T. Machin, *Politics and the Churches in Great Britain, 1869–1921*
    (Oxford: Clarendon Press, 1987), 147.
3. Ibid, 284ff.
4. K.S. Inglis, *Churches and the Working Classes in Victorian England*
    (London: Routledge & Kegan Paul, 1963), 74ff; K.D. Wald, *Crosses on the
    Ballot: Patterns of British Voter Alignment Since 1885* (Princeton, NJ:
    Princeton University Press, 1983), 64–5, 172–7.
5. D.M. Fahey, 'The Politics of Drink: Pressure Groups and the British Liberal
    Party, 1883–1908', *Social Science*, 54 (1979), 76–85.
6. Wald, *Crosses on the Ballot*, 173; Inglis, *Churches and the Working
    Classes*, 74.
7. M. Pugh, *The Making of Modern British Politics, 1867–1939* (New York:
    St. Martin's Press, 1982), 68–9.
8. E. Halevy, *Imperialism and the Rise of Labour* (New York: Barnes &
    Noble, 1961), 381.
9. M. Kinnear, *The British Voter* (London: B.T. Batsford, 1968), 34ff. notes
    the intensity of the issue in 1910.
10. B. Keith-Lucas, *The English Local Government Franchise* (Oxford: Oxford
    University Press, 1952), 215.
11. Halevy, *Imperialism and the Rise of Labour*, 201–7.
12. K.O. Morgan, *Rebirth of a Nation: Wales, 1880–1980* (New York: Oxford
    University Press, 1981), 37–8, 58.
13. Machin, *Politics and the Churches in Great Britain*, 260–73.
14. Ibid, 289.
15. A. Fox, *History and Heritage: The Social Origins of the British Industrial
    Relations System* (London: Allen & Unwin, 1985), 170ff.
16. Ibid, 182.
17. H.A. Clegg, A. Fox and A.F. Thompson, *A History of British Trade Unions
    since 1889*, Volume I: 1889–1910 (Oxford: Oxford University Press, 1964),
    414.
18. G.D.H. Cole, *British Working Class Politics, 1832–1914* (London:
    Routledge & Kegan Paul, 1950), 189–90.
19. H. Pelling, *A History of British Trade Unionism* (London: Macmillan,
    1963), 125–30.
20. Fox, *History and Heritage*, 187; Halevy, *Imperialism and the Rise of
    Labour*, 246ff; E.H. Hunt, *British Labour History, 1815–1914* (Atlantic
    Highlands, NJ: Humanities Press, 1981), 307–10.

21. C. Andrew, *Her Majesty's Secret Service* (New York: Viking, 1986), 34–85.
22. Clegg, Fox and Thompson, *A History of British Trade Unions since 1889*, 329.
23. L. Hannah, *The Rise of the Corporate Economy: The British Experience* (Baltimore: Johns Hopkins University Press, 1976), 8–24.
24. E.J. Hobsbawm, *Labouring Men: Studies in the History of Labour* (New York: Basic Books, 1964).
25. Clegg, Fox and Thompson, *A History of British Trade Unions since 1889*, 83; Hunt, *British Labour History*, 295ff.
26. Hobsbawm, *Labouring Men*; R.Q. Gray, 'The Labour Aristocracy in the Victorian Class Structure', in F. Parkin (ed.), *The Social Analysis of Class Structure* (London: Tavistock, 1974), 19–38; R. Gray, *The Aristocracy of Labour in Nineteenth-Century Britain, c. 1850–1914* (London: Macmillan, 1981).
27. H.C.G. Matthew, R.I. McKibbin and J.A. Kay, 'The Franchise Factor in the Rise of the Labour Party', *The English Historical Review*, 91, 361 (October 1976), 723–52; N. Blewett, 'The Franchise in the United Kingdom, 1885–1918', *Past and Present*, 32 (December 1965), 27–56.
28. Cole, *British Working Class Politics*, 85ff.
29. Ibid, 147.
30. J. Saville, 'Trade Unions and Free Labour: The Background to the Taff Vale Decision', in A. Briggs and J. Saville (eds), *Essays in Labour History* (London: Macmillan, 1960), 317–50.
31. Morgan, *Rebirth of a Nation: Wales*, 40–2.
32. If we turn our attention to the technical features of Figure 5.1, we see the Weiner simplex model for the component change processes of the Conservative vote across the eight elections of the period. The attraction of the Weiner simplex models lies in their capacity to decompose the vote across time into short and long run components of a trend. This decomposition appears in the coefficients linking the observed or manifest variables to the latent variables. In the Weiner simplex process, the first latent vote variable in the series will capture all the variance or changes up to that point in time, subsequent latent vote variables represent the continuity and change from the preceding latent vote variable. The manifest variable coefficients display the relative contributions to that continuity and change. For example, for the 1885 latent vote variable the coefficient linking the 1885 observed vote captures the variance up to that point in time; the coefficient from the 1886 election captures the continuity linking the 1885 election to the 1886 election. Similarly, for the 1886 latent vote variable, the coefficient for that election captures the additional variance contributed for that election after removing the effects of the 1885 election, while the coefficient for the 1892 election captures the continuity between 1886 and 1892. This process then proceeds through the eight elections. The size of the coefficients indicates the extent of the lingering effects of previous observations on subsequent observations and the size of the changes from election to election. The paths linking the socio-economic and organisational latent variables to the Weiner simplex process represent the former's capacity to account for the latter.

Figure 5.1 presents this information for the Conservatives. The model does a competent job of accounting for the variance in the simplex process with predictability ranging around 22 per cent. The model is quite good at reconstructing the original data matrix generating high fit statistics. The Bentler-Bonett coefficient is 0.88 for the reconstructed missing value data and 0.54 for the other data sets.

33. J.J. McArdle and M.S. Aber, 'Patterns of Change within Latent Variable Structural Equation Models', in A. von Eye (ed.), *Statistical Models in Longitudinal Research*, Volume I: *Principles and Structuring Change* (New York: Academic Press, 1990), 188.

34. R. Quinault, 'Joseph Chamberlain: A Reassessment', in T.R. Gourvish and A. O'Day (eds), *Later Victorian Britain, 1867–1900* (New York: St. Martin's Press, 1988), 69–92.

35. The Weiner simplex model for the Unionist vote between 1885 and 1910 is also quite successful since it generates fit statistics of 0.90 and 0.51 for the reconstructed and non-reconstructed missing data.

36. Wald, *Crosses on the Ballot*, 213.

37. J.F. Glaser, 'English Nonconformity and the Decline of Liberalism', *American Historical Review*, 63, 2 (January 1958), 363.

38. G. Dangerfield, *The Strange Death of Liberal England*, Reprint (London: MacGibbon & Kee, 1935).

39. Ibid, 16.

40. P.F. Clarke, *Lancashire and the New Liberalism* (Cambridge: Cambridge University Press, 1971); H. Pelling, *Popular Politics and Society in Late Victorian Britain* (London: Macmillan, 1968), 101ff; N. Blewett, *The Peers, The Party and the People: The General Election of 1910* (London: Macmillan, 1972).

41. Pelling, *Popular Politics and Society*, 119–20.

42. Wald, *Crosses on the Ballot*, 205.

43. Ibid, 214–15.

44. G.S. Jones, 'Working-Class Culture and Working-Class Politics in London, 1870–1900: Notes on the remaking of a Working Class', *Journal of Social History*, 7, 4 (Summer 1974), 498.

45. Hunt, *British Labour History*, 151ff.

46. Inglis, *Churches and the Working Classes*, 120ff.

47. Cole, *British Working Class Politics*, 180–1.

48. On the increasing isolation of the Liberals in single party districts of the peripheral Nonconformist middle classes, see D. Urwin, 'Toward a Nationalisation of British Politics?: The Party System, 1885–1940', in O. Buesch (ed.), *Waehlerbewegung in der Europaeschen Geschichte* (Berlin: Colloquium Verlag, 1980), 240–2, 252.

The model provides a good fit to the data (Bentler-Bonett = 0.87 for the reconstructed missing values and 0.529 for the non- reconstructed data) as well as a sizeable proportion of the variance in the vote latent variables. For the Liberals the model accounts for about 30 per cent of the latent vote variance in each of the elections. For Labour the predictive success increased dramatically from zero in 1885 to about 30 per cent by 1910. The success for the Lib-Labs increases from about 18 per cent to about 30 per cent across the period. Overall, the model is statistically successful and theoretically interesting.

6 CHALLENGES TO DOMESTIC EMPIRE IN LATE VICTORIAN POLITICS

1. Lord Salisbury, (unsigned), 'Disintegration: Speeches of the Right Hon. W.E. Forester, M.P., at Devonport and Stonehouse', *The Quarterly Review*, 156, 312 (1883), 559–95.
2. P. Smith, *Lord Salisbury on Politics* (Cambridge: Cambridge University Press, 1972), 26.
3. Ibid, 87.
4. David Cannadine, *The Decline and Fall of the British Aristocracy* (New Haven, CT: Yale University Press, 1990), 37ff.
5. P. Smith, *Disraelian Conservatism and Social Reform* (London: Routledge & Kegan Paul, 1967), 205.
6. M. Pugh, *The Tories and the People, 1880–1935* (Oxford: Basil Blackwell, 1985), 13.
7. E.J. Hobsbawm, 'Mass-Producing Traditions: Europe, 1870–1914', in E. Hobsbawm and T. Ranger (eds), *The Invention of Tradition* (Cambridge: Cambridge University Press, 1983), 263–308; E.J. Hobsbawm, *Nations and Nationalism since 1780: Programme, Myth and Reality* (Cambridge: Cambridge University Press, 1990), 101–30.
8. For a review, see E.S. Wellhofer, 'Core and Periphery: Territorial Dimensions in Politics', *Urban Studies*, 26 (1989a), 340–55.
9. E.S. Wellhofer, 'Models of Core and Periphery Dynamics', *Comparative Political Studies*, 21, 2 (July 1988), 281–307.
10. E.S. Wellhofer, '"Two Nations": Class and Periphery in Late Victorian Britain, 1885–1910', *American Political Science Review*, 79, 4 (December 1985), 977–93.
11. D. Urwin, 'Territorial Structures and Political Development in the United Kingdom', in S. Rokkan and D. Urwin (eds), *The Politics of Territorial Identity* (Beverly Hills, CA: Sage, 1982), 31–7.
12. W.D. Rubinstein, 'The Victorian Middle Classes: Wealth, Occupation, and Geography', *Economic Historical Review*, second series, 30, 4 (November 1977), 620.
13. M. Hechter, *Internal Colonialism: The Celtic Fringe in British National Development, 1536–1966* (Berkeley, CA: University of California Press, 1975), 209; C.C. Ragin, 'Class, Status and "Reactive Ethnic Cleavages": The Social Bases of Political Regionalism', *American Sociological Review*, 42, 3 (June 1977), 438–50; D. Urwin, 'Towards a Nationalisation of British Politics?: The Party System, 1885–1940', in O. Buesch (ed.), *Waehlerbewegung in der Europaeschen Geschichte* (Berlin: Colloquium Verlag, 1980), 225–58; K.O. Morgan, Rebirth of a Nation: Wales, 1880–1980 (New York: Oxford University Press, 1980), 94–118; Urwin, 'Territorial Structures and Political Development in the United Kingdom';

238 *Notes*

D. Urwin, 'The Price of a Kingdom: Territory, Identity and Centre-Periphery in Western Europe', in Y. Meny and V. Wright (eds), *Centre-Periphery Relations in Western Europe* (London: Allen & Unwin, 1985), 151–70.

14. Rubinstein, 'The Victorian Middle Classes', 620–1.
15. C.H. Lee, 'Regional Growth and Structural Change in Victorian Britain', *Economic History Review*, 34, 3 (August 1981), 442–3, 449, 450ff.
16. For a example, see B. Thomas, 'The Migration of Labour into the Glamorganshire Coalfield (1861–1911)', *Economica*, 10 (November 1930), 275–94.
17. Urwin, 'Territorial Structures and Political Development in the United Kingdom', 33.
18. Lee, 'Regional Growth and Structural Change in Victorian Britain', 450.
19. Ibid, 451.
20. W. Christaller, *Central Places in Germany* (Englewood Cliffs, NJ: Prentice-Hall, 1966); C.A. Smith, 'Regional Economic Systems: Linking Geographical Models and Socio-economic Problems', in C.A. Smith (ed.), *Regional Analysis* Volume I: *Economic Systems* (New York: Academic Press, 1976a), 3–63; C.A. Smith, 'Exchange Systems and the Spatial Distribution of Elites: The Organisation of Stratification in Agrarian Societies', in Smith (ed.), *Regional Analysis*, Vol. II: *Social Systems* (New York: Academic Press, 1976b), 309–74.
21. E.J. Hobsbawm, *Industry and Empire* (New York: Pantheon Books, 1968), 252–76, 289, 291.
22. Wellhofer, '"Two Nations"', 986–9.
23. Rubinstein, 'The Victorian Middle Classes', 602–23; Urwin, 'Towards a Nationalisation of British Politics?'; Lee, 'Regional Growth and Structural Change in Victorian Britain'.
24. For the constituent units, see K.D. Wald, *Crosses on the Ballot: Patterns of British Voter Alignment Since 1885* (Princeton, NJ: Princeton University Press, 1983), 143.
25. J.S. Hurt, *Elementary Schooling and the Working Classes, 1860–1918* (London: Routledge & Kegan Paul, 1979), 158.
26. K.S. Inglis, *Churches and the Working Classes in Victorian England* (London: Routledge & Kegan Paul, 1963), 330ff.
27. E.R. Wickham, *Church and People in an Industrial City* (London: Lutterworth Press, 1957), 155.
28. F.M.L. Thompson, *The Rise of Respectable Society: A Social History of Victorian Britain, 1830–1900* (Cambridge, MA: Harvard University Press, 1988), 140.
29. Ibid, 141.
30. Ibid, 10.
31. Inglis, *Churches and the Working Classes*, 334; also see R.F. Wearmouth, *Methodism and the Struggle for the Working Classes, 1850–1900* (Leicester: Edgar Backus, 1954), 111; Thompson, The *Rise of Respectable Society*, 327–8.
32. H. Pelling, *Popular Politics and Society in Late Victorian Britain* (London: Macmillan, 1968), 120.
33. Wellhofer, '"Two Nations",' 977–93.

34. A. Fox, *History and Heritage: The Social Origins of the British Industrial Relations System* (London: Allen & Unwin, 1985), 239–46; see also Pelling, *Popular Politics*, 82–100.
35. Urwin, 'Territorial Structures and Political Development in the United Kingdom', 41, 45–6.
36. E. Halevy, *Imperialism and the Rise of Labour* (New York: Barnes & Noble, 1961), 188–9.
37. All relationships between the socio-economic variables and the Unionist vote are stronger in the periphery than in the country-wide model. Those for the Liberals are about the same, with Roman Catholic opposition stronger in the periphery. The models provide a good fit to the data and the results of the reproduced missing value data are confirmed in the alternative models of these processes. Tests of coefficient stability are also successful. The explained variances are all at respectable levels (in the 40–50 per cent range for the major parties).
38. Halevy, *Imperialism and the Rise of Labour*, 99–110; M. Pugh, *The Making of Modern British Politics, 1867–1939* (New York: St. Martin's Press, 1982), 102–10.
39. T. Boyle, 'The Liberal Imperialists, 1892–1906', *Bulletin of the Institute of Historical Research*, 52 (1979), 51–5.
40. H.C.G. Matthew, *The Liberal Imperialists: The Ideas and Politics of a Post-Gladstonian Elite* (Oxford: Oxford University Press, 1973), 151.
41. K.O. Morgan, *The Age of Lloyd George* (London: George Allen & Unwin, 1971), 119.
42. Matthew, *The Liberal Imperialists*, 152.
43. Ibid, 282; R.R. James, *The British Revolution: British Politics, 1880–1939* (London: Hamish Hamilton, 1976), 146–9.
44. Pelling, *Popular Politics and Society*, 86, 94; E.J. Feuchtwanger, *Democracy and Empire: Britain 1865–1914* (London: Edward Arnold, 1985), 242–4; Matthew, *The Liberal Imperialists*, 90.
45. Matthew, *The Liberal Imperialists*, 226–64.
46. Ibid, 56.
47. Ibid, 293.
48. L.E. Davis, and R.A. Huttenback, *Mammon and the Pursuit of Empire: The Political Economy of British Imperialism, 1860–1912* (Cambridge: Cambridge University Press, 1986), 272.
49. Matthew, *The Liberal Imperialists*, 51ff.
50. Halevy, *Imperialism and the Rise of Labour*, 189–210.
51. E. Halevy, *The Rule of Democracy* (New York: Peter Smith, 1952), 64–76.
52. H.F. Moorhouse, 'The Political Incorporation of the British Working Class: An Interpretation', *Sociology* 7, 3 (September 1973), 341–59; C. Chamberlain, 'The Growth of Support for the Labour Party in Britain', *British Journal of Sociology*, 24, 4 (December 1973), 474–89; P.F. Clarke, 'Liberals, Labour and the Franchise', *The English Historical Review*, 92, 364 (1977), 582–9; H.C.G. Matthew, R.I. McKibbin and J.A. Kay, 'The Franchise Factor in the Rise of the Labour Party', *The English Historical Review*, 91, 361 (October 1976), 723–52.
53. Once again the technical results for the models support the above analysis. Overall goodness-of-fit statistics are excellent in all models and reproduced

with the various data sub-sets. The explained variances again are in the range of 40 to 50 per cent for the larger parties. The coefficients are stable and remain significant in the presence of various control variables.

7 PHILOSOPHERS, PORTERS, PARSONS AND PARVENUS

1. K. Marx and F. Engels, *On Britain* (Moscow: Foreign Languages Publishing House, 1953), 499–500, 522–3.
2. M. Cowling, *1867: Disraeli, Gladstone and the Revolution: The Passing of the Second Reform Bill* (Cambridge: Cambridge University Press, 1967); J.P.D. Dunbabin, 'Electoral Reforms and their Outcome in the United Kingdom, 1865–1900', in T.R. Gourvish and A. O'Day (eds), *Later Victorian Britain, 1867–1900* (New York: St. Martin's Press, 1988), 93–126.
3. The egregious consequences of specialisation were the concern of numerous commentators including Smith himself, who feared the loss of a sense of any common good resulting from a constantly narrowing perspective of specialised labour. On the other hand, some held that the ever widening web of mutual, functional dependencies inherent in the market would bind society together. For a review of such arguments, see A.O. Hirschman, *The Passions and the Interests: Political Arguments for Capitalism Before its Triumph* (Princeton, NJ): Princeton University Press, 1977); E.S. Wellhofer, 'Contradictions in Market Models of Politics: The Case of Party Strategies and Voter Linkages', *European Journal of Political Research*, 18, (1990), 9–28.
4. Adam Smith, *An Inquiry into the Nature and Causes of the Wealth of Nations* (New York: The Modern Library, 1937), 15.
5. Ibid, 15–16.
6. E.J. Hobsbawm, *Labouring Men: Studies in the History of Labour* (New York: Basic Books, 1964), 275.
7. R. Gray, *The Aristocracy of Labour in Nineteenth-Century Britain, c. 1850–1914* (London: Macmillan, 1981), 8.
8. A.C. Pigou (ed.), *Memorials to Alfred Marshall* (New York: Augustus M. Kelley, 1966), 105.
9. Marx and Engels, *On Britain*, 23–31.
10. Ibid, 28.
11. Ibid, 529–30.
12. V.I. Lenin, *British Labour and British Imperialism* (London: Lawrence & Wishart, 1969), 118.
13. H. Pelling, *Popular Politics and Society in Late Victorian Britain* (London: Macmillan, 1968), 57.
14. E.P. Thompson, *The Making of the English Working Class* (New York: Pantheon Books, 1964), 234–68; Hobsbawm, *Labouring Men*, 272–315, and Pelling, *Popular Politics*, 37–61.
15. Pelling, *Popular Politics*, 61.
16. G. Crossick, *An Artisan Elite in Victorian Society* (London: Croom Helm, 1978), 251. For an earlier example of this thesis, see T. Tholfsen, 'The

Transition to Democracy in Victorian England', *International Review of Social History*, 6 (1961), 226–8, 244; for a general review see, H.F. Moorhouse, 'The Marxist Theory of the Labour Aristocracy', *Journal of Social History*, 3, 1 (January 1978), 61–82.

17. Crossick, *An Artisan Elite*, 248.
18. C. More, *Skill and the English Working Class, 1870-1914* (New York: St. Martin's, 1980), 230–6. Also see G. Crossick, 'The Petite Bourgeoisie in Nineteenth-Century Britain', in G. Crossick and H.-G. Haupt (eds), *Shopkeeper and Master Artisans in Nineteenth-Century Europe* (London: Methuen, 1984), 62–94, and J. Belchem, *Industrialisation and the Working Class: The English Experience, 1750–1900* (Portland, Oregon: Areopagitica Press, 1990), 218–19.
19. H. Perkin, *The Origins of Modern British Society, 1780–1880* (London: Routledge & Kegan Paul, 1969), 394.
20. Gray, *The Aristocracy of Labour*, 20–9.
21. F.M.L. Thompson, *The Rise of Respectable Society: A Social History of Victorian Britain, 1830–1900* (Cambridge, MA: Harvard University Press, 1988), 198.
22. G.S. Jones, 'Working-Class Culture and Working-Class Politics in London, 1870–1900: Notes on the remaking of a Working Class', *Journal of Social History*, 7, 4 (Summer 1974) 460–508; H. Perkin, The Rise of Professional Society: England Since 1880 (London: Routledge, 1989), 101–15; Belchem, *Industrialisation and the Working Class*, 229–43.
23. Perkin, *The Rise of Professional Society*, 107; Belchem, *Industrialisation and the Working Class*, 211–12.
24. E.H. Hunt, *British Labour History, 1815–1914* (Atlantic Highlands, NJ: Humanities Press, 1981), 158–70.
25. F.M.L. Thompson, *The Rise of Respectable Society*, 199.
26. A recent statement of this position is F.M.L. Thompson's, *The Rise of Respectable Society*.
27. Recent examples of this genre include: Perkin's *The Rise of Professional Society*; Belchem's *Industrialisation and the Working Class*; and most recently, although emphasising an earlier period, E.P. Thompson's *Customs in Common* (London: Merlin Press, 1992).
28. Hobsbawm, *Labouring Men*; Pelling, *Popular Politics*; Moorhouse, 'The Marxist Theory of the Labour Aristocracy', 63; Gray, *The Aristocracy of Labour*, 15–34.
29. Marx and Engels, *On Britain*, 28.
30. Hobsbawm, *Labouring Men*, 181; see also H.A. Clegg, A. Fox and A.F. Thompson, *A History of British Trade Unions Since 1889*, Volume I: *1889–1910* (Oxford: Oxford University Press, 1964), 55ff.
31. L. Hannah, *The Rise of the Corporate Economy: The British Experience* (Baltimore MD: Johns Hopkins University Press, 1976), 10–13; More, *Skill and the English Working Class*, 230–6.
32. These three factors generate a very good fit to the observed data (Bentler–Bonett = 0.814) as well as demonstrating statistical independence from each other.
33. M.J. Cullen, 'The 1887 Survey of the London Working Class', *International Review of Social History*, 20, 1 (1975), 48–60.

34. E.J. Hobsbawm, *Workers: Worlds of Labour* (New York: Pantheon Books, 1984), 27–8.
35. For example, Pelling, *Popular Politics*, 16–17; A.J. Lee, 'Conservatism, Traditionalism and the British Working Class, 1880–1918', in D.E. Martin and D. Rubinstein (eds), *Ideology and the Labour Movement* (London: Croom Helm, 1979), 84–102; Hunt, *British Labour History*, 270–1; F.M.L. Thompson, *The Rise of Respectable Society*, 326–7.
36. G.D.H. Cole, *British Working Class Politics, 1832–1914* (London: Routledge & Kegan Paul, 1950), 175–99.
37. Moorhouse, 'The Marxist Theory of the Labour Aristocracy', 79.
38. The technical aspects of the model support the above conclusions. The models provide a good fit to the data with a Bentler–Bonett fit coefficient of 0.9 for the reconstructed missing data and 0.45 for the non-reconstructed data. The coefficients are robust and stable. These results also hold up across models tested against the remaining data sets.
39. Lenin, *British Labour and British Imperialism*, 118.
40. A.E.P. Duffy, 'New Unionism in Britain, 1889–1890: A Reappraisal', *The Economic History Review*, 14 (1961/1962), 319.
41. Pelling, *Popular Politics*, 37–61.
42. Ibid, 99.
43. Weiner simplex models enable us to examine the components of change by decomposing the trend line. As in the Weiner simplex models in Chapter 5, a moving-average change component model fits the data best. Such models generate two loading coefficients for each election: the first component represents the continuity between the elections; the second, the additional impact of the current election. In this manner Weiner simplex models describe a non-linear structure of change in which the coefficients to the latent variables demonstrate the build-up or decay of an across-time dynamic in which the changes are independent, additive and persistent. See Appendix II for a full discussion of these techniques.
44. Further evidence of these interpretations appears in the technical aspects of the model. The LV loadings for Labour demonstrate little change between 1885 and 1895, but marked increases after 1900. The across-time changes for unskilled general labour also conform to the earlier findings: unskilled general labour shows little political activity. The model provides a good fit to the data with a Bentler-Bonett fit statistic of 0.709 and accounts for respectable proportions of the variance for the Liberal and Labour parties.

8 CONTINUITY AND CHANGE IN THE TRANSITION TO MASS POLITICS

1. A. Gerschenkron, *Bread and Democracy in Germany* (Berkeley, CA: University of California Press, 1943).
2. B. Moore, *Social Origins of Dictatorship and Democracy* (Boston, MA: Beacon, 1968).
3. S.M. Lipset and S. Rokkan (eds), *Party Systems and Voter Alignments* (New York: Free Press, 1967).

4. G.D. Luebbert, *Liberalism, Fascism or Social Democracy* (New York: Oxford University Press, 1991); D. Rueschemeyer, E.H. Stephens and J.D. Stephens, *Capitalist Development and Democracy* (Chicago: University of Chicago Press, 1992).
5. Moore, *Social Origins*; Rueschemeyer, Stephens and Stephens, *Capitalist Development and Democracy*.
6. Luebbert, *Liberalism, Fascism or Social Democracy*.
7. For a fuller development of this discussion, see E.S. Wellhofer, "'Men Make Their Own History, But ...'": The New Institutionalism and the Fate of Inter-War Democracy in Europe', *Democratisation*, 1, 2 (Summer, 1994), 323-42.
8. J.G. March and J.P. Olsen, *Rediscovering Institutions: The Organisational Basis of Politics* (New York: Free Press, 1989), 159.
9. J.G.A. Pocock, *Politics, Language and Time: Essays in Political Thought and History* (New York: Anthenum, 1971); J.G.A. Pocock, *The Machiavellian Moment: Florentine Political Thought and the Atlantic Republican Tradition* (Princeton, NJ: Princeton University Press, 1975).

APPENDIX I: UNITS OF ANALYSIS, DATA DESCRIPTION AND SOURCES

1. K.F. Wald, *Crosses on the Ballot: Patterns of British Voter Alignment Since 1885* (Princeton, NJ: Princeton University Press, 1983) 83. For a description of the boundary matching, see ibid, 82ff.
2. Ibid, 126.

APPENDIX II: ANALYTICAL TECHNIQUES

1. P.M. Bentler, 'Multivariate Analysis with Latent Variables: Causal Modelling', *Annual Review of Psychology*, 34 (1980), 434.
2. K.G., Joereskog, 'A General Method of Estimating a Linear Structural Equation System', in A.S. Goldberger and O.D. Duncan (eds), *Structural Equation Models in the Social Sciences* (New York: Seminar Press, 1973) 85–112; G. King, *Unifying Political Methodology: The Likelihood Theory of Statistical Inference* (Cambridge: Cambridge University Press, 1989); L.A. Hayduk, *Structural Equation Modelling with LISREL* (Baltimore, MS: The Johns Hopkins University Press, 1987).
3. P.M. Bentler and D.G. Weeks, 'Linear Structural Equations with Latent Variables', *Psychometrika* 45, 3 (September 1980), 289–308.
4. J. Lohmoeller, *Latent Variable Path Modeling with Partial Least Squares* (Heidelberg: Physica-Verlag, 1989), 28–9.
5. K.D. Wald, *Crosses on the Ballot: Patterns of British Voter Alignment Since 1885* (Princeton, NJ: Princeton University Press, 1983); M. Hechter, *Internal Colonialism: The Celtic Fringe in British National Development, 1536–1966* (Berkeley, CA: University of California Press, 1975).

6.   J.J. McArdle and M.S. Aber, 'Patterns of Change within Latent Variable Structural Equation Models', in A. von Eye (ed.), *Statistical Models in Longitudinal Research*. Volume I: *Principles and Structuring Change* (New York: Academic Press, 1990), 151–224.

7.   Wald, *Crosses on the Ballot*, 149.

8.   J.J. McArdle and D. Epstein,' Latent Growth Curves with Developmental Structural Equations', *Childhood Development*, 58 (1987), 110–33.

9.   Lohmoeller, *Latent Variable Path Modelling*, 52–5.

10. P.M. Bentler and D.G. Bonett, 'Significance Tests and Goodness of Fit in the Analysis of Covariance Structures', *Psychological Bulletin*, 88, 3 (November 1980), 588–606; L.R. Tucker and C. Lewis, 'A Reliability Coefficient for Maximum Likelihood Factor Analysis', *Psychometrika*, 38, 1 (March 1973), 1–10; see also L.R. James, S.A. Mulaik and J.M. Brett, *Causal Analysis: Assumptions, Models and Data. Studying Organisations: Innovations in Methodology No. 1* (Beverly Hills, CA: Sage, 1982) 151–6; and J.C. Loehlin, *Latent Variable Models* (Hillsdale, NJ: Lawrence Erlbaum Associates, 1987), 54–67.

11. B.R. Hertel, 'Minimising Error Variance Introduced by Missing Data Routines in Survey Analysis', *Sociological Methods and Research*, 4, 4 (May 1976), 459–74.

12. Lohmoeller, *Latent Variable Path Modeling*, 53–5; K.A. Bollen, *Structural Equations with Latent Variables* (New York: Wiley, 1989), 257.

13. Lohmoeller, *Latent Variable Path Modeling*, 55, 216; Bollen, *Structural Equation Models*, 277.

14. C.W. Ostrom, *Time Series Analysis: Regression Techniques*, Sage University Paper series on Quantitative Applications in the Social Sciences (Beverly Hills, CA: Sage, 1978).

15. M.B. Jones, 'Practice as a Process of Simplification', *Psychological Review*, 69, 4 (1962), 274–94; R. Short, J. Horn and J.J. McArdle, 'Mathematical-Statistical Model Building in Analysis of Developmental Data', in R.N. Emde and R.J. Harmon (eds), *Continuities and Discontinuities in Development* (New York: Plenum, 1984), 384.

16. L.A. Guttman, 'A New Approach to the Study of Factor Analysis: The Radex', in P.F. Lazarfeld (ed.), *Mathematical Thinking in the Social Sciences* (Glencoe, IL: Free Press, 1954), 216–384.

17. McArdle and Aber, 'Patterns of Change within Latent Variable Structural Equation Models', 176–84.

18. Ibid, 184–91.

19. Ibid, 187.

20. Ibid, 184.

21. K.G. Joereskog, 'Estimation and Testing of Simplex Models', *The British Journal of Mathematical and Statistical Psychology*, 23 (November 1970), 128–9.

22. W.S. Robinson, 'Ecological Correlations and the Behaviour of Individuals', *American Sociological Review*, 15 (June 1950), 351–3.

23. J.L. Hammond, 'Two Sources of Error in Ecological Correlations', *American Sociological Review*, 38, 5 (December 1973), 772.

24. L.I. Langbein and A.J. Lichtman, *Ecological Inference*, Sage University Papers on Quantitative Applications in the Social Sciences (Beverly Hills,

CA: Sage, 1978); James, Mulaik and Brett, *Causal Analysis*, 64–71. For a fuller treatment of these arguments, see E.S. Wellhofer, 'The Comparative Method and the Study of Development, Diffusion, and Social Change', *Comparative Political Studies*, 22, 3 (October 1989b), 315–42; E.S. Wellhofer, 'Confounding Sources of Variance in the Macro-Analysis of Electoral Data', *European Journal of Political Research*, 19 (1991), 425–40.

Bibliography

ALDCROFT, D.H. (1968). 'British Industry and Foreign Competition, 1875–1914', pp. 11–36 in D.H. Aldcroft (ed.), *The Development of British Industry and Foreign Competition*. Toronto: University of Toronto Press.

ANDERSON, P. (1974). *Lineages of the Absolutist State*. London: New Left Books.

ANDREW, C. (1986). *Her Majesty's Secret Service*. New York: Viking.

ARMSTRONG, W.A. (1972). 'The Uses of Information About Occupation', pp. 191–310 in E.A. Wrigley (ed.), *Nineteenth Century Society*. Cambridge: Cambridge University Press.

BAIN G.S. and R. Price (1980). *Profiles of Union Growth*. Oxford: Basil Blackwell.

BANKS, J.A. (1978). 'The Social Structure of Nineteenth Century England as Seen Through the Census', pp. 179–223 in R. Lawton (ed.), *The Census and the Social Structure*. London: Frank Cass.

BELCHEM, J. (1990). *Industrialisation and the Working Class: The English Experience, 1750–1900*. Portland, Oregon: Areopagitica Press.

BENDIX, R. (1964). *Nation-Building and Citizenship*. New York: Doubleday.

BENTLER, P.M. (1980). 'Multivariate Analysis with Latent Variables: Causal Modelling', *Annual Review of Psychology*, 34, 419–56.

BENTLER, P.M. and D.G. Bonett (1980). 'Significance Tests and Goodness of Fit in the Analysis of Covariance Structures', *Psychological Bulletin*, 88, 3 (November), 588–606.

BENTLER, P.M. and D.G. Weeks (1980). 'Linear Structural Equations with Latent Variables', *Psychometrika*, 45, 3 (September), 289–308.

BLEWETT, N. (1965). 'The Franchise in the United Kingdom, 1885–1918', *Past and Present*, 32 (December), 27–56.

BLEWETT, N. (1972). *The Peers, The Party and the People: The General Election of 1910*. London: Macmillan.

BLUMER-THOMAS, I. (1965). *The Growth of the British Party System*, two volumes. New York: Humanities Pres.

BOLLEN, K.A. (1989). *Structural Equations with Latent Variables*. New York: Wiley.

BOOTH, C. (1902). *Life and Labour of the People of London*. London: Macmillan.

BOWLEY, A.L. (1900). *Wages in the United Kingdom in the Nineteenth Century*. Cambridge: Cambridge University Press.

BOWLEY, A.L. (1937). *Wages and Income in the United Kingdom since 1860*. Cambridge: Cambridge University Press.

BOYLE, T. (1979). 'The Liberal Imperialists, 1892–1906', *Bulletin of the Institute of Historical Research*, 52, 48–82.

BRIGGS, A. (1956). 'Middle-Class Consciousness in English Politics, 1780–1846', *Past and Present*, 9 (April), 65–74.

246

BRIGGS, A. (1960). 'The Language of "Class" in Early Nineteenth-Century England', pp. 43–73 in A. Briggs and J. Saville (eds), *Essays in Labour History*. London: Macmillan.

BRIGGS, A. (1979). 'The Language of "Mass" and "Masses" in Nineteenth-Century England', pp. 62–83 in D. Martin and D. Rubinstein (eds), *Ideology and the Labour Movement*. London: Croom Helm.

BUTLER, D.E. (1968). *The Electoral System in Britain Since 1918*. Oxford: Clarendon Press.

BUTLER, D.E. (1986). *The Electoral System in Britain Since 1918*. Westport, CT: Greenwood Press.

BUTLER, D.E. and J. Cornford (1969). 'United Kingdom', pp. 330–51 in S. Rokkan and J. Meyrait (eds), *International Guide to Electoral Statistics*. Paris: Mountonord.

CANNADINE, D. (1983). 'The Context, Performance and Meaning of Ritual: The British Monarchy and the "Invention of Tradition", *c.* 1820–1977', pp. 101–64 in E. Hobsbawm and T. Ranger (eds), *The Invention of Tradition*. Cambridge: Cambridge University Press.

CANNADINE, D. (1990). *The Decline and Fall of the British Aristocracy*. New Haven, CT: Yale University Press.

CARLYLE, T. (1986). 'Past and Present', pp. 55–80 in E. Jay and R. Jay (eds), *Critics of Capitalism: Victorian Reactions to 'Political Economy'*, Cambridge: Cambridge University Press.

CHADWICK, M.E.J. (1976). 'The Role of Redistribution in the Making of the Third Reform Act', *The Historical Journal*, 19, 3, 665–83.

CHAMBERLAIN, C. (1973). 'The Growth of Support for the Labour Party in Britain', *British Journal of Sociology*, 24, 4 (December), 474–89.

CHARLESWORTH, A. (ed.) (1983). *An Atlas of Rural Protest in Britain, 1548–1900*. Philadelphia: University of Pennsylvania Press.

CHRISTALLER, W. (1966). *Central Places in Germany*. Englewood Cliffs, NJ: Prentice-Hall.

CLARK, G.S.R.K. (1967). *An Expanding Society: Britain, 1830–1900*. Cambridge: Cambridge University Press.

CLARKE, P.F. (1971). *Lancashire and the New Liberalism*. Cambridge: Cambridge University Press.

CLARKE, P.F. (1977). 'Liberals, Labour and the Franchise', *The English Historical Review*, 92, 364, 582–9.

CLEGG, H.A., A. Fox and A.F. Thompson (1964). *A History of British Trade Unions Since 1889*, Volume I: *1889–1910*. Oxford: Oxford University Press.

COLE, G.D.H. (1950). *British Working Class Politics, 1832–1914*. London: Routledge & Kegan Paul.

COLLEY, L. (1986). 'Whose Nation? Class and National Consciousness in Britain, 1750–1830', *Past and Present*, 113 (November), 97–117.

CONACHER, J.B. (ed.) (1971). *The Emergence of British Parliamentary Democracy in the Nineteenth Century*. New York: Wiley.

CORNFORD, J. (1963). 'The Transformation of the Conservative Party in the Late Nineteenth Century', *Victorian Studies*, 7 (September), 35–66.

CORNFORD, J. (1964). 'The Adoption of Mass Organisation by the British Conservative Party', pp. 400–24 in E. Allardt and Y. Luttussen (eds),

248 *Bibliography*

Cleavages, Ideologies and Party Systems. Helsinki: Transactions of the Westermark Society.

CORRIGAN, P. (1977). 'Feudal Relics or Capitalist Monument? Notes on the Sociology of Unfree Labour', *Sociology*, 11, 3 (September), 435–63.

COUSINS, J.M. and R.L. Davis (1974). '"Working Class Incorporation" – A Historical Approach with Reference to the Mining Communities of S.E. Northumberland, 1840–1890', pp. 275–98 in F. Parkin (ed.), *The Social Analysis of Class Structure*. New York: Methuen.

COWLING, M. (1967). *1867: Disraeli, Gladstone and the Revolution: The Passing of the Second Reform Bill*. Cambridge: Cambridge University Press.

COX, G.W. (1987). *The Efficient Secret: The Cabinet and the Development of Political Parties in Victorian England*. Cambridge: Cambridge University Press.

CROSSICK, G. (1978). *An Artisan Elite in Victorian Society*. London: Croom Helm.

CROSSICK, G. (1984). 'The Petite Bourgeoisie in Nineteenth-Century Britain', pp. 62–94 in G. Crossick and H.-G. Haupt (eds), *Shopkeeper and Master Artisans in Nineteenth-Century Europe*. London: Methuen.

CULLEN, M.J. (1975). 'The 1887 Survey of the London Working Class'. *International Review of Social History*, 20, 1, 48–60.

DANGERFIELD, G. (1935). *The Strange Death of Liberal England*. Reprint. London: MacGibbon & Kee.

DAVIDSON, R. (1985). *Whitehall and the Labour Problem in Late-Victorian and Edwardian Britain*. London: Croom Helm.

DAVIS, L.E. and R.A. Huttenback (1986). *Mammon and the Pursuit of Empire: The Political Economy of British Imperialism, 1860–1912*. Cambridge: Cambridge University Press.

DEANE, P. and W.A. Cole (1962). *British Economic Growth, 1688–1959*. Cambridge: Cambridge University Press.

DREYFUS, H.L. and P. Rabinow (1982). *Michel Foucault: Beyond Structuralism and Hermeneutics*. Chicago: University of Chicago Press.

DUFF, D. (ed.) (1980). *Queen Victoria's Highland Journals*. Exeter: Webb & Bower.

DUFFY, A.E.P. (1961/1962). 'New Unionism in Britain, 1889–1890: A Reappraisal', *The Economic History Review*, 14, 306–19.

DUNBABIN, J.P.D. (1963). 'The "Revolt of the Field": The Agricultural Labourers' Movement in the 1870s', *Past and Present*, 26 (November), 68–97.

DUNBABIN, J.P.D. (1974). *Rural Discontent in Nineteenth Century Britain*. New York: Holmes & Meier.

DUNBABIN, J.P.D. (1983). 'Agricultural Trade Unionism in England, 1872–94', pp. 171–3 in A. Charlesworth (ed.), *An Atlas of Rural Protest in Britain, 1548–1900*. Philadelphia: University of Pennsylvania Press.

DUNBABIN, J.P.D. (1983). 'The Welsh Tithe War, 1886–95', in A. Charlesworth (ed.), *An Atlas of Rural Protest in Britain, 1548–1900*. Philadelphia: University of Pennsylvania Press.

DUNBABIN, J.P.D. (1988). 'Electoral Reforms and their Outcome in the United Kingdom, 1865–1900', pp. 93–126 in T.R. Gourvish and A. O'Day (eds), *Later Victorian Britain, 1867–1900*. New York: St. Martin's Press.

DUNKLEY, P. (1982). *The Crisis of the Old Poor Law in England, 1795–1834*. New York: Garland Publishing.

ENGELS, F. (1971). *The Condition of the Working Class in England*. Oxford: Basil Blackwell.

FAHEY, D.M. (1979). 'The Politics of Drink: Pressure Groups and the British Liberal Party, 1883–1908', *Social Science*, 54, 76–85.

FEUCHTWANGER, E.J. (1968). *Disraeli, Democracy and the Tory Party*. Oxford: Clarendon Press.

FEUCHTWANGER, E.J. (1985). *Democracy and Empire: Britain 1865–1914*. London: Edward Arnold.

FOUCAULT, M. (1977). *Discipline and Punish*. New York: Pantheon Books.

FOX, A. (1985). *History and Heritage: The Social Origins of the British Industrial Relations System*. London: Allen & Unwin.

FRASER, D. (1981). 'The English Poor Law and the Origins of the British Welfare State', pp. 9–31 in W.J. Mommsen (ed.), *The Emergence of the Welfare State in Britain and Germany, 1850–1950*. London: Croom Helm.

GARVIN, T. (1980). 'Decolonisation, Nationalisation, and Electoral Politics in Ireland, 1832–1945', pp. 259–80 in O. Buesch (ed.), *Waehlerbewegung in der Europaeschen Geschichte*. Berlin: Colloquium Verlag.

GASH, N. (1977). *Politics in the Age of Peel*. Hassocks, Sussex: Harvester Press.

GAZELEY, I. (1989). 'The Cost of Living for Urban Workers in Late Victorian and Edwardian Britain', *Economic History Review*, Second Series, 52, 2, 207–21.

GERSCHENKRON, A. (1943). *Bread and Democracy in Germany*. Berkeley, CA: University of California Press.

GILBERT, B.B. (1966). *The Evolution of National Health Insurance in Great Britain: The Origins of the Welfare State*. London: Michael Joseph.

GIROUARD, M. (1979). *The Victorian Country House*. New Haven, G: Yale University Press.

GLASER, J.F. (1958). 'English Nonconformity and the Decline of Liberalism'. *American Historical Review*, 63, 2 (January), 352–63.

GRAY, R.Q. (1974). 'The Labour Aristocracy in the Victorian Class Structure', pp. 19–38 in F. Parkin (ed.), *The Social Analysis of Class Structure*. London: Tavistock.

GRAY, R.Q. (1981). *The Aristocracy of Labour in Nineteenth-Century Britain, c. 1850–1914*. London: Macmillan.

GRIFFEN, R. (1890). *Essays in Finance: Second Series*. London: G. Bell.

GUTTMAN, L.A. (1954). 'A New Approach to the Study of Factor Analysis: The Radex', pp. 216–384 in P.F. Lazarfeld (ed.), *Mathematical Thinking in the Social Sciences*. Glencoe, II: Free Press.

GWYN, W.B. (1962). *Democracy and the Cost of Politics in Britain*. London: University of London, The Athlone Press.

HALEVY, E. (1952). *The Rule of Democracy*. New York: Peter Smith.

HALEVY, E. (1961). *Imperialism and the Rise of Labour*. New York: Barnes & Noble.

HALL, S. and B. Schwarz (1985). 'State and Society, 1880–1930', pp. 7–32 in M. Langan and B. Schwarz, (eds), *Crises in the British State, 1880–1930*. London: Hutchinson.

HAMMOND, J.L. (1973). 'Two Sources of Error in Ecological Correlations', *American Sociological Review*, 38, 5 (December), 764–77.

HANHAM, H.J. (1959). *Elections and Party Management*. London: Longman, Green.
HANNAH, L. (1976). *The Rise of the Corporate Economy: The British Experience*. Baltimore: Johns Hopkins University Press.
HARRISON, B. (1976). 'Pubs', pp. 161–90 in H.J. Dyos and M. Wolff (eds), *The Victorian City: Images and Realities*. London: Routledge & Kegan Paul.
HARRISON, B. (1982). *Peaceable Kingdom: Stability and Change in Modern British Politics*. Oxford: Clarendon Press.
HARVIE, C. (1989). 'Scott and the Image of Scotland', pp. 173–92 in R. Samuel (ed.), *Patriotism: The Making and Unmaking of the British National Identity*. Volume II: *Minorities and Outsiders*. London: Routledge.
HAYDUK, L.A. (1987). *Structural Equation Modelling with LISREL*. Baltimore: The Johns Hopkins University Press.
HAYES, W.A. (1982). *The Background and Passage of the Third Reform Act*. New York: Garland Publishing.
HECHTER, M. (1975). *Internal Colonialism: The Celtic Fringe in British National Development, 1536–1966*, Berkeley, CA: University of California Press.
HERTEL, B.R. (1976). 'Minimising Error Variance Introduced by Missing Data Routines in Survey Analysis', *Sociological Methods and Research*, 4, 4 (May), 459–74.
HIMMELFARB, G. (1984). *The Idea of Poverty: England in the Early Industrial Age*. London: Faber & Faber.
HIMMELFARB, G. (1991). *Poverty and Compassion: The Moral Imagination of the Late Victorians*. New York: Knopf.
HIRSCHMAN, A.O. (1977). *The Passions and the Interests: Political Arguments for Capitalism Before its Triumph*. Princeton, NJ: Princeton University Press.
HIRSCHMAN, A.O. (1986). 'Rival Views of Market Society', pp. 105–41 in A.O. Hirschman, *Rival Views of Market Society and Other Recent Essays*. New York: Viking.
HOBSBAWM, E.J. (1960). 'Custom, Wages and Work-load in Nineteenth Century Industry', pp. 113–39 in A. Briggs and J. Saville (eds), *Essays in Labour History*. London: Macmillan.
HOBSBAWM, E.J. (1963). *Primitive Rebels: Studies in Archaic Forms of Social Movements in the 19th and 20th Centuries*. New York: Frederick A. Praeger.
HOBSBAWM, E.J. (1964). *Labouring Men: Studies in the History of Labour*. New York: Basic Books.
HOBSBAWM, E.J. (1968). *Industry and Empire*. New York: Pantheon Books.
HOBSBAWM, E.J. (1983). 'Mass-Producing Traditions: Europe, 1870–1914', pp. 263-308 in E. Hobsbawm and T. Ranger (eds), *The Invention of Tradition*. Cambridge: Cambridge University Press.
HOBSBAWM, E.J. (1984). *Workers: Worlds of Labour*. New York: Pantheon Books.
HOBSBAWM, E.J. (1990). *Nations and Nationalism since 1780: Programme, Myth and Reality*. Cambridge: Cambridge University Press.
HOSKINS, W.G. (1957). *The Making of the English Landscape*. London: Hodder & Stoughton.
HUME, J.R. and M. Oglethorpe (1986). 'Engineering', pp. 136–9 in J. Langton and R.J. Morris (eds), *Atlas of Industrialising Britain, 1780–1914*. London: Methuen.

HUNT, E.H. (1981). *British Labour History, 1815–1914*. Atlantic Highlands, NJ: Humanities Press.
HUNTER, J. (1976). 'The Making of the Crofting Community', Unpublished PhD Dissertation, Edinburgh University, Edinburgh.
HUNTER, J. (1983). 'The Highland Land War, 1881–1896', pp. 179–82 in A. Charlesworth (ed.), *An Atlas of Rural Protest in Britain, 1548–1900*. Philadelphia: University of Pennsylvania Press.
HURT, J.S. (1979). *Elementary Schooling and the Working Classes, 1860–1918*. London: Routledge & Kegan Paul.
HUTCHISON, T.W. (1953). *A Review of Economic Doctrines, 1870–1929*. Oxford: Clarendon Press.
INGLIS, K.S. (1963). *Churches and the Working Classes in Victorian England*. London: Routledge & Kegan Paul.
JAMES, L.R., S.A. Mulaik and J.M. Brett (1982). *Causal Analysis: Assumptions, Models and Data. Studying Organisations: Innovations in Methodology No. 1*. Beverly Hills, CA: Sage.
JAMES, R.R. (1976). *The British Revolution: British Politics, 1880–1939*. London: Hamish Hamilton.
JEFFERIES, R. (1992). Hodge and His Masters. Stroud: Alan Sutton.
JOERESKOG, K.G. (1970). 'Estimation and Testing of Simplex Models', *The British Journal of Mathematical and Statistical Psychology*, 23 (November), 121–45.
JOERESKOG, K.G. (1973). 'A General Method of Estimating a Linear Structural Equation System', pp. 85–112 in A.S. Goldberger and O.D. Duncan (eds), *Structural Equation Models in the Social Sciences*. New York: Seminar Press.
JONES, A. (1972). *The Politics of Reform, 1884* (Cambridge: Cambridge University Press).
JONES, D.J.V. (1983). 'The Rebecca Riots, 1839–1844', pp. 165–71 in A. Charlesworth (ed.), *An Atlas of Rural Protest in Britain, 1548–1900*. Philadelphia: University of Pennsylvania.
JONES, G.A. (1966). 'Further Thoughts on Franchise, 1885-1918'. *Past and Present*, 34 (July), 134–8.
JONES, G.S. (1974). 'Working-Class Culture and Working-Class Politics in London, 1870–1900: Notes on the remaking of a Working Class', *Journal of Social History* 7, 4 (Summer), 460–508.
JONES, M.B. (1962). 'Practice as a Process of Simplification', *Psychological Review*, 69, 4, 274–94.
KEARNEY, H. (1989). *The British Isles: A History of Four Nations*. New York: Cambridge.
KEITH-LUCAS, B. (1952). *The English Local Government Franchise*. Oxford: Oxford University Press.
KING, G. (1989). *Unifying Political Methodology: The Likelihood Theory of Statistical Inference*. Cambridge: Cambridge University Press.
KINNEAR, M. (1968). *The British Voter*. London: B.T. Batsford.
LANGAN, M. (1985). 'Reorganising the Labour Market: Unemployment, the State and the Labour Movement, 1880–1914', pp. 104–25 in M. Langan and B. Schwarz (eds), *Crises in the British State, 1880–1930*. London: Hutchinson.
LANGAN, M. and B. Schwarz (eds) (1985). *Crises in the British State, 1880–1930*. London: Hutchinson.

252   *Bibliography*

LANGBEIN, L.I. and A.J. Lichtman (1978). *Ecological Inference.* Sage University Papers on Quantitative Applications in the Social Sciences. Beverly Hills, CA: Sage.

LEE, A.J. (1979). 'Conservatism, Traditionalism and the British Working Class, 1880–1918', pp. 84–102 in D.E. Martin and D. Rubinstein (eds), *Ideology and the Labour Movement.* London: Croom Helm.

LEE, C.H. (1981). 'Regional Growth and Structural Change in Victorian Britain', *Economic History Review*, 34, 3 (August), 438–52.

LEE, C.H. (1986). *The British Economy Since 1700: A Macroeconomic Perspective.* Cambridge: Cambridge University Press.

LENIN, V.I. (1969). *British Labour and British Imperialism.* London: Lawrence & Wishart.

LEVI, L. (1885). *Wages and Earnings of the Working Classes.* London: J. Murray.

LEVY, S.L., ed. (1928). *Industrial Efficiency and Social Economy by Nassau W. Senior*, two volumes. New York: Henry Holt.

LINDERT, P.H. and J.G. Williamson (1983). 'Reinterpreting Britain's Social Tables, 1688–1913', *Explorations in Economic History*, 20 (January), 94–109.

LIPSET, S.M. and S. Rokkan (eds) (1967). *Party Systems and Voter Alignments.* New York: Free Press.

LIVELY, J. and J. Rees (eds) (1978). *Utilitarian Logic and Politics.* Oxford: Clarendon Press.

LOEHLIN, J.C. (1987). *Latent Variable Models.* Hillsdale, NJ: Lawrence Erlbaum Associates.

LOHMOELLER, J. (1989). *Latent Variable Path Modeling with Partial Least Squares.* Heidelberg: Physica-Verlag.

LOVEJOY, A.O. (1936). *The Great Chain of Being: A Study of the History of an Idea.* Cambridge, MA: Harvard University Press.

LOWELL, A.L. (1898). 'Oscillations in Politics', *The Annuals*, 12 (July), 69–97.

LUBENOW, W.C. (1971). *The Politics of Government Growth: Early Victorian Attitudes Toward State Intervention, 1833–1848.* Hamden, CT: Archon Books.

LUEBBERT, G.D. (1991). *Liberalism, Fascism or Social Democracy.* New York: Oxford University Press.

MACHIN, G.I.T. (1987). *Politics and the Churches in Great Britain, 1869–1921.* Oxford: Clarendon Press.

MACKENZIE, R.T. and A. Silver (1967). 'The Delicate Experiment: Industrialism, Conservatism and Working-Class Tories in England', pp. 115–25 in S.M. Lipset and S. Rokkan (eds), *Party Systems and Voter Alignments: Cross-National Perspectives.* New York: Free Press.

MAEHL, W.H. (1975). 'The Northeastern Miners' Struggle for the Franchise, 1872–74', *International Review of Social History*, 20, 2, 198–219.

MARCH, J.G. and J.P. Olsen (1989). *Rediscovering Institutions: The Organisational Basis of Politics.* New York: Free Press.

MARSHALL, T.H. (1964). *Class, Citizenship and Social Development.* Garden City: Doubleday.

MARX, K. and F. ENGELS (1953). *On Britain.* Moscow: Foreign Languages Publishing House.

MATTHEW, H.C.G. (1973). *The Liberal Imperialists: The Ideas and Politics of a Post-Gladstonian Elite.* Oxford: Oxford University Press.

MATTHEW, H.C.G., R.I. McKibbin and J.A. Kay (1976), 'The Franchise Factor in the Rise of the Labour Party', *The English Historical Review*, 91, 361 (October), 723–52.

MATTHEWS, R.C.O., C.F. Feinstein and J.C. Odling-Smee (1982). *British Economic Development, 1856–1973*. Stanford, CA: Stanford University Press.

MCARDLE, J.J. and M.S. Aber (1990). 'Patterns of Change within Latent Variable Structural Equation Models', pp. 151–224 in A. von Eye (ed.), *Statistical Models in Longitudinal Research*. Volume I: *Principles and Structuring Change*. New York: Academic Press.

MCARDLE, J.J. and D. Epstein (1987). 'Latent Growth Curves with Developmental Structural Equations', *Childhood Development*, 58, 110–33.

MCCORD, N. (1967). 'Some Difficulties of Parliamentary Reform', *The Historical Journal*, 10, 4, 376–90.

MCLEOD, H. (1986). 'Religion', pp. 212–17 in J. Langton and R.J. Morris (eds), *Atlas of Industrialising Britain, 1780–1914*. London: Methuen.

MEWS, S. (1988). 'The General and the Bishops: Alternative Responses to Dechristianisation', pp. 209–28 in T.R. Gourvish and A. O'Day (eds), *Later Victorian Britain, 1867–1900*. New York: St. Martins' Press.

MILL, J. (1819/1978). 'Essay on Government', pp. 53–96 in J. Lively and J. Rees (eds), *Utilitarian Logic and Politics*. Oxford: Clarendon Press.

MILL, J.S. (1986). 'Principles of Political Economy with some of their Applications to Social Philosophy', pp. 114–36 in E. Jay and R. Jay (eds), *Critics of Capitalism: Victorian Reactions to 'Political Economy'*. Cambridge: Cambridge University Press.

MOORE, B. (1968). *Social Origins of Dictatorship and Democracy*. Boston, MA: Beacon.

MOORHOUSE, H.F. (1973). 'The Political Incorporation of the British Working Class: An Interpretation', *Sociology*, 7, 3 (September), 341–59.

MOORHOUSE, H.F. (1978). 'The Marxist Theory of the Labour Aristocracy', *Journal of Social History*, 3, 1 (January), 61–82.

MORE, C. (1980). *Skill and the English Working Class, 1870–1914*. New York: St. Martin's Press.

MORGAN, K.O. (1971). *The Age of Lloyd George*. London: George Allen & Unwin.

MORGAN, K.O. (1980). *Wales in British Politics, 1868–1922*. Cardiff: University of Wales Press.

MORGAN, K.O. (1981). *Rebirth of a Nation: Wales, 1880–1980*. New York: Oxford University Press.

MORGAN, P. (1983). 'From Death to a View: The Hunt for the Welsh Past in the Romantic Period', pp. 43–100 in E. Hobsbawm and T. Ranger (eds), *The Invention of Tradition*. Cambridge: Cambridge University Press.

O'LEARY, C. (1962). *The Elimination of Corrupt Practices in British Elections, 1868–1911*. Oxford: Clarendon Press.

OSTROGORSKI, M. (1902). *Democracy and the Organisation of Political Parties*, two volumes. New York: Macmillian.

OSTROM, C.W. (1978). *Time Series Analysis: Regression Techniques*. Sage University Paper series on Quantitative Applications in the Social Sciences. Beverly Hills: CA: Sage.

PELLING, H. (1963). *A History of British Trade Unionism*. London: Macmillan.

PELLING, H. (1965). *The Origins of the Labour Party*. Oxford: Clarendon.
PELLING, H. (1968). *Popular Politics and Society in Late Victorian Britain*. London: Macmillan.
PERKIN, H. (1969). *The Origins of Modern British Society, 1780–1880*. London: Routledge & Kegan Paul.
PERKIN, H. (1989). *The Rise of Professional Society: England Since 1880*. London: Routledge.
PERKIN, H. (1991). 'Interfere! Don't Interfere!', *The Times Literary Supplement*, 22 November, 25.
PIGOU, A.C. (ed). (1966). *Memorials to Alfred Marshall*. New York: Augustus M. Kelley.
POCOCK, J.G.A. (1971). *Politics, Language and Time: Essays in Political Thought and History*. New York: Anthenum.
POCOCK, J.G.A. (1975). *The Machiavellian Moment: Florentine Political Thought and the Atlantic Republican Tradition*. Princeton, NJ: Princeton University Press.
POLANYI, K. (1957). *The Great Transformation*. Boston: Beacon Press.
PORRITT, E. (1911). 'Barriers Against Democracy in the British Electoral System', *Political Science Quarterly*, 26, 1 (March), 1–31.
PUGH, M. (1982). *The Making of Modern British Politics, 1867–1939*. New York: St. Martin's Press.
PUGH, M. (1985). *The Tories and the People, 1880–1935*. Oxford: Basil Blackwell.
QUINAULT, R. (1988). 'Joseph Chamberlain: A Reassessment', pp. 69–92 in T.R. Gourvish and A. O'Day (eds), *Later Victorian Britain, 1867–1900*. New York: St. Martin's Press.
RAGIN, C.C. (1977). 'Class, Status and "Reactive Ethnic Cleavages": The Social Bases of Political Regionalism', *American Sociological Review*, 42, 3 (June), 438–50.
RIMINGLER, G.V. (1971). *Welfare Policy and Industrialisation in Europe, America, and Russia*. New York: Wiley.
ROBB, J.H. (1942). *The Primrose League, 1883–1906*. New York: Columbia University Press.
ROBINSON, W.S. (1950). 'Ecological Correlations and the Behaviour of Individuals', *American Sociological Review*, 15 (June), 351–7.
ROKKAN, S. (1961). 'Mass Suffrage, Secret Voting and Political Participation', *European Journal of Sociology*, 2, 132–52.
ROKKAN, S. and D. Urwin, eds (1982). *The Politics of Territorial Identity: Studies in European Regionalism*. Beverly Hills, CA: Sage Publications.
ROKKAN, S. and D. Urwin (1983). *Economy, Territory, Identity: Politics of European Peripheries*. Beverly Hills, CA: Sage Publications.
ROSE, M.E. (1972). *The Relief of Poverty, 1834–1914*. London: Macmillan.
ROWNTREE, B.S. (1910). *Poverty: A Study of Town Life*. London: Macmillan.
RUBINSTEIN, W.D. (1977). 'The Victorian Middle Classes: Wealth, Occupation, and Geography', *Economic Historical Review*, second series, 30, 4 (November), 602–23.
RUESCHEMEYER, D., E.H. Stephens and J.D. Stephens (1992). *Capitalist Development and Democracy*. Chicago: University of Chicago Press.

SALISBURY, Lord (unsigned) (1883). 'Disintegration: Speeches of the Right Hon. W.E. Forester, M.P., at Devonport and Stonehouse', *The Quarterly Review*, 156, 312, 559–95.

SAVILLE, J. (1960). 'Trade Unions and Free Labour: The Background to the Taff Vale Decision', pp. 317–50 in A. Briggs and J. Saville (eds), *Essays in Labour History*. London: Macmillan.

SEYMOUR, C. (1915). *Electoral Reform in England and Wales: The Development and Operation of the Parliamentary Franchise, 1832–1885*. New Haven, CT: Yale University Press.

SHORT, R., J. Horn and J.J. McArdle (1984). 'Mathematical-Statistical Model Building in Analysis of Developmental Data', pp. 371–401 in R.N. Emde and R.J. Harmon (eds), *Continuities and Discontinuities in Development*. New York: Plenum Publishing.

SIMON, A. (1975). 'Church Disestablishment as a Factor in the General Election of 1885', *Historical Journal*, 18 (December), 791–820.

SMITH, A. (1937). *An Inquiry into the Nature and Causes of the Wealth of Nations*. New York: The Modern Library.

SMITH, C.A. (1976a). 'Regional Economic Systems: Linking Geographical Models and Socioeconomic Problems', pp. 3–63 in C.A. Smith (ed.), *Regional Analysis*: Volume I: *Economic Systems*. New York: Academic Press.

SMITH, C.A. (1976b). 'Exchange Systems and the Spatial Distribution of Elites: The Organisation of Stratification in Agrarian Societies', pp. 309–74 in C.A. Smith (ed.), *Regional Analysis*, Vol. II: *Social Systems*. New York: Academic Press.

SMITH, P. (1967). *Disraelian Conservatism and Social Reform*. London: Routledge & Kegan Paul.

SMITH, P. (1972). *Lord Salisbury on Politics*. Cambridge: Cambridge University Press.

TAYLOR, A.J.P. (1972). *Laissez-faire and State Intervention in Nineteenth-century Britain*. London: Macmillan.

TAYLOR, A.J.P. (1976). *Essays in English History*. Harmondsworth, Middlesex: Penguin.

TAYLOR, R. (1975). *Lord Salisbury*. London: Allen Lane.

THANE, P. (1988). 'Late Victorian Women', pp. 175–208 in T.R. Gourvish and A. O'Day (eds), *Later Victorian Society, 1867–1900*. New York: St. Martin's Press.

THOLFSEN, T. (1959). 'The Origins of the Birmingham Caucus', *Historical Journal*, 2, 2, 161–84.

THOLFSEN, T. (1961). 'The Transition to Democracy in Victorian England', *International Review of Social History*, 6, 226–48.

THOMAS, B. (1930). 'The Migration of Labour into the Glamorganshire Coalfield (1861–1911)', *Economica*, 10 (November), 275–94.

THOMPSON, E.P. (1964). *The Making of the English Working Class*. New York: Pantheon Books.

THOMPSON, E.P. (1992). *Customs in Common*. London: Merlin Press.

THOMPSON, F.M.L. (1988). *The Rise of Respectable Society: A Social History of Victorian Britain, 1830–1900*. Cambridge, MA: Harvard University Press.

TREVOR-ROPER, H. (1983). 'The Invention of Tradition: The Highland Tradition of Scotland', pp. 15–42 in E. Hobsbawm and T. Ranger (eds), *The Invention of Tradition*. Cambridge: Cambridge University Press.

TUCKER, L.R. and C. Lewis (1973). 'A Reliability Coefficient for Maximum Likelihood Factor Analysis', *Psychometrika*, 38, 1 (March), 1–10.

URQUHART, R.G. (1988). 'The Autonomy of Commerce in Eighteenth Century British Political Economy', Unpublished PhD Dissertation, New School for Social Research, New York.

URWIN, D. (1980). 'Towards a Nationalisation of British Politics?: The Party System, 1885–1940', pp. 225–58 in O. Buesch (ed.), *Waehlerbewegung in der Europaeschen Geschichte*. Berlin: Colloquium Verlag.

URWIN, D. (1982). 'Territorial Structures and Political Development in the United Kingdom', pp. 19–74 in S. Rokkan and D. Urwin (eds), *The Politics of Territorial Identity*. Beverly Hills, CA.: Sage Publications.

URWIN, D. (1985). 'The Price of a Kingdom: Territory, Identity and Centre-Periphery in Western Europe', pp. 151–170 in Y. Meny and V. Wright (eds), *Centre-Periphery Relations in Western Europe*. London: Allen & Unwin.

WALD, K.D. (1983). *Crosses on the Ballot: Patterns of British Voter Alignment Since 1885*. Princeton, NJ: Princeton University Press.

WALLERSTEIN, I. (1983). *Historical Capitalism*. New York: New Left Books.

WATSON, G. (1973). *The English Ideology: Studies in the Language of Victorian Politics*. London: Allen Lane.

WEARMOUTH, R.F. (1954). *Methodism and the Struggle for the Working Classes, 1850–1900*. Leicester: Edgar Backus.

WELLHOFER, E.S. (1984). 'To "Educate Their Volition to Dance in Their Chains": Enfranchisement and Realignment in Britain, 1885–1950, Part I: The Decay of the Old Order', *Comparative Political Studies*, 17, 1 (April), 3–33.

WELLHOFER, E.S. (1985). '"Two Nations": Class and Periphery in Late Victorian Britain, 1885–1910', *American Political Science Review*, 79, 4 (December), 977–93.

WELLHOFER, E.S. (1988). 'Models of Core and Periphery Dynamics', *Comparative Political Studies*, 21, 2 (July), 281–307.

WELLHOFER, E.S. (1989a). 'Core and Periphery: Territorial Dimensions in Politics', *Urban Studies*, 26, 340–55.

WELLHOFER, E.S. (1989b). 'The Comparative Method and the Study of Development, Diffusion, and Social Change', *Comparative Political Studies*, 22, 3 (October), 315–42.

WELLHOFER, E.S. (1990). 'Contradictions in Market Models of Politics: The Case of Party Strategies and Voter Linkages', *European Journal of Political Research*, 18, 9–28.

WELLHOFER, E.S. (1991). 'Confounding Sources of Variance in the Macro-Analysis of Electoral Data', *European Journal of Political Research*, 19, 425–40.

WELLHOFER, E.S. (1994). '"Men Make Their Own History, But ...": The New Institutionalism and the Fate of Inter-War Democracy in Europe', *Democratisation*, 1, 2 (Summer), 323–42.

WICKHAM, E.R. (1957). *Church and People in an Industrial City*. London: Lutterworth Press.

WILLIAMS, T. (1989). 'The Anglicisation of South Wales', pp. 193–206 in R. Samuel (ed.), *Patriotism: The Making and Unmaking of the British National Identity.* Volume II: *Minorities and Outsiders*. London: Routledge.

Index

and Roman Catholic working class,
93, 124, **148**
and social and economic progress,
44
and 'Strange Death' question, 95,
124
and support in the periphery, 147
and trade union support, 96, 122
and trade unions, 91
and unchurched working class, 95,
128
and working-class support, 122
changes in support for, 133
changing social base of, 94
decline of and Nonconformism, 124
decline of and religion, 127
decline of and working class, 128
effectiveness of party organisation,
94
in Wales, 94
interpretations of decline of, 124
LVPA models of support for, 92,
121, 128
Nonconformist working class and,
185
on class and national divisions, 45
religion and the working class, 126
support for and declining turnout,
133
Lib-Labism
and labour aristocracy, 184
and Labour Party, 98, 128
and Liberal Party, 96
and New Unionism, 97
and Roman Catholic working class,
128
and support in the periphery, 148
and trade unions, 128
challenges to, 97
LVPA models of support for, 98,
128

Marshall, Alfred
on labour aristocracy, 169
on social and economic progress, 44
Marx, Karl
on classical republican problem, 11
on division of labour and labour
aristocracy, 170

on Irish–English working-class
antagonism, 55
on labour aristocracy, 169
on language of class, 8
on suffrage expansion and socialism,
11
Mill, J.S.
and implications of the Poor Law
reforms for democracy, 26
effects of capitalism and democracy,
10
on democracy and civil society, 9
treatment of the poor, 6

National Liberal Federation
and Liberal Party, 94
weakness of, 65
Nationalism
and Nonconformism in Wales, 53
and religion, 13, 14, 53
as challenge to Empire, 52
creation of, 52
Highland land war, 53
language of, 11
religion, language and geography,
12
rise of in rural areas, 53
Scottish and Welsh, 13
Welsh Tithe War, 53
New Institutionalism
applied to British transition to
democracy, 195–6
definition of, 193
New Unionism
and labour aristocracy, 173
and Labour Party, 96
and Lib-Labism, 97
employers' response to, 109
rise of, 110
Nonconformis, **144**
Nonconformism
and Conservative Party, 85, 90
and education, 51, 107
and entertainment, 106
and establishment, 50
and Liberal Party, 91, 95, 111, 124,
133, 184
and the working class, 54, 61
and Unionist support, 83, 90, 116

264

Index